President 2012
Patriot or Puppet for Billionaires

David Tippie

Dedication

I owe a great deal of gratitude to President Ronal Reagan, who I have studied a great deal and his way of thinking about government pleases me very deeply. Such as when he would make statements like: Government is not the solution to your problems, Government is the cause of your problems.

The very reason I wrote this book was after pondering what Reagan always said to his PR staff and that was to help put everything in 30-second sound bites. He studied many things and the media was one of those. He saw that the media had already created that 30-second environment to the public and they were used to getting things quickly and may not take the time to listen to anything at length.

So in keeping with that train of thought I decided to make certain each of the issues making up my entire platform were thoroughly mapped out in this book so each issue could be understood and could be referred to at any time. Then the 30-second sound bites could be employed through this reference point and the media who are normally not on the side of the conservatives who deliberately spin sound bites in the opposite direction could be held accountable by referencing this book.

Let's Win One FOR THE GIFFER.

Contents

Chapter 6, P-83, The Middle Class Has Shrunk in America

Chapter 7, P-99, 2012 Presidency

Chapter 8, P-135, White Americans Voted For the First Black President

Chapter 9, P-161, Education Through Progressive Communism

Chapter 10, P-171, What is a Conditioned Response?

Chapter 11, P-191, If We Don't Stand for Something, We Will Fall for Anything

Chapter 12, P-197, Who is David Tippie

Introduction

My name is David Tippie, and I am running for President of the United States in 2012. I chose to place my name in the hat against those who are beholden to their huge money backers. I will not be beholden to no person, group or organization. My entire presidency will be for the fourth branch of government (shunned by today's politicians and government) and that fourth branch is the American people. We the people will return our government back to a government of the people, by the people and for the people.

I see ambition as being high jacked by the left. To get everyone to focus on their issues as being moral such as entitlements, they had to slowly refer to entitlements as a human right. Where hard work is penalized and apathy is rewarded. They selected a more sinister word for the word ambition inherent to those folks who wanted to provide the best life they could for their families through their hard work and ambition and that sinister word that replaced ambition was Greed.

Ambition is a constructive force. It is part of what defines "greatness". It builds companies, expands the economy, creates jobs, and increases wealth for others as well as the ambitious themselves. It is the pursuit of an idea, and is driven by the imagination; the success or failure of the ambitious lies mainly in their own energy, strength and ingenuity. When someone is breaking the law in some manner and collecting money or wealth our judiciary system should be applied just as for any other criminal. The far left will say the criminal was greedy so they can re-apply the word greed to further their agenda to anyone who has worked hard and got a well deserved good life for their families.

I love our country and I love Americans who love our country. You will find in this book how I define American patriot, which is very important and you will also find what I intend to do with those imposters here who hate our wonderful country. We are the land of the free because our country is the home of the brave. Can we return to our Republic with Liberty and Justice for all without Revolt? How have the puppets for billionaires worked for you so far?

At this very moment, no other country needs or disserves our help until we can recover from the madness, which we are now in the middle of in this year 2011. The world needs a strong healthy and financially stable America; they don't need a weak America.

I am not the deliverer of "Hope & Change", then to ask you to wait and find out what change really means; read this book and agree or disagree because I leave no stone unturned, it is for you the American patriot, to judge me and decide if you want me for your president. I have never invented any words or phrases so I owe everything I have come to believe to someone else.

Like most of you my education came from my research even opposing views are important to educating yourself. I cannot keep track of how many websites and articles I have read and gleaned talking points from.

End of book is my thanks.

Chapter 1

American Politics, No longer Business as Usual

Everyone knows that building a national organization or movement through the World Wide Web, television, and in various other media outlets is expensive and demands a methodical approach.

However, 2012 is going to bring about the NEW AMERICAN leaders who are not multimillionaires, who love their country, and who refuse to let America be thrown over the cliff, as seems to be happening today in 2011.

Those in power see that the only way to control Americans is to destroy the economy and make Americans beholden to other countries and to reduce our country to third-world status. I discuss in this book information about who Obama surrounds himself with as well as what Obama studied and who his mentors were, as well as his professors. After reading my book I do not think it will be hard for you to come to this same conclusion.

On a Wednesday in 2011, Sen. Judd Gregg, Republican from New Hampshire told CNBC that if the US government does not act soon to reduce the deficit and debt, it will become like Greece in a few years.

The new rising patriots are not looking for a political posture to make them richer; they are just like you and me—they love our country and are going to stop the malignant political and financial destruction of America.

When we vote for those with money and fame or vote for past politicians, we get what we deserve. How has it worked so far?

While freedom rings, our flag still flies, thanks to the soldiers on the ground and our pilots in the skies; soldiers salute the flag with honor and pride, and some get buried under it.

Soldiers give their all doing what they must to ensure that our families and theirs remain free and safe. To those in uniform, or those who must remain invisible because of their tasks, we will thankyou with our vote for the patriot, which is what will ensure we stay strong and free. We are going to start voting for those who understand that our country must become strong once more.

Our pledge to you, our beloved soldiers, is that you will not have served or died in vain. Now we must all become soldiers, in a manner of speaking, to right the terrible wrongs those in power have created.

Obama wanted a Civilian Defense Force equivalent in power with our military. Why do you suppose he wants this? We already have a military and the finest in the world. Do you suppose it is because he feels it necessary to prepare for the conservative threat which he sees coming his civilian defense will have been given the liberal license to rage against the conservative threat which he feels is his only way that he has a chance of staying in office. You can hear Obama's speech about it–copy and paste this: http://www.youtube.com/watch?v=Tt2yGzHfy7s&feature=player_embedded

In 1776, Nathan Hale, before being executed by the British at the age of twenty-one, is reported to have said, "I regret that I have but one life to give for my country."

Loving America is the main ingredient one needs to be America's leader; as a matter of fact, it should be a prerequisite, so that our country will not ever again be shamed by a leader such as Obama who apologizes for American arrogance to Europe. Here is that message on youtube: http://www.youtube.com/watch?v=0PcWNZGsBHY

On Boomeryearbook.com you can go and read a comment by Joseph J. Kusnell: An open letter to Obama: Dear Mr. President: It is not America that is arrogant; it is you who are arrogant. Go to the website there is more.

Often we get in our own way, because of how the average American thinks. Average Americans do not have huge amounts of money and fame, so they tend not to like those who have the same financial status as they themselves have. Typical Americans tend to be jealous of their neighbors, who may have accomplished something they themselves have not, such as getting a new car or moving to a bigger house.

These same petty jealousies exist if our neighbor runs for political office; we may secretly choose not to vote for him because of these petty jealousies. After all, your neighbor looks just like you, has zero fame, and is financially equal to you as well.

Yet we continually see illegal acts being perpetrated, day in and day out, by those we elected who had the fame and fortune we did not; Charlie Rangle for one, that supports this argument, which you will read about later.

We came from an era in which royalty ruled over lives when we were serfs, and for some reason we have a hard time believing that an average patriotic American is not a serf and is who we should be electing to political office, because that patriot truly represents the American voting patriot and he never sells our country out because he is willing to die for it.

Why can't we learn that Joe the plumber or Joe or Jane the business person would have made a better president or congressman than the career politicians who are simply puppets for those billionaires who spent their money to put them in office? Was it not amazing how George Soros appeared back in American and Obama amassed a billion dollars to run again for office? We can certainly understand that those billionaire puppeteers (only pointing to one-others later) have hidden agendas and do not have our country at heart, like the true patriot American does and will always have for his country? How many political scandals does it take to wake up the American voter?

Who Was Ralph Nader

Ralph Nader ran on zero dollars and got twenty five percent of the votes even though he was out of touch with the mainstream conservative voter. I use him to relate only to one thing (zero dollars spent campaigning). Why couldn't we, the voting public, get more than fifty percent of the vote in 2012 with the right Patriot candidate? Let me introduce you to a simple businessman who is a God-loving, America-loving patriot and a conservative, opposite Nader politically, who will have one thing in common with Nader and that is, he ran on a zero dollars campaign budget and therefore not beholden to any billionaires. We can get behind our candidate like that and disregard the billions of dollars spent on television ads paid for by the politicians and their supporters. Why not read a book like the one you are now reading: one that outlines the platform for America so there will be no surprises like we got from Obama and you simply decide up or down if you want the candidate, by reading his book? No campaign contributors, no special interest groups which he must be beholden to, just clean, clear-thinking patriot, just like you.

Supporters who believed in Nader brought him the venues so he could present his platform and show the millionaires and billionaires that American courage and patriotism are back and that we do not have to buy votes.

Let's do that again with the majority and show those billionaire puppeteers that we are going to take back control and provide a government that is of the people, by the people, and for the people, just as our patriot founders did from England. The Tea Party forming today exemplifies our forefathers throwing the tea off the ships in Boston Harbor.

So that you can begin to think as I do, I have written this book to declare my beliefs, not the bullet points you get from politicians. Their answer to most questions is often something like, "We are going to make sure" or "We are going to try and do" this or that. Never do they hone in on anything specific. This is due to the many years of giving the voting public words in order to get elected or re-elected as career politicians.

In this book I tell it exactly as I see it and I do not need a teleprompter.

Ralph Nader's attempt failed because he did not think like the mainstream majority of conservatives who are the God-loving, America-loving patriots, which means you and me conservatives who demand less government intrusion in our lives.

It would mean a great deal to the beginning of this movement which is designed as the campaign, if each reader would consider, at the very least, to review all subject matter, and mail your thoughts to all your contacts and constituents and ask them to purchase my book to help the drive toward 2012.

Always remember my contact is my website: www.LiveLonger123.com

The following principals and American values should be what all candidates' platforms represent in the next 2012 election cycle if they think like the majority of conservatives do. We love our country and want it to be safe, secure and debt free once again.

No person's insistence of an idea makes it engaging until it meets with approval and scrutiny of their constituents; remember my website and contact me with your thoughts.

I think the same way as the majority of conservatives do, so I believe that if you are conservative you will appreciate this platform by the time you finish reading this book.

My intention with this book is to display the most positive platform: and it is my attempt to build an organized movement that is as strong and as fired-up as is the Tea Party.

You will see when I introduce the plan that it has much more than just merit. Each issue has depth and does not leave you hanging.

Professionals in each area of expertise of my plan are invited to step in with their opinion or give their objections, just as long as they follow up with their suggestions, which must be conservative and promote the same values (possibly in a shorter version) that would further my original goal as long as their intent is not left-wing liberal.

And second, to create a base of brave, mentally strong Americans who have had enough of politics as usual will appreciate what I have to say enough to spread my words and to get others to read my book. These readers will become part of our base to help get our patriot, (of course that would be me) who will be returning America to a constitutional form of government, when elected as your president in 2012.

Constitutional/Conservative

C/Conservative is defined as smaller government with less government inter-vention in our personal lives. It also means to reduce spending and balancing the budget, all the while eliminating the deficit by living within our means.

Also and this is major, to remove support for other nations, at least until we become strong again and have the budget to enable America to be more charitable. Foreign entanglements and nation-building were not among the founders' original intentions.

We are using every tax dollar collected and borrowing $3.97 billion every day to pay for all of the government programs and agencies which are increas-ing our national debt. This was reported n an op-ed March 2011, by U.S. Sena-tors, Saxby chambliss, Republican of Georgia and Mark Warner, Democrat of Virginia.

I have chosen the Wikipedia explanation from the beginning of our country until today, to discuss our national debt:

http://en.wikipedia.org/wiki/United_States_public_debt

Begins: The United States has had public debt since its inception. Debts incurred during the American Revolutionary War and under the Articles of Confederation led to the first yearly reported value of $75,463,476.52 on January 1, 1791. From 1796 to 1811 there were fourteen surpluses and only two deficits. The first dramatic growth-spurt of the debt occurred because of the War of1812. In the first twenty years following the War of 1812, eighteen surpluses were experienced and the United States paid off 99.97 percent of its debt.

The second dramatic growth spurt of the debt occurred because of the Civil War. The debt was just $65 million in 1860, but passed $1 billion in 1863 and had reached $2.7 billion following the war. In the following forty seven years America returned to the practice of running surpluses during times of peace experiencing thirty six surpluses and only eleven deficits. During this period fifty five percent of the U.S. national debt was paid off.

The next period of major growth in debt came during WWI reaching $25.5 billion at its conclusion. It was followed by eleven straight surpluses and saw the debt reduced by thirty six percent.

Social programs enacted during the Great Depression and the buildup and involvement in World War II during the Roosevelt and Truman presidencies in the 1930s and 1940s caused the largest increase at that time - a sixteen fold increase in the gross public debt from $16 billion in 1930 to $260 billion in 1950. When Roosevelt took office in 1933, the national debt was almost $20 billion; a sum equal to twenty percent of the U.S. gross domestic product (GDP). During its first term, the Roosevelt administration ran large annual deficits between two and five percent of GDP. By 1936, the national debt had increased to $33.7 billion or approximately forty percent of GDP.

After this period, the growth of the gross public debt closely matched the rate of inflation where it tripled in size from $260 billion in 1950 to around $909 billion in 1980. Gross debt in nominal dollars quadrupled during the Reagan and Bush presidencies from 1980 to 1992. The net public debt quintupled in nominal terms.

In nominal dollars the net public debt rose and then fell between 1992 and 2000 from $3T in 1992 to $3.4T in 2000. During the administration of President George W. Bush, the gross public debt increased from $5.7 trillion in January 2001 to $10.7 trillion by December 2008. Under Barack Hussein Obama, the debt increased from $10.7 trillion to $14.2 trillion by February 2011. Based on the 2010 U.S. budget, total national debt will nearly double in dollar terms between 2008 and 2015 and will grow to nearly one hundred percent of GDP. END Wikipedia http://en.wikipedia.org/wiki/United_States_public_debt

If you do the math insofar as spending from Bush and Obama that is $5-trillon in eight years under Bush, which is inexcusable and unacceptable and then there is a $4-trillion increase in one year under Obama, which is not only inexcusable and unacceptable it should be an impeachable offense in my view. This kind of spending behavior for a president is finished.

I like to use practical knowledge to explain certain things like how much money we spend on illegal aliens and send to foreign countries? This data is not something that the government keeps track on a regular basis, or at least does not make it readily available to the public; but there have been studies on this topic, albeit not of late statistics, mostly from research institutions, scholars and academics reported in various media outlets, such as: The Remittance Marketplace (2004) - Pew Hispanic Research on this website, which by their words is by no means scientific: http://pewhispanic.org/files/reports/28.pdf

Billions in Motion: Latino Immigrants, Remittances, and Banking, the Pew Hispanic Center/Multilateral Investment Fund (2002) on this website: http://pewhispanic.org/reports/report.php?ReportID=13

Financial Access for Immigrants: The Case of Remittances (Bernanke speech) on this website: http://www.federalreserve.gov/boarddocs/speeches/2004/200404162/default.htm

For more recent data, you might go to the economic statistics agency of the specific government and look for the figures. In the Philippines for example, remittances are classified as Net Factor Income from Abroad and you can find the data broken down by source countries from the National Statistical Coordination Board for the United States. You must be your own judge, but in my view these are upwards of the trillion dollar mark of borrowed dollars and taxed dollars to support illegals and other countries? America is a giant family and therefore must act like a family.

A family that is in debt over its head does not find legal or illegal ways to get another credit card just to give money to a person who is begging on the street. The family must come first.

Other countries need America to be strong and not on a path of self-destruction, which we are on now. What good are we to them or ourselves if we lose our sovereignty and our dollar turns to dust?

Look at it from this angle: If you had a house that was under water insofar as debt to value and you were having trouble making the payments and were very near to foreclosure and the repo man was hooking up to your vehicle and you were finding it difficult to put food on the table to feed your family it, would be the same if you do the math insofar as spending from Bush and Obama which is $5-trillon in eight years under Bush, which is inexcusable and unacceptable and then there is a $4-trillion increase in one year under Obama, which is not only inexcusable and unacceptable it should be an impeachable offense in my view. This kind of spending behavior for a president is finished.

There is no difference in that analogy of a family than it is for our leaders who are shipping money overseas with our country about to default. All of our families are going to suffer greatly if we do.

How we might reverse the damages created by the politicians controlled by their contributors will be the agenda for this book. You won't find me dodging any issue. Prepare yourself, because I am not politically correct, either I am honest.

Chapter 2

Is It Probable That Someone Who is Not a Multi-millionaire Could Become President?

Let's find out together, shall we?

This movement is searching for like-minded people who are brave and willing to become part of the organizational team; they must be capable of removing the petty jealousies, as I have mentioned, and to do the right thing for America.

I need you to become a proud soldier to undertake needed activity before the 2012 election. You need to place your vote to remove career politicians from office and put true patriots in their place, which will be by default, helping our patriot to become a known conservative candidate for president.

If the lifer Republican politicians do not wish for our patriot to represent them, then our patriot will run as an Independent, and you can help, if you would be so kind, by creating venues for our patriot to stay in the news and to win the presidency in 2012 for we, the people.

I believe that people who try to do something and fail are infinitely better off than those who try to do nothing and succeed at it.

Think of that when deciding to get on board to help stop the sinking of the ship called America.

Experiencing failure is inevitable on our journey to be successful. But every defeat is merely another step to victory when the passion is great. Americans always find that the number of times they succeed is in direct proportion with the number of times they fail and yet keep trying.

America will not be judged by the number of times it has failed, but by the number of times the people succeed and get strong once again.

Failure to some is nothing but education; nothing but the first step to change—not the change this administration has brought, but something thoroughly explained as I have attempted to do in this book, which by default, is better and safer than the unknown; as well as using past successes of others for our future goals mentioned in this book that are much more prosperous for America.

Our efforts will, by default, return our country to being the most respected, powerful, and prosperous country in the world.

Americans cannot be winners and be afraid to lose a battle. This organization that you and I are creating is asking for like-minded people to come together to help refine the plan and continue with this long overdue movement to take back America from those who sell it and bow to our enemies.

There is not a single mainstream candidate who has indicated that he or she has what it takes for the necessary steps to keep our country from self- destruction. All are searching for the buzz words that get them on television and they all sense that our population has been voting for the guy who has the most money and fame and appears in front of them most on television.

The Federal Government Mandate

I believe that the federal government has one major task, to protect the life, liberty, and property of Americans, and that it should accomplish this task by returning to the ethics of our original republic and by protecting the Constitution where the states govern all else, for example, by closing down government agencies and setting term limits. Politics should not be a job for many years, it should be your time to help make our country great for four to eight years, and then go get a job.

The protection for the American people can be viewed as closing down redundant government agencies as well as those agencies not directly called for by our Constitution and getting government out of private lives, and by stopping lobbyist from bribing politicians, by punishing the politicians and such illegal activity because career politicians are all too tempted to accept bribes; the Charlie Rangel story is the best way to support this statement.

Throwing out the lifelong politicians and setting term limits are one way of pushing the start button on removing this temptation.

One needs only to examine the American Association of Retired Persons (AARP) to expose the corruptions and collusion between elected government officials or appointed bureaucrats and special interest groups, as well as big business.

AARP organizers cancel listening session after participants refuse to keep their comments quiet. You can listen to it here: http://www.breitbart.tv/aarp-reps-cancel-listening-session-after-participants- refuse-to-keep-their-comments-quiet

Now that the House of Representatives hearings have revealed how AARP's support of the new health care law will put over a billion dollars into AARP's pockets, the Association of Mature American Citizens (AMAC), the little David that came out against the Goliath of AARP 18 months ago, is poised to make huge inroads.

Similar information I am speaking of is played on YouTube here: http://www.youtube.com/watch?feature=player_embedded&v=kMrfZpTJwDc

AARP stands to earn $1 billion from Obamacare; AMAC stands to gain millions of members!

AMAC had only 5,000 members less than two years ago. Now it has over130,000 paid members and growing rapidly.

I have been slowly introducing myself as our patriot candidate and If I am elected, special interest groups will not be allowed to influence our laws even if I must accomplish it through Executive Order.

We live in the land of the free only because of the brave! Stand up with me! It is a difficult road, but our country is at stake!

Progressivism Reduced Learning in "Schools"

While President Obama has much to do with it, we have fallen in world status due to the years of progressivism that have removed prayer and the pledge to our flag from our schools, and we have reduced teaching standards to accommodate the lowest learner so that we are now 17th in educational status in the world. Progressivism has replaced individual initiative with the entitlement attitude; that, I believe was the plan of the true puppet masters who are in control of the career politicians.

After all, you can't control the everyday lives of successful people; you can only control those people if they are beholden to you. What better way to accomplish that than to constantly give people something to remove their desire to work for it?

Hugo Chavez in Venezuela is a master at this bait and switch disguise. Hugo Chavez Frias was reelected by an overwhelming nearly two to one margin over his only serious rival on December 3, 2006 giving him a mandate to proceed with his agenda to build a socialist society in the 21st century on a Bolivarian model designed to meet the needs of the current era in Venezuela and Latin America overall. Read more about it here: http://www.information-clearinghouse.info/article17158.htm

Saul Alinsky pioneered a method of helping poor and working-class people organize themselves to improve their communities. Combining urban social theories he had learned at the University of Chicago with street smarts he had earned growing up in that city's Jewish ghetto, Alinsky first worked in prisons and as a juvenile delinquency researcher; then, starting in crime-ridden Chicago neighborhoods in the late 1930s.

Saul Alinsky is considered to be the founder of modern community organizing in America. His ideologies are truly at the core of progressivism in our country today.

The political left holds a 1960s-bred agenda of anticapitalism implemented through undisguised authoritarian socialism to which our current imitation of a president is an adherent; this is not just in my opinion, but the opinion of thousands.

His actions are proof enough for me that he is for outright world socialism, which in my view, as well as in the minds of many, is scientifically planned and directed by billionaire puppet masters. All this is being accomplished while true red, white and blue-blooded God-loving American patriots have been lulled to sleep hearing the words that they are going to be taken care of by the government.

Obama's socialistic and anti-capitalism agenda eloquently described by Greg Ransom of PrestoPundit: you have to go to this website he did a good job: http://prestopundit.wordpress.com/2008/04/07/barack-obama-hid-his- fathers-socialist-and-anti-western-convictions-from-his-readers/

Greg Ransom of PrestoPundi Begins: There's a big mystery at the heart of Barack Obama's book Dreams for My Father: A Story of Race and Inheritance. What was Barack Obama doing seeking out Marxist professors in college? Why did Obama choose a Communist Party USA member as his socio- political counselor in high school? Why was he spending his time studying neo- colonialism and the writings of Frantz Fanon, the pro-violence author of "the "Manifesto of the Communist Party" which is a Communist Manifesto of neo- colonialism", in college? Why did he take time out from his studies at Columbia to attend socialist conferences at Cooper Union?

Obama's Book Dreams of My Father

If there is a mystery at the heart of Barack Obama's book Dreams for My Father, one thing is not left as a mystery, the fact that Barack Obama organized his life on the ideals given to him by his Kenyan father. Obama tells that, "All of my life, I carried a single image of my father, one that I tried to take as my own."

(p. 220) And what was that image? It was the father of my dreams, the man in my mother's stories, full of high-blown ideals (p. 278). What is more, Obama tells that, it was into my father's image that I packed all the attributes I sought in myself. And also, that I did feel that there was something to prove to my father in his efforts at political organizing. (p. 230) Obama stakes out the following positions in his attacks on the paper produced by Mboya's Ministry of Economic Planning and Development:

1. Obama advocated the communal ownership of land and the forced confiscation of privately controlled land, as part of a forced development plan, an important element of his attack on the government's advocacy of private ownership, land titles, and property registration. (p. 29)

2. Obama advocated the nationalization of European and Asian owned enterprises, including hotels, with the control of these operations handed over to the indigenous black population. (pp. 32 -33)

3. Obama advocated dramatically increasing taxation on "the rich" even up to the one hundred percent level, arguing that, there is no limit to taxation if the benefits derived from public services by society measure up to the cost in taxation which they have to pay (p. 30) (my comment inserted here: Do you recall the earlier mention of his $4-trillion spending in his first year in office? continuing with Greg Ransom's reporting: and that, Theoretically, there is nothing that can stop the government from taxing one hundred percent of income so long as the people get benefits from the government commensurate with their income which is taxed.(p. 31)

4. Obama contrasts the ill-defined and weak-tea notion of African Socialism negatively with the well-defined ideology of scientific socialism, i.e. communism. Obama views African Socialism pioneers like Nkrumah,

Nyerere and Toure as having diverted only a little from the capitalist system. (p. 26)

5. Obama advocates an "active" rather than a "passive" program to achieve a classless society through the removal of economic disparities between black Africans and Asian and Europeans. (p. 28) While we welcome the idea of a prevention of class problems, we should try to cure what has slipped in. We need to eliminate power structures that have been built through excessive accumulation, so that not only a few individuals shall control a vast magnitude of resources, as is the case now, so long as we maintain free enterprise one cannot deny that some will accumulate more than others. (pp. 29 to 30)

6. Obama advocates price controls on hotels and the tourist industry, so that the middle class and not only the rich can afford to come to Kenya as tourists. (p. 33)

7. Obama advocates government owned and operated model farms as a means of teaching modern farming techniques to farmers. (p. 33)

8. Obama strongly supports the governments assertion of a non-aligned status in the contest between Western nations and communist nations aligned with the Soviet Union and China. (p. 26) END Greg Ransom's article (check it out for yourself). http://prestopundit.wordpress.com/2008/04/07/barack-obama-hid-his-fathers-socialist-and-anti-western-convictions-from-his-readers/

Entitlement attitude

Those expecting government entitlements accept the fact that the government will be furnishing those entitlements by taking money from those who it considers to be the selfish working people who pay taxes. Remember the word greed that has been substituted for ambition, earlier mentioned.

Taking from the haves and giving it to those who chose not to work for it will be a thing of the past, which all Americans will begin to see was the start of our destruction when the patriot David Tippie is elected president.

This is what has happened to our society. This also results from the fact that there are fewer fathers around the dinner tables to instill family values; even less frequently are those family values displayed by the children because they did not come from a family that sat together around that dinner table.

Look at the results of lowered teaching methods used today that teach school children only the very basics. Also look at the caving-in to the politically correct to apply the separation of church and state in our schools, which inspired the removal of prayer, and the pledge to the flag in our schools, as well as in our everyday society and media. We have experienced the removal of the expression "Merry Christmas, replaced by Happy Holidays; so as not to offend any other religion.

I am a Christian and have explained in this book that Christianity was woven into the fabric of our Constitution by our founders. It is appalling that those we elect can discard our founding values. I believe separating our children from our founding faith has been the catalyst in creating the rise of criminal behavior that is increasing from one generation to the next.

When I say this next thing, I am not speaking at all to the left-wing activists who are intent on destroying America by destroying it from the inside by collapsing the economy to then be more capable of controlling people. I might add that they are accomplishing that destruction with skill. I am speaking only to the God-loving America-loving patriots, just like myself:

You patriots know we have to return to our family values and stop this madness; it will not be accomplished by the cowards who maintain political correctness; it will be accomplished by the brave—the same type of patriot founded our country.

In fact, the destruction of capitalism in America by the swelling of the welfare rolls to the point of collapsing our economy and then implementing socialism by nationalizing many private institutions, is the plan, and is in action right now. The action brought on by the global elite (who pull the strings of its puppets, like Obama). To add more than a semblance of credibility to this statement and not to elaborate on the greed of wall street (remember greed is criminal intent—not ambition) and insider bailouts, which in the opinion of many, ruined millions of middle-class people's lives or the wars which I disagree with that are dragging our country into debt as well; all of this you can research for yourselves and form your own opinions; the following article sums up what I am referring to: http:// goblr.com/watch/2401883/worldview_radio_ obama_destroying_the#title

Brannon Howse of Worldview Radio interviewed author James Simpson. Entitled, Barack Obama is Destroying Our Economy on Purpose; Howse's interview of Simpson concentrated on Columbia University professors Richard Andrew Cloward and Frances Fox Piven who wrote an article in 1966 for The Nation magazine. The article was published on May 2, 1966 and laid out what is now known as the Cloward-Piven Strategy. The plan calls for the destruction of capitalism in America by swelling the welfare rolls to the point of collapsing our economy and then implementing socialism by nationalizing many private institutions, explains a synopsis on the Worldview Radio web-site."Cloward and Piven studied Saul Alinsky just like Hillary Clinton and President Obama. END, again you can do your own research.

The elitists' agenda is to consolidate power and destroy all opposition globally. That agenda has nothing to do with liberating anyone. When there is a show of opposition in some war, even if the elitist refuse to call it war; they tend to finance both sides. Those hidden from view, who are pulling the strings, have shrewdly understood that collapsing economies by whatever means, including war, will accomplish their goals. Behind the scene corruption is explained fairly well in the website: economic crisis: http://economic- crisis. us/2010/01/goldman-sachs-tens-billions-dollars-economic-collapse- america

Investment banking giant Goldman Sachs has become perhaps the most prominent symbol for everything that is wrong with the U.S. financial system, but most Americans cannot even begin to explain what Goldman Sachs does or how it has made tens of billions of dollars from the economic collapse of America. The truth is that what Goldman Sachs did was fairly simple, and there may not have even been anything illegal about it (although it is now being investigated by the SEC among others).

The following is how Goldman Sachs made tens of billions of dollars from the economic collapse of America in four easy steps:

Step 1: Sell mortgage-related securities that are absolute junk to trusting clients at vastly overinflated prices.

Step 2: Bet against those same mortgage-related securities and make massive bets against the U.S. housing market so that your firm will make massive profits when the U.S. economy collapses.

Step 3: Have ex-Goldman executives in key positions of power in the U.S. government so that bailout money can be funneled to entities, such as AIG that Goldman had made these failure bets with, so that Goldman can get paid after the housing crash and so it winds up winning the bets.

Step 4: Collect the profits - Goldman Sachs is having its most successful year and will end up reporting approximately $50 billion in revenue for 2009.

So is it right for the biggest fish on Wall Street to make tens of billions of dollars by betting that the U.S. housing market will collapse? My injection: Now this is what should be the determination of the meaning of greed is; not hard working people with the ambition to exceed for their families, END my injection.

Back to economic crisis: You see when you are talking about a financial giant the size of Goldman Sachs, the line between betting that something will happen and making something happen gets blurred very quickly.

Not that Goldman Sachs was the only one betting against the housing market. According to the New York Times, firms like Deutsche Bank and Morgan Stanley also created mortgage-related securities and then bet that they would fail.

See this website for more: http://economiccrisis.us/2010/01/goldman-sachs-tens-billions-dollars-economic-collapse-america

Enter the Federal Reserve

There is no difference from any of the elitists other tactics than that from the undercover banking attacks on the world economy, such as the Federal Reserve is involved in.

To me the agenda explained further on, is destroying our country. The elitists in our government and those outside of government who control it are aggressively accomplishing the collapse of the economy in America. Beginning with the granting of the Fed the control of the monetary systems of all nations is the key to implementing iron-fisted control over the world. Reducing America to a third-world status will make American's more controllable.

The Federal Reserve's contribution to the destruction of our country is dealt with in detail further on, under the title: The Federal Reserve is an unelected Body.

Logistics Must Be Considered

Perhaps it comes down to a question of logistics. Gerald Celente, the CEO of Trends Research Institute, is renowned for his accuracy in predicting future world and economic events

Celente's logistics in the details of the socioeconomic chain of events are tending toward collapse in our country and supported by people like Gerald Celente, who predicted the 1987 stock market crash and the fall of the Soviet

Union

So many other crises may occur, an opinion shared by many as to when, where and to what extent is not clear. Some say months, some say it will be years before our country collapses under the economic pressures; one related event is of course the election of 2012: will it be for a patriot or another puppet?

Tax Code

Absolutely no tax-and-spend ideology will be permitted.I am the patriot which I refer to as our patriot to become president and I will use everything in the arsenal of the president, including standing in the well of the Senate and browbeating those who are still trying to sink our country.

The United States is going to do exactly what every family must do in times of economic crisis—to live within its means.

However, everybody is going to pay their taxes in our patriot administration; the tax code will be simplified to a flat tax displayed in four tiers: five percent for those earning $50,000 per year or less, fifteen percent for those earning above $50,000 to a maximum of $175,000, and twenty percent for those above $175,000 to a maximum of $250,000. All above that bracket will pay a flat twenty five percent, no deductions.

Over many decades, companies have found loopholes as well as ways to lobby for the loopholes, to escape taxes. General Electric, to name only one has spent tens of millions of dollars in lobbyists' fees to push for changes in tax laws for more generous depreciation schedules on jet engines and things like green energy "credits for its wind turbines.

But the most lucrative of these measures allows GE to operate a vast leasing and lending business abroad with profits that face little foreign taxes and no American taxes, as long as the money remains overseas. In the new administration, all business here, as well as those who seek to export to our country, will be subject to the same flat tax rate, period.

Import-Export

If you are from another country and you wish your products sold in America, you are going to pay the flat tax rate. If you are a U.S. company who chooses to manufacture in other countries, you will be subject to the flat tax rate. If you choose to do all of your manufacturing inside the Unite States, your tax rate will be reduced substantially.

If you are a company outside the United States that sells a product to America and your product is determined to be toxic or detrimental in some way to the health of Americans, you will pay all restitution and any such product category manufactured by you will be banned from entry to the United States.

If you are a country that has been found to have stolen intellectual property, you will be banned from sales of that product to America.

If you are a country that wishes to export to the United States and terrorists are found to be from your country or illegal drug drugs are being brought into the United States by your citizens, then your country will pay for the removal, safety, and restabilization of Americans who were harmed by your countrymen. You will have to provide acceptable proof that your country is doing all things necessary and acceptable to the United States to stop terrorist or drug related activity in the United States.

The Federal Reserve is an Unelected Body

The Federal Reserve, while unelected, is an omnipotent, benevolent entity that can print money at will and distribute money to any country, undetected by Americans. The Fed is in one sense, our dictators. What would I be called if I printed money and distributed it undetected? Does counterfeiter come to mind?

The Bilderberg Group, Bilderberg conference, or Bilderberg Club is an annual, unofficial, invitation-only conference of approximately-120 to 140 guests from North America and Western Europe, most of whom are people of influence. About one-third is from government and politics, and two-thirds from finance, industry, labor, education and communications. If you have ever done any research on the New World Order or the Builderbergs (which I refer to collectively as they or their, further on) you may recognize the following: The Fed is an integral part of the their plan for world domination, which in part is responsible for the dumbing down of the average American so that their deceit can remain hidden from public view and so that they can say there is nothing the average American should worry about. In other words: Don't pay any attention to that man behind the curtain; just pay attention to what I am telling you. This is similar to The Wizard of Oz.

They (remember the meaning above of "they") might as well say to you: After all, hasn't our plan of dumbing you and your children down, taken full effect by now?

Do Others Owe You Money?

There are those in our country who have been duped into thinking they are entitled to what others earn. Therefore hard work and integrity are a thing of the past and will be replaced by the belief that government should be the answer to all of life's problems.

True God-loving American patriots are woven from better fabric than the elitists have anticipated, and we will not relinquish our inalienable rights to control our government, nor will we be reduced to serfs again, as we were under the beginning English monarchy so many years earlier, when those governing masters saw themselves as being much better than the peasants.

Enough Is Enough

Without a doubt, true red, white, and blue-blooded Americans—who are in the majority, by the way—have stated that enough is enough and have formed the Tea Party, banding together in their rejection of government control and to our government returning America to a form of monarchy rule.

We cannot let the actions of these true American patriots go without our support. These are Americans who have been awakened, as in the awakening of the sleeping giant in all of us. This is going on today in the Tea Party movement.

We must all become soldiers now and do the right things to take back control of our country and fire the monarchy-style government or what I refer to as billionaire puppets, which are today's politicians who often only line their own pockets.

All of those on the far left, and yes, largely union people, and the minorities who have that entitlement attitude do not care what price America has to pay to accomplish their bidding, no matter what is happening to our country.

A great many Americans want more, but without earning it. They believe the government owes them because, for whatever reason, the government started giving them things, way back there until today, where forty nine percent are on food stamps and receive housing subsidies which has taken away their will to achieve for themselves, as I have pointed out and continue substantiating throughout this book.

Those same entitlement seekers find fault with America because they don't get enough entitlements; unlike the red, white and blue-blooded American patriots who work to build America.

Entitlement seekers blame the government for their problems. At this point in our cultural history, enough people have been misinformed and misled that they are prepared to sell America to whoever offers them the most advantages.

To these people, I suggest visiting any one of the third world countries and see if this is the life you expect to have given to you; I think we all know what that answer would be. And quite possibly, we could transform them into red, white and blue-blooded working Americans who believe in achieving their own success and therefore we would stop drowning our country in debt.

White Americans Voted for the Black Man

Some white Americans who voted for the first black man did so not for his values or business savvy (no one knew about him) or his love for our country (future disappointment); they had no clue if that existed. At the very least it is fair to say they did not read any of Obama's books or review who he surrounds himself with (but that is for you to decide). Some whites voted for Obama to relieve something burdensome or painful that has been implanted in them from those who make a living keeping the past in the present as though we were responsible for the past. Can anyone say Al Sharpton or Jesse Jackson, to name only two?

The liberal media did not do any checking of the past or his legitimacy for the first black man running for President; had they reviewed his or his wife's printed views they may have prevented what was to come. I believe that some whites only thought that this would somehow stop the review of our ancestral past. Many whites, who voted for the first black for the most part, may have been indulging their sense of spiritual purging or cleansing, which will never be accepted as atonement by the racists who make their living on racism. Racist make their living inventing new and improved racist vileness; as long as they can be invited to keep it front and center on television, they can keep making a fortune on the backs of their fellow blacks, who fail to see what is before them.

We got an ACORN political organizer not a well-respected black man. The Association of Community Organizations for Reform Now (ACORN).

Although white or black voters had nothing to do with Colin Powell seeking or choosing not to seek the Whitehouse, had he chosen to seek the presidency with his experience, our country would have been better off for it.

Looking to heal old wounds, in the place of the most respected man in America at the time black or white, Colin Powell, who did not run, we got a community organizer instead, Obama as the first black man to become President. If we had Colin Powell as our choice for that first black man for President he would have blasted Obama out of the picture and it would have changed America alright, but not the change we got from the anointed one (to quote Sean Hannity of Fox News). Instead of being handed a true respected champion, we were handed a community organizer backed by puppet master billionaires, who have an agenda of reducing America to the third-world country status as I have earlier pointed to; we were in such a hurry to vote for the black man, no one wanted to take the time to research him. Shirle Chishom, Jesse Jackson and Al Sharpton were known's and the research was all around when they ran for president and lost but I think because of the un-known we could make up our own past for Obama, after all he could read his teleprompter well.

Chapter 3

Honest, Trustworthy Patriots Did Not Bring us to Where We Are Today

I do not care how far back you care to go, politics has always had money and corruption at its core. I believe that if we install term limits for all in congress, like the presidency has, this will help to bring our country back to the people; less time for politicians to learn to take bribes.

As president I believe we have to make learning and understanding the Constitution of the United States of America a lifetime discipline, for both our school-age children and ourselves in order to pursue understanding of the original intent of the founding fathers in our Republic. I will do whatever I can to get this agenda back in our schools.

I discuss at length the Democracy verse our original Republic in this book and the return to our Republic is my goal. I believe we must stop allowing the Democracy, which is the majorly of elected officials or the appointed judges to determine the framer's meanings. Our Constitution and our Republic insures our rights as Americans, changing the meaning of our Constitution to suit the electorate in charge absent the people's choice would be Anti-American. We must put these ideologies and determinations before the people who will be affected most by the outcome.

Keep in mind that in the United States almost nobody who reads, writes, or does arithmetic well, gets much respect, they are referred to as nerds (a person who is accomplished in science or technical pursuits but is seen to be socially unattractive); so kids would rather be game players and talkers and thanks to the no child left behind that reduced teaching to the weakest student now we are seventieth in the order of world class education in some categories. That well educated people consistently get rewarded has not provided a better school environment, the focus is more on sports and games.

Comparing the American economy's direction toward implosion to a train ride, which is the train that we are now on that is headed over the cliff, although it serves free lunches to those poor entitlement souls; if we don't change train conductors, that gravy-train will be hurled over the cliff and there are no entitlement programs at the bottom. A change in mindset (self achievement over entitlement) at the 2012 election would be a win win for everybody.

Part of this vast amount of entitlement voters are the forty four million food stamp recipients (one out of every seven U.S. citizens or one out of every two households), and this entitlement-prone group of people does not want to see its gravy train end. These people do not like looking outside the train either. Thankfully this group of folks does not always vote. However I am trying to include them by asking them to change their mindset now to self achievement to become part of the win win group.

We Only Want Americans

The left is always playing the race card to keep that part of it's voting bloc focused on the wrong issues. The race card, like an overused credit card, is now rejected.

I plainly state that I need you to stand up and be strong with me. Again I want only those who see themselves as Americans. If your skin color affects your commitment to be a patriotic red, white and blue- blooded American, then sit this out; you are on the other team.

However, no matter what your skin color, if you are a God-loving true American patriot who truly wants to save our country then support our patriot (by now you know that is me) who will be elected president in 2012. It is you I represent and it is you who must help me take our country out of the jaws of these America haters.

We have to see the plot to destroy from within as mentioned and to those patriots who have been on this tilting scale who can see the light outside the train, we welcome you aboard; please bring your own sack lunch, like the rest of us.

I keep reminding people that when you are on your computer, nothing happens until you push the start button. Any one thing may seem small in the context of the massive number of problems that exist, and which we must address, but as many issues that we can start to dismantle at one time, the better off we will be. I mention several of those issues in the base of my platform presented later in my book. We must push that start button and become soldiers.

What Becoming Soldiers Means

Becoming a soldier means to return to our original republic that consists of the proud and the free once more. When you are a soldier, it does not matter what your skin color is; being a soldier just means that you love our country and are willing to make the ultimate sacrifice for it.

It is the soldier, not the reporter, who has insured Americans have the freedom of the press.

It is the soldier, not the poet, who has insured Americans have the freedom of speech.

It is the soldier, not the politician, who ensures our right to life, liberty, property and the pursuit of happiness.

It is the soldier who salutes the flag, who serves beneath the flag, and whose coffin is draped by the flag the same flag that the left has removed from our schools.

Cutting Government Waste

In 2012 when elected president I will close federal departments that are not specified with a federal responsibility in the Constitution, such as the departments of Education, Health, Housing, the Interior, Recreation, and many others that fit this description.

As reported by several news outlets; Federal Judge Jeffrey White rebuked the USDA for its continual approval of new genetically modified seeds produced by a company called Monsanto without proper environmental impact studies; a violation of the National Environmental Policy Act.

The USDA continues to run over the legal system in approving GM products, such as the well-known GM sugar beet and corn crops. The USDAs rationale for its approval seems to be: a GM sugar beet or corn ban might cause sugar and corn prices to rise. I cannot wait for the beginning of this housecleaning, which by default will save small farmers and will improve the health of Americans at the same time.

A probing environmental impact evaluation of roundup-ready sugar beets would most likely not be very harsh, since appointed governmental, none-lected, bureaucrats are in support of the huge Monsanto monopoly. Monsanto would be allowed to do its own studies; which could produce skewed outcomes.

Cross-pollination and roundup resistant super weeds are just a couple of the Monsanto-wrought problems, not to mention the cross-pollination of the GM corn to surrounding farmland.

This is a ridiculous and illegal act that Monsanto is allowed to do by the government: to sue farmers who are the recipients of the bee's crosspollination of their natural corn crops. The bees bring the GM corn pollen over the fence to the farmers natural corn crops, without the farmers knowledge and consent (of course how could you keep a bee from doing that anyway?); which in my view, Monsanto violates the right of the farmer who is trying to grow natural corn.

Like political office seems to be, laws as well seem to be for the highest bidder in our country.

Laws do not seem to be able to be purchased because with more money from a different lobbyist it can be changed so I guess the best words that apply are: laws are rented; so the laws tend to sway in the direction of the large companies with the most money.

As it stands now, Monsanto can take the farmers property if the bees take the pollen from the patented manmade GM corn crops and pollinate the crops of the farmer who is trying to grow natural corn; the farmer must then forfeit his property to Monsanto. This is theft by lobbyist, in my view.

The USDA has obviously circumvented the legal system too many times, such as backing these ridiculous claims by Monsanto. The USDA finally decided some environmental impact studies are in order.

In a seemingly passive-aggressive act of childish defiance, the USDA is allowing the genetically modified organisms (GMO) industry to conduct its own impact studies, unless of course that industry wants to pay third-party researchers to do it (it is the GMO industry's choice) and I don't ever see that happening, because the GMO industry could not control the outcome.

Judge White wants the USDA to better protect the environment, but the USDA is doing the exact opposite in the name of not being too burdensome to the GMO industry. This stinks and it must stop, no matter what. When I get elected in 2012 I will do all things within my power to punish elected and nonelected bureaucrats over agencies that govern others who take something (bribes) in exchange for their favoritisms.

The USDA should and will be dismantled and farmers who have their crops contaminated with genetically modified pollen will have the right to sue the GMO industry for contamination of their natural crops.

Those who are responsible for the genetically altered seeds being planted will be liable, not the organic farmer; plus, we will push for laws to restrict GMO cross-pollination, which would mean that farmers who are growing organic crops would be allowed to actually produce them without contamination or be compensated by the GMO companies, not just those who purchase their seeds for planting. GMOs are banned in several foreign countries today because those foreign countries such as Japan understand the danger they present.

When closing government agencies, as president I will sell the equipment, furniture, vehicles, etc., and have the states be responsible for and profit from the buildings, parks and land contained within their jurisdiction, yet the asset remains federal to help support the value of the dollar.

As president I will remove the federal government from management of resources in each of these areas federally owned in every state completely. It will eliminate the regulators number one (reducing the tax burden and lower the deficit), and the regulations from the funding, so that states have the funding without mandates. They can decide which "entitlements to continue or to cut, depending on their budget. Local political jobs will be at stake if office-holders do not conform to their constituents' wishes and operate within the states means.

As president I will return to free choice in healthcare and not be influenced by the drug manufacturers, which are backed by government bureaucrats such as the FDA. You cannot have a monopoly in the United States without government support and that support will be slanted by those who have the most money. This will be abolished.

We have voted millionaires and billionaires as well as lifelong politicians into office for decades. Why?

We have been voting them into office blindly once they place enough ads on TV. The ones with the most money, who could entertain us the most, got elected, when a Joe the plumber, who actually loves our country, would have been the better and wiser choice. For instance, the Democrats controlled the presidency and both houses for a time, and they passed a healthcare plan against the wishes of the majority of people. Because their vote does not cut any entitlements to their voting bloc, who favors entitlements, it was appreciated by their far-left voting bloc.

However, it infuriates the majority and inflates our daily borrowing from other countries, who are beginning to see themselves as the owners of America and Americans.

We Borrow $3.97 Billion per Day

The $3.97-billion dollars per day borrowing, as outlined in the first chapter, accumulates an insurmountable debt for our children and grand children and will seal the fate for the demise of America. Check out the U.S. National Debt Clock here: http://www.brillig.com/debt_clock/

This mounting debt severely limits your choices, not just in healthcare, but overall. Drugs are at the forefront of this health-care program and absent from it are recognizable natural and preventatives, due to the drug company monopoly, which has driven up healthcare costs in our country for many years.

As reviewed on healthcare.gov http://www.healthcare.gov/law/provisions/preventive/index.html

Prevention as reviewed in the new obamacare are not the same nor are they recognized as preventive in the natural health and wellness industry that does not believe in such things as vaccines or radiation exams. They would be more inclined to use Thermography exams and natural Rejuvenis OSH Silver to fight bacteria and virus. Here is some of what the government healthcare sees as prevention: For example, depending on your age, you may have access at no cost to preventive services such as:

- Blood pressure, diabetes, and cholesterol tests
- Many cancer screenings, including mammograms and colonoscopies
- Counseling on such topics as quitting smoking, losing weight, eating healthfully, treating depression and reducing alcohol use
- Counseling and screening to ensure healthy pregnancies
- Regular well-baby and well-child visits, from birth to age 21

The healthcare system does not allow drug competition from outside of our country, reinforcing the US drug companies' monopoly. Bernie

Sanders, U.S. Senator for Vermont was the only senator to vote against a Food and Drug Administration bill in 2007 and he said he did so because the bill failed to legalize importation of lower-priced drugs. Senator Sanders has cosponsored the Pharmaceutical Market Access and Drug Safety Act (S.1232) which, if passed would allow U.S. licensed pharmacies and drug wholesalers to import these much lower cost drugs and help end the monopoly that has caused the healthcare costs in America to sky rocket. This bill did not pass and did not become law in the 2009-2010 congress.

When government has sunk Americans into an un-repayable debt, a goal the government is pursuing at warp speed, it can then tell the American people that they must give up American assets to foreign countries, as well as American sovereignty to other countries to whom we owe money, because we have no choice.

We then would become slaves or serfs, as we were in the beginning under England, and assume third-world status.

This alone should be empowering to the brave to become soldiers with me and stop this madness now in the 2012 election. An American slang expression fits quite nicely here: "Throw the bums out." We must return to our republic.

Republic versus Democracy

Why do I believe strongly in our republic over democracy?

In short, the difference between a republic and a democracy is that a republic is a political unit governed by a charter, while a democracy is a government whose prevailing force is always that of the majority in power, no matter what the charter represents.

Perhaps one of the difficulties in defining these two words stem from the fact that many people have been lulled to sleep on this subject and consider them to be synonyms, which the terms are not; they are no more alike than an apple and an orange, and yet they are often used interchangeably.

The difference between a republic and a democracy lies in the ultimate source of official power. In the case of a republic, it lies with a charter such as our Constitution. The American Constitution writers in 1787, who we refer to as our founders, focused on limiting the power of government and on the potential danger of the new absolute ruler, Congress, and the power of federal government institutions generally.

This they sought to achieve not only through constitutional provisions and the Bill of Rights, but also through the celebrated checks and balances whereby two houses, and the president as executive, were to exercise discipline and restraint over one another. The judiciary was also put in place to act as a restrictive force; indeed, in earlier times the U.S. Supreme Court has traditionally seen itself as the ultimate discipline over government power and champion of the citizen against government excesses. This un-biasness does not exist today due to the fact that these judges are selected and appointed by who ever happens to be president at the time the position becomes vacant, therefore political influence of the sitting president affects who is nominated as the judge for that vacancy.

This has proven to reduce the judiciary to nothing more than partisanship politics which is why I believe the justices should become elected officials by the people and have term limits.

I believe the founders did not see this potential problem or they would have seen to it that the people had the ultimate choice as to who was replaced as a justice, through the voting process.

As your president 2012 I will do all in my power to remove the political-naming process and replace it with the voting process when a judge seat is vacated.

Plus, as your president I will do all in my power to get term limits installed for both houses of government to a maximum of twelve years, to be served in four-year increments, only after being re-elected in each four-year cycle.

Now for Democracy

In a democracy, power lies with the rule of the majority in power, so government can change overnight. This in my view is why the Democrats want to make it easier for illegals to vote. Illegal Immigrants tend to vote Democrat because Democrats are more willing to let them stay for their vote. For that reason it makes illegal immigration a win for Democrats that can count on the illegal immigrants' vote to help them stay in power.

A recent example of how a political majority can rule without following the wishes of the majority of the American people is when the Democrats shoved the healthcare bill down America's throat. This goes back to that old saying I mentioned, we need to throw the bums out before they ruin life as we have come to know it in what I see to be forced democracy.

As a republic we have certain inalienable rights from our Constitution and Bill of Rights that no elected group should be able to tamper with.

Slowly the progressive's are trying to close the chapter of our republic. The government of the United States that has reduced our citizen rights by transforming our republic into a democracy is a definite government, confined to specified objects. It is not like the state governments or our original republic, where powers are more general. For example charity is not part of the legislative duty of the government in a republic.

They want to convince the public that we should only focus on democracy and they accomplish that with entitlement programs. Progressives have deliberately confused the public into thinking it is the same as saying republic.

The names republican may have originated from those who believe in our republic. The name democrat may have been considered to characterize a person who believes in a democracy form of government. Both parties got lost in the power and money-grabbing attitudes of lifelong politicians, both Republican and Democrat, who simply became puppets for special interest groups that helped them, get elected. Replacing republic with democracy had to be accomplished by giving government hand outs to a voting bloc, which made a centralized view of government where an elected political majority rules, no matter what the majority of Americans wanted, or no matter what their charter which was originally put in place to protect the people states. No protection of the people by their charter from the rule of its elected official's best defines a democracy.

Adding to the confusion is the fact that there are different types of democracies in the world. In a representative democracy, citizens elect people to represent their interests in the government (which is that adapted by a democratic America), even though they may change their perspective once elected. After being elected these representatives (who are suppose to be representing their constituents) determine among themselves how issues are decided (which seems to favor the far-left Democrats in today's America) since the president is a democrat and the democrats control the senate and the Republicans have only control of the house since November 2009. A Democrat monopoly in a democracy form of government represents absolute power, and the popular statement has always been that absolute power corrupts absolutely.

In a republic, people may vote for their representatives but the federal government, as well as the states responsibilities, are limited, insofar as interfering in private lives, because they are clearly bound by a charter that the federal or state government should not enter into or attempt to change in any way, as they are doing so often in our democratic democracy today.

Democracy is failing America, and we can't just blame all of it on the politicians and the corporations. People actually vote for their own self-destruction by electing professional liars to represent them.

At its core, the democratic process of electing representatives is a popularity contest. The voters inevitably end up supporting whichever lawmakers offer the best handouts at the moment, regardless of the long-term consequences to the nation. Voting, in other words, is a contest based on short-term rewards rather than long-term vision. Not surprisingly, when the voters go to the polls, they tend to elect the person who promises them the most right now. "Democracy is the worst form of government", Sir Winston Churchill once said...except for every other form of government. But Mr. Churchill was only exposed to our republic; he did not live in it. Our republic is the best form of governing in the world because of its safe-guards for the people.

Freedom is realized by the willingness of the people to live by the dictates of the charter, which is the Constitution, Bill of Rights and our Declaration of Independence. The Constitution protects the individual's rights, not the federal government's rights. In a republic, the people control the federal and state governments.

The detailed organization of the government for a republic can vary widely and look more like a dictatorship. In most cases, the head of state, as it exists in France for example, is appointed not elected and referred to as the president. I have chosen Wikipedia's description which parallels many I have reviewed, which is the government of the French Republic is a semi-presidential system. In the case of some republics, however, such as Switzerland and San Marino, the head of state is actually a committee of several persons in aggregate.

Republics without a charter can be led by a head of state that retains many characteristics of a dictator or monarchy due to the lack of a specific charter, and in some instances the so called president may rule for the duration of his life.

So the charter is the most important document to decide on in the young republic, and our founding fathers accomplished this beautifully, determining individual's rights and establishing long-term governance by federal and state-elected officials.

The Framers had the greatest minds in the world and created the best documents in the world that gave direction to form the best government, but do you think the framers thought of everything? The answer is certainly no; term limits for an example for all elected officials, which failed to ensure that the people who were elected to government and appointed to the judicial branch as well as leaving out that the judicial branch of government should also be elected by the people and not appointed by the president and confirmed by congress, which would have ensured that all of government remained a body that represents the people.

I believe these oversights have influenced and play an important role in the failing of our governing body, which is reflected in the huge deficits we face today as well as other critical issues.

The first Amendment states: Congress shall make no law respecting an establishment of religion, or prohibiting the free exercise thereof; or abridging the freedom of speech, or of the press; or the right of the people peaceably to assemble, and to petition the government for redress of grievances.

How many of these can you name have been broken with just this sitting president in 2011?

Someone needs to advise the current head of our country of this Amendment. Daryl Hannah was arrested in 2011 outside the White House after refusing police orders to leave a sit-in pro-test by environmentalists. Now whether I agree or disagree with the environmentalists, they have a right to be there.

Nothing will substitute for personal responsibility and will include taking responsibility for whom we elected and recognizing that we are the root cause of our government, good or bad.

I suppose you could say the root cause is lack of participation, or lack of responsibility, or ignorance or partial knowledge or even learned helplessness or maybe you could sum them all up into one word, apathy. But still whose fault is that? Did you vote? Do we allow what we complain and blame the government most about of that which is happening to ourselves, due to apathy? Look in the mirror and ask yourself, whose fault is it? If you voted for Obama then tell yourself that you are now going to become responsible in 2012 and vote him out of office.

Obama is walking a fine line between pretending to care about the republic while in reality; he is trying to rip it to shreds.

Budget Deficits

The Democrats seem to be claiming that the budget deficits are just a ruse that Republicans are making up to turn the country toward conservatism. The Democrats know they are on the Titanic and are sinking fast, so they will stop at nothing to try to stay afloat.

If elected president in 2012 I will support the governor of Wisconsin's effort in 2011 plan to reduce the public employees unions choke hold on job creation in our country. This represents the will of the strong majority of Americans and our free enterprise system. Since union money automatically supports democratic candidates I guess that would leave me out, but since I am going to not be beholden to anyone, their money is not needed. God knows the everyday American does not support a union worker being paid twice or three times what the private sector would receive for the same task in our free enterprise system that is the number one cause of companies fleeing America in 2011. Also costing jobs in our country is the union worker being guaranteed such things as tenure no matter what his performance as well as lifetime pensions and insurance and other benefits completely absent to the private sector. It is this type of over indulgence by union bosses that has caused companies to move to a right-to-work state, as well as to move out of America.

Unions had a job to do when Americans were not educated, unions stood up for the worker. That standing up for the worker fell to the depths of destroying jobs in America, due to money and corruption by those union bosses. American education and our free enterprise system must be rebuilt in each state, so jobs once again begin to come to and stay in America.

Left-wing progressives would be quick to state that the right-to-work states are also called by names like Indonesia, China, Japan, and Korea, where even better deals may be had than in the USA. But they fail to point out that, "Made in America" was once the most sought-after product label in the world and it was the unions that destroyed this by inflating our products by the unions ridicules demands placed on the companies they worked for who were left with no other choice. You or I would not start a company in America where the employee and not free enterprise dictates what companies pay them.

The elimination of some or, at least enough Democrats to make unions irrelevant will mean a thoroughly conservative America in every issue of political governance, so that we can begin job creation and the reversal of the damages the Democrats and unions have caused to date.

This does not mean that because someone hangs out their shingle saying they are Republican that they should automatically win; but this means that every mother's son and daughter running for office will be held accountable from this day forward for their actions, as well as their inactions. As an elected official, your duty toward America and Americans never stops. We will take back our republic that has been devalued and destroyed by the majority rule of the progressive democracy, and government won't get our guns in the interim.

Gun Control

Barack Obama and his band of what I respectfully refer to as ill-chosen team-mates who do not have the best interests of America at heart are playing to the demands of the far-left yet again by trying to establish gun control.

Michael Moore the film producer appeared on MSNBC's Rachel Maddow Show, a program that is as far-left as you can get. Moore expressed his bewilderment as to why the United States is such a violent country and wondered aloud why anyone would want to own a gun. According to Moore, people only own guns because they're racist and afraid of people of color.

Patriots of all colors can only hope he will visit the border states and hopefully take up residence near the border. We believe he could then learn firsthand why we own guns, which is to protect ourselves and our families from those who will have guns no matter what the law states.

Those on the far-left who are in favor of gun control spread propaganda to imply that those who chose to own guns are actually saying that the great United States of America grants them, the free citizens of America, a right to kill other people at will. For those ill-informed folks, I will attempt to educate them in the following manner.

Fundamental Rights

The United States is governed by a set of laws called the Constitution; I referred to it earlier as a charter. The Constitution is a document written by outcasts of England who settled here. It sets forth the nation's fundamental laws; it establishes the form of the national government; and it defines the rights of the American people.

It also lists the aims of the government and the methods of achieving them that were brought about by the Revolutionary War. Remember the first time we the people, the serfs, the peasants, the little people, said enough is enough and threw the tea into that Boston harbor? Or the war for independence is also a good example. When we say enough is enough we mean it.

Chapter 4

Revolutionary War and Independence

After the states won independence in the Revolutionary War (1775–1783), they faced the problems of peacetime government.

Although the states were very different from each other, the founders knew that in order to grow and prosper as well as to make our country safe, the states needed each other.

Delegates from each state met to produce a plan for unity, which was initially submitted to the Second Continental Congress on July 12, 1776.

These men had a big task ahead of them. How was the legislature going to be structured? Some wanted representation to be based on population, which was referred to as the Virginia Plan. Others wanted equal representation; this was called the New Jersey Plan.

Rodger Sherman proposed a legislature with two parts. States would have equal representation in the Senate, although the population of states would determine representation in the House.

After a lot of debate, this Great Compromise was agreed upon. On September 17, 1787, the Constitution of the United States was finally accepted by the delegates.

The second amendment of the U.S. Constitution states: "A well regulated militia, being necessary to the security of a free state, the right of the people to keep and bear arms, shall not be infringed." Of course a well regulated militia is our national guard which is set up to protect Americans from outlaw gangs or dangerous illegal immigrants and the like, but that does not infringe the right of the people to keep and bear arms to protect themselves and their families from those the militia miss, which seem to be quite a number. Does this clear it up for you Mr. Moore?

Just as a side-note, referring to a worst-case scenario, do you think the farmers and ranchers who are left to defend themselves from the Mexican drug cartel and other illegal aliens want to be told they may not own guns?

Again Mr. Moore, we suggest you move down along the border so this will become clearer to you.

We were a sound Republic in the beginning and therefore our rights as guaranteed by the Constitution could not be compromised. But somewhere along the way, the progressives started polluting the minds of Americans, saying that democracy was the same thing as a republic, and slowly began to infringe on the rights of all Americans, due to that democracy shift, where the majority of elected officials rule, no matter what the Constitution states.

More Review of Republic versus Democracy

Perhaps one of the difficulties in defining these two words stems from the fact that many people consider them to be synonyms, as I said earlier. But they are not interchangeable.

The difference between a republic and a democracy lies in the ultimate source of official power. In the case of a republic, it lies with a charter as previously mentioned; in a democracy, power lies with the rule of the elected majority of politicians, so government can change quickly because the majority of politicians rule in a democracy (their decision does not have to represent the will of the people). As a republic, through our charter, we have certain inalienable rights from our charter, charter or Constitutional amendments, as well as the Bill of Rights, the Declaration of Independence and all of which, no group should be able to eliminate.

As stated earlier, slowly the progressive's are closing the chapter of our republic while we remain oblivious to their actions, because they have convinced some of the people that we should only focus on democracy. Slowly changing direction toward this popular ideology that is slowly reforming what we fought to free ourselves from in our past, which was a monarchy.

To remain credible with what I am stating I will put some issues out to consider:

Most of the problems the progressive left has with the Constitution are in the Bill of Rights. The left often claims that the First Amendment erects a wall of separation between church and state, which I for one believe it does no such thing. Christian beliefs were woven in the fabric of the Constitution because our framers were deeply religious.

However expressing some specifics that I see progressives are trying to change, I would look at:

Article I, Section 8 of the Constitution, which is another drawback for progressives that lists 17 specific powers granted to the Congress. Progressives believe that the general welfare of the United States clause, in the first line of section 8, gives Congress power outside of its seventeen enumerated powers and progressives want people to just take their word for it that any power progressives desire over America and Americans is fare game. Section 8 applies only to the day-to-day functioning of the federal government, and not to the citizens of the United States.

The Second Amendment provides the individual citizen of the United States a right to bear arms, which the progressives must abolish if they are to eventually gain total control of Americans.

Progressives on the Supreme Court believe that the Fifth Amendment, specifically the Kelo vs. New London decision, which was a case involving the use of eminent domain to transfer land from one private owner to another to further economic development, declares that private property can be taken for public purpose. What does that mean? Progressives believe that is whatever the government declares it to be. For instance the lower-middle-class riverfront homes that were torn down in New London, Connecticut are long gone due to this decision.

The Ninth and Tenth Amendments says rights are enumerated or in other words, specifically granted to the central government in the Constitution do not deny, or the word the framers used was, disparage, the rights reserved by the people. Powers not specifically delegated to the federal government belong to the individual states and to the people is what the Tenth Amendment is clear about.

The determination of our rights such as (abortion, prayer in school, gun control, land use planning, election laws, etc. are in the hands of the progressive left wing liberal justices who make their determination through the Ninth Amendment. I am for everyone to be engaged in learning the Constitution so atrocities like the removal of our rights cannot be accomplished by the stroke of a pen.

Our Founders very much feared creating a government that had too many aspects of a pure democracy. They feared the destructiveness that a majority might have in trying to make everyone equal and controllable and in the process taking away property, rights of property, and with it our basic freedoms which the founders considered God given Freedoms. There is that word "God" in the Constitution again. The founding fathers very much feared the development of the Robin Hood mentality we are seeing today: soak the rich and give to the poor. It is a democratic drift toward socialism, and final dictatorship.

You recall earlier when I mentioned the book Obama had written, remember in chapter 2 when on page 29 of the book: Dreams For My Father; where he advocates the communal ownership of land and the forced confiscation of privately controlled land, as part of a forced development plan? And on page 30 where he advocates dramatically increasing taxation on the rich even up to the one hundred percent level, arguing that, there is no limit to taxation if the benefits derived from public services by society measure up to the cost in taxation which they have to pay? And on page 33 he advocates price controls on hotels and the tourist industry and he advocates government owned and operated model farms?

With Constitutional education this would be increasingly more difficult for the progressive left wing to accomplish as though they were retuning America to monarchy rule.

Nancy Pelosi is a great example of this return to monarchy attitude: with her now famous statement: "We have to pass the healthcare bill so we can find out what is in it." Implying that you little people should not concern yourself with political matters, just leave them in our capable hands.

In a republic protected by a charter, like our Constitution, people may vote for their representatives on the federal, state and local levels, but as the charter dictates, even the state and local responsibilities are limited from entering into the personal lives of citizens, because they are clearly bound by our charter that the federal government must follow and not enter into as well. Freedom is realized by the willingness of the people to live by the dictates of that charter. We started out doing this from our Founding Fathers which thousands of Americans are providing the evidence of a steady decline, to where government is entering our lives, more and more each day with hundreds of regulatory agencies.

The republic's charter protects the individual's rights and assures these rights may not be changed by the elected federal, state or local officials and certainly not the appointed judiciary.

We must once again adapt the mindset of our brave soldiers. As soldiers we must stop this government encroachment into our daily lives and force the government to return to our charter by banding together and voting for only those patriots who put our country first.

When you say, "I pledge allegiance to the flag of the United States of America and to the republic for which it stands", this does not mean a body of citizens democratically represented. The Founding Fathers, in their infamous wisdom, knew that a democracy would ultimately lead to the same kind of tyranny that the colonies suffered under King George III. No matter how hard the progressive left-wing liberals try to substitute the words, our Framers did not intend our republic to be a democracy. Then the pledge continues: one nation, under God, (no matter how hard the left-wing liberal progressives try to remove God, he keeps showing up even in 1954 (with one nation under God); then the pledge itself (written in 1892) continues– indivisible, with liberty and justice for all." When it comes to our republic I live by the statement from Patrick Henry: Give me liberty or give me death.

Gun Control, Further Debate

Debate not just the Michael Moore interview earlier mentioned but through the years there has been an ongoing debate over the Second Amendment and how it should be interpreted. The issue that is being debated even today is whether the American government has the right to regulate guns. Obama's word for changing our Constitution is modernize; meaning, allowing the government the legitimacy of revising the Second Amendment, claiming that it is outdated and invalid.

Most Americans believe that the amendment should be interpreted to guarantee citizens free access to firearms so as to be able to defend themselves and their families against the criminals who will have and keep guns, despite the interpretation of the Constitution.

For those on the progressive left who state that gun control is necessary to keep guns away from children. I say parents should be aware of their child's violent tendencies if there are any and become responsible once again, which has been part of the fabric of our past.

Responsibility starts with the parents, first around the dinner table instilling family values. Tough love should be rediscovered and implemented in our families, as well as fathers staying in the lives of their children until the children can become productive citizens who are capable of taking care of themselves. Then your job as a parent is completed.

Those for gun control say that some burglaries actually happen with the intent of stealing your legal firearms; therefore the freedom to purchase guns should be curtailed or eliminated.

I state, as do millions of American patriots that criminals would be looking to burglarize anyway and they would not be successful at getting our firearms or anything else for that matter; the reason for this is, that we have our guns to protect our family and property.

If you were being burglarized and you had no gun to protect yourself, your family or your property, then if you lose your life or the life of family member, it becomes your fault for not caring enough for your family and property to choose to protect it by being a gun owner.

Our elected patriot president (that would be me) will ensure that law-abiding Americans will certainly be able to own and use their guns to protect themselves and their family and property.

The Failure of Modern Public Education

One great reference for research is: http://www.multicon- sole.com

Part of the loss of values in our country is in the failed educational system. While critics tend to rely on the three-decades-long decline of the Scholastic Aptitude Test (SAT) to document the dumbing down of American education, it is equally alarming that our performance against the students of other industrialized countries has fallen.

By virtually every measure of achievement, American students lag far behind their counterparts in Asia and Europe, especially in math and science. Moreover, the evidence suggests that American students are falling farther and farther behind, now at seventeenth in the world.

We live in a time of educational crisis linked to an even greater social crisis. Our nation ranks at the bottom of nineteen industrial nations in reading and writing, and at the bottom with arithmetic.

More important in our student population seems to be narcotics. The world's narcotics economy is based upon our consumption of this commodity.

If we didn't buy so many powdered dreams the business would collapse and schools are an important sales outlet. Our teenage suicide rate is the second highest in the world, and suicidal kids are rich kids for the most part, not the poor. Just looking at some of the privileged actors and actresses tells part of that story.

From the progressive point of view, schools are intended to produce, through the application of formulas, formulaic human beings whose behavior can be predicted and controlled so they will grow into adults who can be controlled. For those of you who are not familiar with the word, "progressive," I am certain by reading this book you will get the sense of who progressives really are.

In a national order in which the only successful people are independent, self- reliant, confident, and individualistic, that most have not learned to be so in public schools. Very few believe anymore that scientists are trained in science classes or politicians in civics classes or poets in English classes. The truth is that schools don't really teach anything except how to obey orders.

Because of the progressive movement for the past one hundred years, progressives have be developing a community life policy and government public school teaching agenda that will feed dependency and weakness, to keep them dependent, weak and controllable and thus the public educated mass will stay weak and dependant which by default, will make them irrelevant and more controllable as adults. Therefore, as a result of this process well-schooled people in government supported public schools are taught to be irrelevant.

Most-not all of the public-schooled people tend to do well at selling things like film and razor blades, push paper and talk on telephones, or sit mindlessly before a flickering computer terminal, but insofar as producing a thinking person who learns everyday, which increases productivity and ensures independence, a great many of these human beings are becoming useless; useless to others in a team-working capacity, as well as being useless to themselves and possibly still living at home with parents. I want to make learning the most admired thing on the planet and I will do everything in my power when elected president to cause this to take place. Don't you just love programs like "Are You Smarter Than A Fifth Grader?"

Only those who were protected from the public school system by educating themselves outside of the public school environment and those who were taught by self-sustaining adult parents in spite of their own education in public schools, can learn to truly think for themselves and to become relevant, independent, successful individuals.

Only 40 percent of U.S. high school graduates enroll directly in college, and of those who do, only four in ten finish in four years. Only thirty one percent of college graduates in America are prose-literate, meaning they can read and understand a newspaper.

The traditional government-operated school is not the only way to educate children, and it has clearly proven it is not the best way. If not private schools funded by the students parents then the charter schools are one of the newer alternatives to traditional public schools–they are publicly funded schools with private boards often staffed by idealistic members of the communities they serve. They run on about eighty percent of the budget of a traditional public school, but recent studies show they do a better job of educating children than public schools if you cannot afford private schools.

This is why I believe in privatizing schools and removing the union atmosphere from teaching, where tenure is more important than the teaching talent. Private schools will succeed where teaching merit is allowed to be rewarded the most and the poor productivity from teachers can be panelized by termination. And the people can deal with the absurdities that exist in public schools by choosing not to send their kids there. It is absurd and anti-life to be part of a system that compels you to sit in confinement with people of exactly the same age and social status because of a no child left behind policy.

That system effectively cuts you off from the immense diversity of life, excelled learning ability and the synergy of variety; it cuts you off from your own past and from a far improved future, sealing you in a continuous present; much the same way as an environment of watching television. Everyone loves to hear about the teenager who is enrolling in a particular University due to their educational excellence.

It is absurd and counterproductive to move from cell to cell at the sound of a gong for every day of your natural youth in public schools, in an institution that demands that you only learn to the weakest student's ability. Letting our children excel above their age group to allow them to learn around older students that are at the level of the younger students IQ, creates an atmosphere for everyone to excel.

But keep in mind that in the United States almost nobody who reads writes, or who does arithmetic well, gets the attention of athletes. Academics are viewed as nerdy as I have earlier reviewed. Since athletic skills can provide a route into college for working-class kids, who would not otherwise get in because they are students mostly well below the average ability and not academically motivated and are effectively employed full-time in their sporting careers, they will continue to lack academic skills.

As a result we have devolved to a land of talkers and game players; we pay talkers and game players the most money and admire talkers and game players the most; and so our children talk constantly and their dreams are of being a game player, following the public models on television are extreme.

It is very difficult to teach the basics anymore, because they really aren't basic to the original basics of our society, which we've allowed to devolve with the progressives in control; and the progressives are doing everything in their power to cause America to devolve; starting with education and then our economy.

What Happened to Our Economy Must Never Happen Again

This review is from Rolling stone Politics by Matt Taibbi http://www.rollingstone.com/politics/news/the-people-vs-goldman-sachs-20110511 because it nails it the best in my view: From tech stocks to high gas prices, Goldman Sachs has engineered every major market manipulation since the Great Depression—and they're about to do it again! What you need to know is the big picture: If America is circling the drain, Goldman Sachs has found a way to be that drain via an extremely unfortunate loophole in the system of Western democratic capitalism. American founders never foresaw that in a society governed passively by free markets and free elections that organized illegal greed always defeats disorganized democracy through the bribing of the unelected government regulators. End of review.

I was amazed at: The Rise of American Fascism http://www.rational-revolution.net/articles/rise_of_american_fascism.htm was pointed out in the following:

The Pledge of Allegiance was written in 1892 by Francis Bellamy. The Pledge reinforced the idea of one nation, something important to many after the Civil War. For most of history a salute, such as "Hail Caesar" or "Heil Hitler" was to the leader. Americans took to saluting the flag of the United States; one country, one God, one language and one flag. It seemed to be that all were supportive. But behind the scenes would tell a different story. The nefarious word laissez-faire describes an environment in which transactions between private parties are free from state intervention, including restrictive regulations, taxes, tariffs and enforced monopolies.

As America became more industrialized, laissez-faire practice presented more and problems. Men like J.P. Morgan, John Rockefeller and Andrew Carnegie owned huge shares of America's economy. J.P. Morgan was arguably the most powerful man in the country during the height of his career, with far more influence than even the president of the United States. A small handful of men controlled virtually all of the financial capital in the country to the degree that people realized that in many ways the government was not in charge of the country and this small group of private citizens was in charge. These individuals had no oversight or democratic responsibilities to the people, they were beholden, basically, to no one; similar to the banking institutions, including the Federal Reserve, today.

The bank's unprecedented reach and power has enabled it to turn all of America into a giant pump-and-dump scam; all the money that you're losing is going somewhere, and in both a literal and a figurative sense, places like Goldman Sachs is where it's going.

Goldman positions itself in the middle of a speculative bubble; selling investments that proved to be worthless and all the while hedging those investments so it could capitalize on failures that could occur in the future. End of The Rise of American Fascism review.

Combine this with the fact that I point out in this book where the Fed allowed banks to stop holding ten percent for a cushion on loans they provide to customers, which I refer to as a bank having to have skin in the game in case of a disaster like the savings and loan crisis and without skin in the game you have a recipe for pending disaster.

Cap and Trade

This is a brand-new commodities market where the main commodity to be traded is guaranteed to rise in price over time. The volume of this new market will be upwards of a trillion dollars annually, which is all smoke and mirrors.

Porter Stansberry of Stansberr & Associates Investment research posted on CARE2 http://www.care2.com/news/member/246963792/2700248

In the report Stansberry says debts don't just disappear and bailouts have big consequences. Basically, for many years now, our government has been borrowing so much money, short-term and long term loans that very soon our country will no longer be able to afford even the interest on these loans. As the banking system collapsed in 2008, all of the bad debts were absorbed by the world's governments. For example, when Fannie Mae and Freddie Mac collapsed in the summer of 2008, the U.S. government responded by simply guaranteeing all of their outstanding debt.

Since then these companies have recorded hundreds of billions of losses – all of which were passed along to the government. Yes, you can still get mortgages today. And yes, Freddie and Fannie are still in business. But costs associated with these programs are piling up at the U.S. Treasury – and they are enormously expensive.

These losses and trillions in other private obligations are now the responsibility of the U.S. government. The problem is, even before this crisis, our government was deeply in debt. With each additional commitment we sink further and further into debt... closing in upon the moment that we can simply no longer afford even the interest payments on our obligations. The Congressional Budget Office (CBO) states that a debt default by the U.S. government would be inevitable – were it not for one simple anomaly the one thing that has saved the United States so far, which is our country's unique ability to simply print more money. The U.S. government has one very important weapon to use in this crisis: It is the only debtor in the world who can legally print U.S. dollars. And the U.S. dollar is what's known as "the world's reserve currency." The dollar forms the basis of the world's financial system. It is what banks around the world hold in reserve against their loans.

That is a secret that most politicians don't understand: As things stand now, the U.S. government can't go broke in any ordinary sense of the word because it can simply print dollars to pay for its bad debts. That might sound pretty good at first. Since we can always just print more money, what is there to worry about? America is the only country in the world that doesn't have to pay for its imports in a foreign currency.

Let's say you're a German and you want to buy oil from Saudi Arabia. You can't just pay for your oil in German marks (or the new euro currency), because the oil is priced in dollars. So you have to buy dollars first, and then buy your oil. And that means the value of the German currency is of great importance to the German government. To maintain the value of its currency Germans must produce at least as much as they consume from around the world, otherwise the value of its currency will begin to fall, causing prices to rise and its standard of living to decline. We can consume as much as we want without worrying about acquiring the money to pay for it, because our dollars are accepted everywhere around the word. In short, for decades now, we haven't had to produce anything or export anything to get all the dollars we needed to buy all the oil (and other goods) our country required. All we had to do was borrow the money and, we did loads of it. End of Porter Stansberry's review.

Without a new direction America is headed over the cliff. Help me, (David Tippie) get elected president in 2012 so I can apply the brakes to the speeding train we are all on.

Most Americans do not know the history of our money in America and have ceded all control over their financial futures to an elite international cabal of bankers with another, more sinister agenda. Most Americans gave their financial control to a local broker who has as much concern about investing their money as throwing a pair of dice.

I like what Warren Buffett said about brokers, he said the average person with even remedial skills can beat any performance from a broker. One reason the average person can beat a broker is that the money you are investing is your own money and not someone else's. End of Buffet.

boomantribune.com and msnbc.msn.com continue to have some logical answers on our financial disaster.

Reported on msnbc.com by John Schoen: The dangers of the steady rise in U.S. debt should be alarming after back-to-back warnings from sources such as insiders like Fed chairman Ben Bernanke and others such as Hillary Clinton.

Clinton and investment guru Warren Buffett both stated: Since the country is so far in debt, where is all this money they are talking about spending, coming from?

What does Hillary now think about what she said back then, as she is now part of the Obama program, is not known?

Everyone knows the American debt money is borrowed, but from whom? boomantribune.com and msnbc.msn.com continue to have some logical answers.

The money is borrowed from buyers of treasury securities, which are basically a big batch of IOUs that are auctioned off every three months. As the auction date approaches, the treasury figures out how much it will need to pay off old interest debt plus cover the government's latest round of new over-spending.

When the auction day comes, buyers submit bids in the form of the interest rate they are willing to accept. You can choose to make a competitive bid (you ask for a specific rate) or a non-competitive bid (you agree to accept the average rate of other winning bids).

When all the bids are in, the treasury starts at the bottom, taking the lowest bids until it has collected enough money to cover that round of borrowing and over-spending.

The money flows in from all over the place: from individual investors and corporations, pension funds and foreign governments around the world.

Basically, anyone with a large amount of cash looking for what is believed to be to date a safe place to put it will be a good candidate for holding U.S. treasury debt.

The biggest chunk, however, about twenty five percent of the 2009 $11.5 trillion total, was held by foreign governments. Japan topped the list in 2008 with $644 billion, followed by China ($350 billion), United Kingdom ($239 billion), and oil-exporting countries ($100 billion). These figures are far greater today; and some of these countries may not have our best interest at heart.

Is it true that the Bank of China currency is gaining, while the American dollar continues to fall?

If so, is it even a remote possibility that America will one day be run by foreign governments through the devaluation of the dollar and the removal of the dollar as the accepted international currency?

Or, could it be that the large purchases of American companies and

American land has already been the forerunner to this?

As a sovereign nation, the United States cannot be run by a foreign government short of an invasion and military occupation; but what if we lose sovereignty?

By relying on foreign governments to maintain our standard of living, we take certain risks. Hillary Clinton told CNBC when she was running for president in 2008 that she saw a slow erosion of our economic sovereignty and she singled out China's big holdings of Treasury debt as an example.

I wonder what she thinks now that she is teamed up with Obama who has spent more in a year and a half than all the other presidents combined, dating back to Washington.

Now that we are in a recession and the economy is tanking fast, along with shrinking tax revenues due to companies exiting the country and I have made my point earlier that I believe it is largely due to union labor bosses, we still have to pay the interest on the borrowed money that we have borrowed and that which we are about to borrow.

Uncle Sam still has to the pay interest on what he borrowed and does not get a break from interest, just like you do not get a break on your mortgage payment when you lose your job.

If we keep spending more and more on interest, the federal budget gets squeezed that much harder when the economy eventually stumbles and falls over the cliff, sovereignty is then at risk.

A major reason we can fund our budget and trade deficits is that the United States is still an incredibly wealthy country with lots of stock, bonds, real estate and companies to sell. Who is buying them? For instance Chrysler used to be in this country, now it is in Italy.

Foreigners now earn more on their U.S. investments than Americans do on their investments abroad. America has used up its bank account and turned to a credit card.

If this financial method spells doomsday for a family, can you see it spelling disaster for our country? And, like everyone who gets in hock, the United States will now experience reverse compounding as we pay ever-increasing amounts of interest on interest. No matter how rich you are, borrowing on top of borrowing is not a great long-term financial plan. End of my use of some of the msnbc and boomer review

I believe that, at some point in the future, U.S. workers and voters will find this annual contribution (of interest payment on the debt) so onerous that there will be a severe political backlash which is why in 2012 electing David Tippie a patriot for president is the first step to real financial reform with actions which I point out in this book.

I say vote only patriots into office and throw out the career politicians who have proven to be nothing more than puppets to their true puppet masters; you know who the politicians are, and who their puppet masters are, as well those special interest groups and large campaign contributors whom the political candidate must be beholden to.

The political tide must be turned from the mindset of voting for the millionaire and billionaire who keep America in the mess it is in, to a mindset of being turned to voting for the patriot who has had enough, just like the average Sue and Joe. The enough is enough statement is made, be it by the Tea Party movement all over this country or by the voters this past Novembers (2010) elections.

We are going to return to a stable economy and less government. End of story. I need your help. Get as many people to purchase this book as possible. Go to my website and contact me to volunteer to help build a national organization. But only do it because you love our country and want to help. My website is: http://www.Livelonger123.com

In my research I have read literally hundreds of articles on the world wide web and I do my very best keeping track of each and I even post most or all that I can recall at the end of this book and on my website for your quick review. Here is my understanding of how the Fed colluded with banks and created the financial disaster we are in now which I have studied for this review. My web- site review of these links is located here: http://livelonger123. com/DavidTippie/ president-2012-Credits-page.htm

I pledge to surround myself with extremely knowledgeable people on every subject who can help put the platform stated in this book in action mode. I promise none will be communists or radicals.

It seems that the Chinese are using up their dollar reserves buying goods and services with them, knowing that the value of the dollar is falling and wanting to get rid of as many greenbacks as they can.

Nations are purchasing gold and silver as I have pointed out earlier. The Fed keeps printing money as if it were going out of style. Something is going on that your government does not want you to know about. Very few journalists have written about it and little or nothing has appeared in the mainstream media. The story could be one of major stories of our time.

The Shanghai Cooperation Organization SCO

There is a crisis involving the American dollar and I agree with Porter Stansberry of Stansberry & Associates Investment research on this issue as I earlier stated as well as this analogy from the Burning Platform on this website: http:// www.theburningplatform.com/?p=7637

Western powers have tried to destroy gold as a backing for currencies for many years; Nixon took the United States off the gold standard. Few know what the Shanghai Cooperation Organization (SCO) really is. Few have been listening and few have been interested in what its mission is and what it has been up to. Some of the members are large oil producers and some, like China, are large oil users. Some have very large U.S. dollar surpluses. Some are large commodity and gold and silver buyers. In fact, members are in a great part responsible for driving these prices higher. It is debatable, but I believe there is a conscious foreign country effort to accumulate gold and silver, and dump dollars, and back foreign currencies with gold, crumbling the dollar.

China and Russia are both large gold producers and for a number of years have been buying up domestic gold and silver production, so that it never reaches the market and therefore does not lower market prices.

If anything, the absence of sales tends to push the markets higher. Russia and India are visible buyers as well. Even Iran with its oil surplus recently announced that it had purchased 340 tons of gold.

All of the foreign countries recent gold purchases are very significant as affiliate SCO members, which have access to the present and ultimate direction of the SCO group. You might say that buying gold has been a protective effort to make it less available which shields SCO members. The undercover gold purchase initiative seems, to be a hedge against the problems generated by dollar policies that I believe have been corrupt. Foreign countries are accumulating gold for the past ten years, but particularly over the past few years.

Reagan's Executive Order as Well as Others

One great and enduring gift from our founders' generation was the inclusion of separation of power principles in the United States Constitution.

You can review many who share this view at the Heritage House http: // www.heritage.org or the http://judiciary.house.gov or many others like http: // commdocs.house.gov

Despite the increased public attention focused on executive orders and similar directives, public understanding regarding the legal foundation and proper uses of such presidential decrees is limited. A couple of references that should indicate that executive orders are not-fix-all or do all, period.

Bill Clinton: A legal memorandum prepared for President Bush (43) accuses Bill Clinton of having abused his presidential powers to issue executive orders, many of which are described as illegal, improper or political; too numerous to go into.

Ronald Reagan: Since 1988 in August when Present Reagan signed the Executive Order creating, the Presidents Group on Financial Markets and the subsidiaries that have grown out of that policy, that the treasury won many if not most of the battles.

Reagan's Executive Order started out looking like it was restraining for the Federal Reserve and would serve to thwart the efforts of the Fed, as well as the US policymakers and other central banks in Europe from being able to continue the blatant suppression of gold and silver prices.

The benefactors of this did not surface immediately, except for raids into derivatives and futures, when it came to hedging and risk management of bad deals intentionally made on Wall Street.

The Fed seemed to temporarily lose control and suppression of gold and silver prices. Nefarious financial perversions by the Fed promote the false illusion of strength in the almighty U.S. Dollar an irredeemable flat currency backed by nothing but a financially bankrupt government.

If you doubt that there is an undercurrent trying to destroy American currency with a gold and silver-backed currency, just review the operations of the SCO. It was an intergovernmental international organization founded in Shanghaion June 14, 2001 by six countries, China, Russia, Kazakhstan, Kyrgystan, Tajikistan and Uzbekistan. Its member states cover an area of over thirty million km2, or about three fifths of Eurasia, with a population of 1.455 billion, about a quarter of the world's total population. Its working languages are Chinese and Russian.

It is only a matter of time before appearances of any control will begin to be visible to the public due to this currency manipulation and very rapid exposure may surface if the dollar is replaced as the international currency by a foreign currency that will be backed by gold and silver, which they are purchasing at breakneck speed.

Since1988, when Present Reagan signed the Executive Order creating the President's Group on Financial Markets, the amount of subsidiaries that have grown out of that policy is amazing; basically benefiting the treasury.

So Reagan has some smut on his Executive Order record in my view as well.

While the mainstream financial press generally dismisses these activities by the Fed as conspiracy theories, preferring the romantic notion that free markets really exist, the working group created by Reagan's Executive Order acts in concert with its agents such as J.P. Morgan and Goldman Sachs. This automatically should raise red flags, as the fox is guarding the hen house.

One of the biggest scams played on the American public through Executive Order came by way of Richard Millhouse Nixon. President Richard Nixon revoked a law that stated: The United States of America cannot borrow any money unless it has that amount of gold in storage at Fort Knox to back up the loan. And you know what has taken place since then.

The reason most business people in the world speak at least some English is because the English language and the American dollars are the common business exchange methods of world commerce. A world reserve currency allows international bankers and governments to invoice trade and denominate foreign debt securities in a common currency, that being the U.S. dollar. Not backed by gold any longer mind you.

In simpler terms using Iran as the example, if Iran sells oil to another country, that country buys the Iranian oil using U.S. dollars. Even though the official currency of that country is the rial the official currency of Iran and not the dollar, the two countries still conduct business in U.S. dollars because they trust the value of the U.S. dollar more than they trust the value of the rial. The same would hold true using any other country for the example.

Before 1944, the world reference currency was the British pound sterling. The transition between pound sterling and U.S. dollar in reserves and its impact for central banks was described after World War II, the international financial system was governed by a formal agreement, the Bretton Woods System. Under this system the US dollar was placed deliberately as the anchor with the U.S. government guaranteeing other central banks that those banks could sell their U.S. dollar reserves at a fixed rate for gold. A currency becomes less stable when the economy of the country issuing the currency becomes less dominant and bankers begin to abandon it for a currency issued by a more stable economy.

The victors of World War II formally discouraged the world from using the currency of Germany and Japan in international trade as an additional means of suppressing their obvious former rivals.

After two consecutive world wars had ravaged the economies of Europe and Asia, the dollar was in the right place at the right time to be adopted as the world's reserve currency. Fortunately for America, it has been used as the primary unit of currency in international trade ever since.

Nixon began the destruction of the dollar

On August 15, 1971, when the United States unilaterally terminated the convertibility of the U.S. dollar to gold when Nixon sidestepped Congress and gave an Executive Order without the knowledge or approval of the American people.

For the last forty years, America has been printing backed only by the American taxpayer some say counterfeit money because our money is not backed by anything other than our word and our sovereignty, which is on shaky ground now.

America sends rivers of American dollars to buy the loyalty of other nations. China is one of Americas largest lenders and trading partners, and China is worried America is about to default on its word due to the insurmountable amount of debt we are accumulating.

If the U.S. dollar is abandoned as the world currency, every nation will be holding worthless world currency. When the whole world clamors to turn in

U.S. dollars for something of tangible value, a massive influx of worthless dollars will flood the U.S. economy causing tsunami-like inflation.

The time to address the Federal Reserve is now. We cannot wait to have our currency abandoned. We take drastic actions which I have called out in this book to eliminate our debt and we have to back our dollar once more with silver and take the printing press away from the Fed, just like John Kennedy did. When you consider the Fed's control of the dollar, it is more in line with a centrally planned economy rather than an economy run by free markets. It all boils down to do we support the Constitution?

The SCO states that now they and the public are winning the war for a fair and free gold and silver market, not connected to the USD currency. The current class-action lawsuits, including RICO, are a testament to the market manipulation in silver. The Racketeer Influenced and Corrupt Organizations Act commonly referred to as the RICO Act, or simply RICO is a United States federal law that provides for extended criminal penalties and a civil cause of action.

If the class-action lawsuit is successful, HSBC and JP-Morgan Chase, who are the major owners of the Fed, are going to be finally prohibited from rigging these markets.

Their officers all belong in jail for the catastrophes in our economy which they are responsible for in the majority, but it seems that elitists never go to jail; they pay fines, and keep right on robbing the public.

Speaking of elitists who seem to fit this bill, one name in the news jumps out is John Edwards. Although he is not connected to the Fed, he can stand right up there in front of you and talk about how he has not broken any laws. Kind of reminds me of Bill Clinton shaking his finger at the TV audience. Of course, all is for a judge and jury to decide.

Other SCO members and observers are accumulating gold as well, albeit in smaller amounts. We might add that other nations observing Russia and China and their gold purchases are buying as well.

These participants must believe that there could be a return to sound money; otherwise they would not be gold buyers. Buying gold is preferable by some to holding U.S. dollars at this point in 2011. Dollars have consistently fallen in value versus other currencies over the last ten years.

Chapter 5

Stop Huge Federal Spending

Much of the banking, financial fact checking in this book came from: Wikipedia. com, freerepublic.com please be my guest and do your own as well.

If I am elected president in 2012, we are going to stop the huge federal spending, reduce the size of government, return power to the states to govern private business and people and back our U.S. dollar by silver once the debt is eliminated and return to a STRONG free economy. We will remove the power to print money from the Fed as JFK did, enforce the banking cushion laws where banks must hold a minimum of ten percent of all that they loan, touched on earlier, as well as more further on and if you want to import to our country you will be subject to the same taxes and guidelines as U.S. businesses. Never again will we have the wild irresponsible spending that has come, dangerously close to destroying our country.

Progressives are working toward the destruction of our country to force a New World Order that does not have the United States of America on top. I will not rest until these terrible wrongs are corrected. I like how this subject is treated in the book titled Progressivism by Arthur S. Link and Richard L. Mc-Cormick.

When the Federal Reserve undertook Quantitative Easing (QE) back in November, 2010, which was sending the money printing press in high gear, the Fed began a program for the second round of the its commitment to buy

$600 billion in US Treasury bonds to keep interest rates low and spur economic growth. The program had a designated endpoint of June of 2011.

There is no question that more and higher inflation is on the way and there is no question that spending our way out of a recession has been tried and failed.

Everyone feels the Inflation now in food, petroleum products, and airline fares and in many other items that we use every day. But we are being told by government there is little or no inflation. No one has a crystal ball but Bob Chapman, the international forecaster, whose analyses is usually very good, is the next best thing, who tracks the continuing implosion of the world economy we could be headed for at a much higher inflation than we have in recorded history. Review Mr. Chapman's views here-by-Steve-Beckow:http://stevebeckow.com/2010/11/continuing-implosion-of- the-world-economy

The Fed's artificial deflation by printing money is a ticking time bomb that is actually spreading inflation. If you have wisely invested in gold or silver you may be spared some of the economic destruction which is about to occur.

This is part of my reasoning for running for president in the fashion I am today, with zero dollars. The politician knows if he or she shouts enough thirty second one liner sound bites on television to the voting public promising entitlements that he or she most likely can get elected or stay in office in that district.

History has provided enough proof that career politicians as well as the Fed's promises are not worth the paper that they are NOT written on. I place everything in writing so you the American people can hold my feet to the fire.

The Fed Chairman Ben Bernanke will print money until America has hyper- inflation. Apparently he thinks he has no way out. Many believe that there is no way to stop what the elitists have put deliberately in motion, without a true patriotic leader who is not afraid to take on every issue we could be doomed. Let us place these burdens on the shoulder a solid America loving patriot president in 2012; David Tippie.

The same errors that were committed during the Great Depression of the1930s are being repeated. Do your own research of history, the Great Depression methods did not work. All who research it feel that the Fed contracted money supply will be what hurls America over the cliff and when the Fed starts the printing press of money cannot have a positive effect.

Brazil Got U.S. Money for Offshore Drilling

Next come tariffs, as an outgrowth of currency wars which are interest and dividend penalties on the inflow of hot, inflationary dollars and retaliatory tariffs, as a result of losing 8.7 million jobs and 430,000 businesses over ten years to free trade, globalization, union bosses, off shoring and outsourcing.

Relive for a moment the billions of dollars that Obama gave to Brazil for their deep-well offshore exploration for oil, which he stopped in America. Had he not stopped this in America this would have created 400,000 high-paying jobs for Americans if it was allowed in American waters. I touch on this again in this book.

At the root of all this is that the Fed is supposed to be saving the U.S. economic and financial structure. It is not doing that, they are saving the banking system and Wall Street instead and these are the villains that caused the problem in the first place. The result of their policy of zero interest rates and easy money is that few are saving.

When I use the word villain and not greed, which means the same to me (criminal), it is because the left-wingers have high jacked the word ambition and substituted the word greed.

Ambition as I state, has been hijacked by the left and their union bosses and replaced by a more sinister word (greed). They wallow in their screams about those greedy old companies and those greedy old rich people (who by the way create jobs).

GREED is not the same as AMBITION

Ambition is healthy. You can be ambitious and still feel good about yourself because you are not a criminal and you prosper for your family. If you work harder than the other employees you are not taking advantage of them if you get selected to move up the ladder of success—no matter how hard they demand to be paid the same as you to their union boss.

Ambition is a constructive force. It is part of what defines greatness. It builds character in humans, builds companies, expands the economy, creates jobs, and increases wealth for many others as well as the ambitious themselves. It is the pursuit of an idea or dream, and is driven by the imagination; the success or failure of the ambitious lies mainly in their own energy, strength and ingenuity.

So—why not choose to work harder and achieve more—rather than to demand more without effort?

Planned destruction by Obama is not written but hypothesized. He has a large enough sample size to conclude he has no intention to honor the oath of office as intended by the Framers. Furthermore, if you put his actions in an equation there is no doubt what the results will be.

So when I say there you have it, planned destruction it is after explaining some action or inaction from Obama. Is it any wonder the SCO members and observers are buying gold on every dip and will not stop doing so until they run out of dollars?

To have an impact on this we must have a strong leader, one who is not looking to simply look good while he is reading his teleprompter, just to get reelected, but a sound patriotic leader who loves America and is willing give his all, including his life if need be, to save it from this impending disaster as well as many others I have and still will touch on in this book.

You are reading my platform and you know that we need tough leadership that we certainly do not have now, however I will prove as your patriotic president which I hope you elect in 2012 is that strong leader and I am asking for your assistance in bringing this message to the country and to support my efforts by getting others to purchase this book from my website and on Amazon. You can begin helping by contacting me via my website http://www. LiveLonger123.com to offer your assistance in building a national movement, to help me, David Tippie get elected in 2012 .

The Fed Was Created in 1913

Please be my guest and do your own research of other media I chose this from Wikipedia, The Federal Reserve System (also known as the Federal Reserve, and informally as The Fed) is the central banking system of the United States. It was created in 1913 with the enactment of the Federal Reserve Act, largely in response to a series of financial panics, particularly a severe panic in 1907. Over time, the roles and responsibilities of the Federal Reserve System have expanded and its structure has evolved.

Events such as the Great Depression were major factors leading to changes in the system. Its duties today, according to official Federal Reserve documentation, are to conduct the nation's monetary policy, supervise and regulate banking institutions, maintain the stability of the financial system and provide financial services to depository institutions for the U.S. government, and foreign official institutions.

The Fed's structure is composed of the presidentially appointed Board of Governors (or Federal Reserve Board), the Federal Open Market Committee (FOMC), twelve regional Federal Reserve banks located in major cities throughout the nation, numerous privately owned U.S. member banks and various advisory councils. The FOMC is the committee responsible for setting monetary policy and consists of all seven members of the Board of Governors and the twelve regional bank presidents, though only five bank presidents vote at any given time.

The responsibilities of the central bank are divided into several separate and independent parts, some private and some public. The result is a structure that is considered unique among central banks. It is also unusual in that an entity outside of the central bank, namely the United States Department of the Treasury, creates the currency used.

According to the Board of Governors (http://www.federalreserve.gov) the Federal Reserve is independent within government in that its decisions do not have to be ratified by the president, or anyone else in the executive or legislative branch of government. However, its authority is derived from the U.S. Congress and is subject to congressional oversight, which seems to be sketchy at best.

Additionally, the members of the board of governors, including its chairman and vice-chairman, are chosen by the president and confirmed by Congress. The government also exercises some control over the Federal Reserve by appointing and setting the salaries of the system's highest-level employees. Thus the Federal Reserve has both private and public aspects.

The U.S. government receives all of the systems annual profits, after a statutory dividend of six percent on member banks' capital investment is paid, and an account surplus is maintained.

The Banking Cushion

Here is what I was referring to earlier when I was referring to the banking cushion that must be enforced: Although under current regulations all depository institutions are required to maintain reserves against transaction (checking) deposits, the reality is they don't and this is what our patriot president will enforce. Referencing Prisonplanet.com:

The purpose of bank reserves is to absorb losses and add stability and liquidity to the financial system in times of crisis and this is non-existent, due to the Fed's relaxing the bank regulations.

The vault cash, so to speak, that banks should use to satisfy reserve requirements is useless in absorbing losses because the cash is indispensable for banking operations such as ATM cash. This is not real cash. The savings and loan crisis of the 1980s and 1990s was the failure of 747 out of the 3,234 savings and loan associations in the United States, but because real cash was used as cushion for these associations, and not money from the imagination, the taxpayers were saved.

In summary, today most depository institutions are satisfying their entire reserve requirement with this imitation vault cash, which they hold to meet the liquidity needs of their customers and would hold even in the absence of reserve requirements because of ATM transactions. For these institutions, reserve requirements are effectively non-existent.

How did we get to the point where U.S. banks are satisfying their reserve requirements with ATM cash?

First, the Federal Reserve has cut reserve requirements to the bone over the last thirty years. In 1990, after the savings and loan crisis, the reserve requirement on all non-transaction accounts (savings, CDs, money markets, etc.) was reduced to zero. Removing all reserve requirements on non-checking accounts has never happened in over a hundred years. Meanwhile, the requirement on transaction deposits (checking accounts) is ten percent, which is near the legal minimum.

However, the reduction of reserve requirements by the Fed does not explain how reserve requirement fell below vault cash (less than three percent of a bank's assets). Something more was needed.

Deposit reclassification is an accounting trick used by virtually the entire financial sector that allows banks to eliminate nearly all their reserve requirements. It splits a checking account into two separate sub-accounts, a transaction (checking) sub-account and a non-transaction (savings) sub-account. This distinction only exists on the bank's books: you will never see these sub-accounts on your bank statements.

Deposit reclassification means that, at any point in time, most of the money in American checking accounts sits in invisible savings sub-accounts. These savings sub-accounts pay no interest but allow banks to avoid reserve requirements by making it seem the same as vault cash. The public is completely unaware of this financial engineering.

By using deposit reclassification, the entire financial sector is already operating without any reserve requirements; this is going to come to a halt in my administration.

From the news.goldseek.com website and my analysis: One reasonable restriction on deposit reclassification is that banks must disclose it to their customers. These disclosures could be in the form of a statement stuffer or buried in the terms and conditions when opening a checking account.

As an example of a disclosure about deposit reclassification, Citibank explains how its checking accounts are maintained; For accounting purposes, all Citibank consumer checking accounts (Regular Checking, Citigold Interest Checking, Interest Checking and Basic Banking Account) consist of two sub-accounts; a transaction sub-account, to which all financial transactions are posted; and a holding sub-account into which available balances above a preset level are transferred daily.

Some of my research is from Prisonplanet.com and my analysis, but as always, do your own research:

Funds will be transferred to your transaction sub-account to meet your transactional needs. For Regular Checking and Basic Banking Account, both sub-accounts are non-interest bearing.for Citigold Interest Checking, and Interest Checking for both sub-accounts that pay the same interest rate.

Transfers can occur on any business day. Transfers to the holding sub-account will be made whenever available balances in the transaction sub-account exceed a preset level.

Transfers from the holding sub-account to the transaction sub-account will be made whenever transaction sub-account balances fall below a predetermined level.

Some of my assumptions and research for the bank reporting referred to, from: news.goldseek.com & www.prisonplanet.com

Because banking regulations limit the number of transfers between these types of sub-accounts, all balances in the holding sub-account will be transferred to the transaction sub-account in the sixth transfer in any calendar month.

Both sub-accounts are treated as a single account for purposes of the client's deposits and withdrawals, access and information (i.e. your statements), tax reporting, fees, etc.

JPMorgan, Bank of America, and the rest of the banking sector are also big users of deposit reclassification. Check the terms and conditions of your checking account. Odds are a large percentage has one of these two sub-accounts or what the industry refers to as Frankenstein monstrosities.

In a banking system with no reserve requirements, everything becomes a systematic risk because financial institutions do not have any buffer to absorb losses.

Even the failure of a small bank becomes enough to bring down the entire financial system. The system is not only broken, it is a giant train wreck waiting to happen.

Savings and Loan Crisis 1980s and 1990s

As noted, the savings and loan crisis could have been as destructive as the financial crisis of today, had it not been for the cushion or reserve that was in place at that time.

Realize that the savings and loan crisis of the 1980s and 1990s was absorbed in large part by bank reserves. The buffer provided reserves that helped limit the cost of bailouts to $105 billion to the taxpayer.

Today, no such buffer exists, and the entire brunt of the bank losses are being transferred to the taxpayer; this handout to the banks is not teaching anything except that dishonesty does not need to stop, in fact the banks are receiving taxpayer money to keep on conducting business as usual.

The lack of any reserve requirements helps explain why current bailouts seem so enormous compared with prior banking crisis and why the banks are asking for more.

Is the Fed-Federal Reserve Aware of the Scheme?

I have studied both news.goldseek.com and .Prisonplanet.com and the following is a combination of both as well as some of my observations. I want you to do your own fact checking as well.

It seems that the Federal Reserve is aware and complicit in this scheme. In order for a bank to begin using deposit reclassification, it first has to obtain Federal Reserve's no objection. So this leads me to believe that the Federal Reserve not only knows of the practice, but has also OK'd every single deposit reclassification program. Or, it would seem that someone or some association would be in serious legal trouble.

It seems that the Federal Deposit Insurance Corporation (FDIC) is also aware of the scheme. It has what it calls a Temporary Liquidity Guarantee Program.

Laws requiring banks and other depository institutions to hold a certain fraction of their deposits in reserve in safe, secure assets have been a part of our nation's banking history for many years. It seems that the rationale for these requirements has changed over time, however, as the country's financial system has de-evolved over the years and knowledge about how reserve requirements affect this system has grown. It is very reasonable that it only took time for it to show up as the disaster it is.

It seems that before the establishment of the Federal Reserve System, reserve requirements were thought to help ensure the liquidity of bank notes and deposits, particularly during times of financial strain.

It makes me recall the old movie "It's a Wonderful Life" and the Bailey Brothers Savings and Loan, when they had the run on their savings and loan. Only this savings and loan run referred to would be a million times worse.

As bank runs and financial panics continued periodically to plague the banking system, despite the presence of reserve requirements, it became apparent that these requirements really had limited usefulness if greater and greater risk was entered into, to make money a larger and larger security blanket would be required but instead banking security blanket was nonexistent.

As a guarantor of liquidity, this security blanket would have to be transferred to the taxpayer which would mingle with Wall Street greedy and create fortunes guaranteed by the taxpayer. Remember my explanation of greed and ambition.

Since the creation of the Fed as a lender of last resort, capable of meeting the liquidity needs of the entire banking system (which is a lie), the notion of and need for reserve requirements as a source of liquidity has all but vanished because requiring it restricted wealth building on Wall Street.

Instead, reserve requirements have devolved into a supplemental tool of monetary policy containing the tricks I pointed out earlier, a tool that reinforces the effects of open market operations that take more risk because of it and discount policy on overall monetary and credit conditions are placed squarely on the backs of the taxpayer and thereby helps the Fed to achieve its objectives, which according to my research was to implement the new world order, concealed from the public eye.

According to the Fed, the notion of and need for reserve requirements has all but vanished, because the Federal Reserve stands ready as a lender of last resort, capable of meeting the liquidity needs of the entire banking system.

Whose money is the Fed using when they are in this ready mode? That's right—yours, the taxpayers money; it is absurdity after absurdity.

Did it ever occur to anyone at the Fed that having to prop up "the entire banking system" with liquidity (as it is doing today was not a good idea, that it produces illegal and the very least, crooked risk taking?

Well if you understand and believe the Fed is part of the progressive new world order, then without a doubt you understand the crookedness. The Fed is certainly aware that it puts the taxpayer on the hook without his knowledge or consent.

Why would not the Federal Reserve just lower reserve requirements instead of allowing checking accounts to be turned into make-believe assets and an accounting nightmare?

Because it could not! The Federal Reserve would have needed an act of Congress to lower reserve requirements below eight percent; so the Fed had to be much sneakier about it.

Why did the Federal Reserve bend the rules so far as to allow banks to escape reserve requirements? I think you begin to get the picture.

Continuing with news.goldseek.com "In June 1993 the Federal Reserve Bulletin explains:" Requiring depositories to hold idle, non-interest-bearing balances is essentially like taxing these institutions in an amount equal to the interest they could have earned on these balances in the absence of reserve requirements."

There you go. The Fed allowed the fox to guard the hen house, so to speak. The Fed let reserve requirements become a joke to eliminate the unfair tax on depositories, which encouraged under-the-table dealing with Wall Street. It is a joke to think that the Fed was ever on the ball and had its priorities straight about protecting the American people; it is clear to me that there was a hidden addenda.

When elected I will use the bully pulpit and every tool available to pass a bill officially lowering reserve requirements to zero and make it illegal for banks to re-classify checking and savings accounts. This would end the farce of deposit reclassification (and hopefully deal a wakeup-blow to this industry which has profited by weakening our financial system).

Furthermore, there would be no adverse impact to eliminating reserve requirements of U.S. banks, as they already do not exist.

Then I would begin the slow process of making the banking system become more accountable and solvent again, by slowly increasing banks reserve cushion back to the original ten percent and if need be raise that some, so that the banking institutions could sustain a crisis as did the savings and loan in that crisis and reduce the temptation to collude with anyone, including Wall Street for illegal deals.

Again, I need your support for our organization. So contact me with your views as to how you can help, just as an America loving patriot who is willing to help me.

Socialism is a Share-the-Wealth Program

I believe the website Jeremiahproject.com points out well.

Socialism as practiced by the progressives, as I have referred to in various parts of this book, is in a nutshell a confidence game to get the people to surrender their freedom to an all-powerful collective. As-a-result, through the legislative process, like sheep going to slaughter, Americans are willingly and slowly sacrificing their life, liberty, property and pursuit of happiness in exchange for the false promises of an increasingly powerful socialist state, constructed through political gifts or entitlement programs.

Patriot for President

Do you have to be a billionaire to run for president? Well, if the right people start thinking about who we have been stuck with for the past however many decades, I think they will see how it has worked out for them so far and there will be a chance for the common businessperson who loves his country and who will stand for no more of the driving our-country-over the cliff political actions and inactions of today. Our country's problems will be irreversible without strong leadership; it is time for the Joes and the Sues to be the senators, representatives and yes, to run for and to become elected president of the United States of America.

As a people we have been lulled into thinking a democracy is the same as a republic but as I have pointed out, this is false.

Our Founding Fathers have provided the documents to form a more perfect union and it has been politicians who have discarded our founding documents. I will be our patriotic president who will restore them again and securing the borders will be one of my tasks.

United States' Borders with Mexico

Mexican borders of our great country are not going to be dangerous after I am elected president. I am going to militarize the borders and place the most up-to-date technology in the hands of our military so that it can defend our borders as well as, protect Americans and their property.

Sheriff Joe Arpaio has come under fierce attack for his courageous stand against illegal aliens. I found the best research on this blog site: barracudabrigade.blogspot.com that seemed to coincide with the television news media as well as agreeing with my own convictions which I comingle here.

The Obama Justice Department worked hand-in-hand with the far-left American Civil Liberties Union to bring a lawsuit against Arizona for passing a tough anti-illegal immigration law. It seems that Obama and his far-left Justice Department lawyers are in full collusion with the ACLU to do everything they can, to stop Arizona's bill SB1070 from becoming law. This new law would seem to have strengthened law enforcement's ability to identify, arrest, and detain those who are in this country illegally.

After all, aren't these federal employees supposed to be acting in the best interest of the citizens of the United States? If the Justice Department and the ACLU are on the same side, where does that leave the majority of Americans? The ACLU collaborated with several far-left extremist organizations to file a lawsuit to block Arizona's tough illegal immigration law. But who would have thought these left-wing organizations would be allowed to team up directly with the Department of Justice? See this blog site for more: barracudabrigade. blogspot.com

Yes I believe that Obama must go, along with all of his radical cronies. The Department of Justice has run a civil rights investigation against Sheriff Arpaio for almost two years now. Because Arpaio has taken the lead over the years by enforcing existing state and federal laws against illegal immigration, Sheriff Arpaio has become the target of attack by radical, left-wing, open borders extremists. He has been sued, picketed, burned in effigy and the Reverend Al Sharpton came to Phoenix twice to march on Sheriff Arpaio's headquarters. It seems that some have even gone so far as to call for Arpaios assassination! And, it has been reported that the Mexican drug cartels have put a $1 Million bounty on his head. Do you begin to see my passion for militerizing the borders.

It seems what these extremists really want are politicians who will look the other way, be silent and allow the charade to continue while ignoring the laws of our land. That, I promise, will never happen, if I am elected president.

If elected, I will not back down. I will not surrender to politicians, (as you are seeing today) and criminals and drug dealers are going to be placed under lock and key! And I certainly will not back down to the far-left ACLU or any other organization! The greater problem of illegals which is being ignored by mainstream media will be a priority when I am elected president.

Deporting Illegal Aliens:

There are approximately 11 to 15 million illegal aliens in our country today and every one of them will be deported if I am elected. The time of big controlling government is over, free enterprise will be encouraged and incentivized, entitlements will be de-incentivized and our beloved country will thrive once more where business wants to be located.

Foreign Aid and Star Wars

Foreign aid will come to a screeching halt under my administration. We are going to help our neighbors by becoming strong and prosperous as a nation once more and able to defend our friends and allies, starting at forty-thousand feet, not with boots on the ground in every country's disputes. And as your president I will further this accomplishment by kick-starting the Star Wars technologies begun under Reagan. We must plan for our future protection and not be vulnerable to what the future is likely to bring.

A look back at our history of conflicts in Afghanistan, Iraq, Kosovo, and Vietnam shows that the U.S. military, while formidably powerful, is not as invincible as the media wants you to believe.

The United States could claim victories in the Iraq and Afghanistan wars based on a strategy of carpet bombing (coupled with a complete lack of opposing air defense). In both these wars, the U.S. forces were aided by local guerilla revolutionaries and multinational coalition forces. This is not acceptable to. There would be no actual victors with the nuclear option, only a massive loss of human lives and property so countries like Iran cannot be allowed to gain that technology.

Restarting Star Wars technology would be the key to gathering intelligence and then further training our first strike professional responders to achieve flawless accuracy. The Navy Seals displayed this type of intelligence and response when they killed Osama Ben Laden and all I could say is, we shall very much improve on these obvious assets for the complete protection of America and Americans. I can only guess, but judging from Obama's past performances where if applied to a mathematical equation, would equal disdain and hate for America. For him to allow the Navy Seals to accomplish this and bring death to those Muslim brothers he has talked about in his book must have something to do with a pending movie. I hear there will be a movie released just before 2012 election that will be all about the Seals operation and how great Obama is. If there is such a movie it would strike me as just another arrogant remark to the American public who he views as less intelligent. Does he think we will ever forget him, the man who bumped Gerald Ford up from being last place insofar as presidents go?

The China Syndrome and Politics

The website archive.org was part of my research as well as friends emailing on the subject who lived there.

China and other foreign countries are putting America in the backseat, which is a step down from the status it has always enjoyed the status of the largest producing nation on earth.

China is poised to blow past the United States and become the largest economy in the world, or is it? Economists are projecting that the Chinese economy could be three times larger than the U.S. economy by mid-century. They say that the age of U.S. economic dominance is ending, and most Americans still do not even understand what is happening.

The U.S. companies, as a result of high union labor wages and plush benefits packages moved their manufacturing to other countries. They increased their profit and still sold products to Americans at the same price or less. As a further result the trickle of jobs and factories leaving the country started to become a flood.

I have liberal friends, who may or may not work for something governed like the post office, who say something generally like this: Consider looking at a somewhat bigger picture. What percentage of American jobs sent overseas were union-based jobs here? What percentage was non-union? What do you do with the fact that in 2010, despite grim economic news in almost every sector of the economy, our revered large corporations had their most profitable year ever? Some companies grew as much as twenty percent! This is not simply a matter of organized labor killing jobs; it is a matter of pure, simple greed and expedience on the part of companies. Blaming unions can be convenient. But the name of the game is greed.

Of course, my answer is as always: Free enterprise does not mean guaranteed success nor shall it ever mean restricted profits. Competition regulates pricing for products and education has eliminated the usefulness of unions. The fact that the flood gates of jobs leaving America were opened because of the union bosses and the six figures per year for a job like driving a bus, did not stop other companies from trying to become as profitable as they could and keep up with competition. For anyone to analyze that efforts to be profitable are simply greed, you have never been in business and fought the battles that more often left you unprofitable. When I am elected president I will simplify the tax code, closing all loop holes and companies, foreign and domestic will pay their share of taxes; all of which is outlined in this book. I don't simply state "trust me, with hope and change," it is here for you to read.

As businesses and jobs fled the country, the U.S. tax base just was not as robust as it had been. The entitlement programs that were in trouble when things were better are now headed for a huge train wreck. I have explained how I will deal with the entitlements in this book if I am elected president.

The federal government, state governments and local governments all started borrowing gigantic amounts of cash from the countries we were sending all of our manufacturing jobs to. China in particular really started to emerge as an economic power-house over the last couple of decades. Most Americans did not care where all of the cheap products were being made and they have no idea what effect it has on our country. I suspect some do not care; that attitude of, "I am entitled to something" has removed the plug from the bottom of the ship of which we are all aboard.

Our government seemed to be having fun running up huge amounts of debt, but eventually bills have to be paid.

All of this borrowing has enabled Americans to enjoy the greatest standard of living in the history of the world, but it has been a false prosperity. The American dream was purchased with borrowed money. In the end, it turns out that it was a good deal for the other countries that got our jobs and we got a bad deal. The Chinese economy has grown seven times faster than the US economy in the past decade; but who realizes the money? Do the workers in China realize it, or some other entity?

Good News Bad News for Our Economy

China is a communist country ruled by one party with an iron grip. The China Communist Party (CCP) party bosses appoint the national, regional and local politicians as well as many private company managers since many private companies are ex-state-owned enterprises (SOE).

Corruption in China is prevalent, rampant even down to lower-ranking employees who are robbing and stealing to survive because of the low wages. One good reference is this website: http://sph.berkeley.edu/news/2010/china- town.php

Laws are all but nonexistent in China; a good reference is this: http://clear-harmony.net/articles/200507/27987.html

Since laws are written to support the communist party and easily manipulated by corrupt local communist bosses. Judges are appointed by the local communist boss and few, if any, understand law; and they are easily bribed to do the communist bosses biding. Please go to this website to read some of these China comments: http://www.businessinsider.com/incredible-facts-about-china-2011-1?slop=1

Banks in China are similar in name only with world banks. Local communist cadres dictate to the banks to lend to their pet projects and of course to their friends, who bribe them. This is not to mention their complete lack of transparency.

No one with a brain trusts the communist government's statistics which are manipulated. And that includes the Chinese people, who take every opportunity to come to America. Auditors and their management can be bribed and money extorted from them, so many of the companies listed on their stock exchange have their numbers cooked.

Most Chinese companies carry multiple books, including one set for taxation and another for slush funds and another for hidden losses.

The Chinese share and commodity appreciation has a lot to do with the communists pumping money into the economy by directing the banks to lend. This kind of stimulus cannot continue indefinitely and never works. We are a prime example for this.

If that type of economy is doing well for its people, why is there such a high suicide rate? Inflation is on the rise; food pricing has gone up twenty percent and factories are facing worker shortages; due to the Chinese people exiting to America and other countries as well as to escape government-controlled population, where certain fetus are mandated to be aborted.

A great deal of real estate is not attractive either, because in China when you buy any of the vacant, hundreds of thousands or so houses, in most of the depressed areas, which they refer to as a flat you are just buying bare walls with a front door and no sinks, toilets, cabinets, flooring, etc, so that housing bubble is expected to pop sooner rather than later.

Finally, as I earlier touched on, the male to-female ratio is widening; Shanghai China has a lopsided male-female ratio, which is caused by government- mandated sex-selection abortions, which is worsening and that ratio is now 120 men for every 100 women.

China seems dime. Even those who have the least in America seem to be much better off than the majority in China. Hard work to build your dreams is non-existent in China.

Chapter 6

The Middle Class Has Shrunk in America

In America, the middle class has shrunk and is coming to resemble the new working poor due in part to government intervention into our lives and government creating a negative environment for companies. However Americas' government intervention creating class warfare is still less intrusive than communistic controls, such as those in China are faced with; this new lowered middle class is still better off than the Chinese worker who is wanting to come to America for its freedoms.

I in the past ten years, as noted, American jobs screamed out of the United States at an ever-accelerating rate of speed. While American workers stood in unemployment lines, major corporations escaped the union bosses' grip and their high wages and plush benefit packages and began to offshore and outsource jobs to third world and other countries.

Why?

They could obtain labor for a dollar-an-hour without any benefits; sometimes even less. And the government allowed tax loop holes for corporations even as they left America. A fare and flat stair step tax is the answer, which I point out under "Tax Code."

Illegal's Cost American Jobs

To add insult to injury while, displacing American workers, the meatpacking, chicken processing, paving, construction, hotel, roofing, landscaping and other trades jobs are being handed over or what I like to call it, "in-sourced" to millions of illegal alien workers.

High labor costs and endless union benefits feed into corporate survival instinct which must include profit, or they could not produce jobs, which people simply labeled greed. Put yourself in the place of the company and ask if you would bother to keep the doors open if there was little profit. If the government would not be continuously breaking the law by allowing the illegal aliens to stay in our country, the corporations would not be trained to illegally hire the illegals. Think about it, the optimal word here "illegal". Both government and company are at fault here and it must be dealt with swiftly.

America's huge manufacturing base and ability to sell products to the world diminished with the rising power of corporations to control taxes, tariffs and commodities markets and to keep money offshore to escape tax; the one in the news of late was General Electric, which built its empire on American soil. However, it has become known as the father of outsourcing.

Respected American Companies Go AWOL

Why do you think companies like General Electric do not get caught hiding money offshore? Cleverly pointed out on these websites: http://www.commondreams.org/view/2011/03/25 and http://www.allvoices.com/contributed-news/5551496-corporations-like-ge-and-exxon-pay-no-taxes : because what they do is legal and because they paid enough money into political action committees and other organizations to make sure they gained tax breaks and other benefits from a corrupt Congress.

One of America's largest banks (Bank of America) eliminated 5,000 jobs while outsourcing another 1,250 jobs to India. It hardly seems right to have America in the name. The bank announced it would cut another 12,000 jobs in the next two years. Employees were given severance pay on condition they train their overseas replacements. Have any of you experienced a phone call where you had been directed to call to rectify some problem? And when speaking to the person you found it rather difficult to explain the problem or to get resolution.

American Telephone and Telegraph (AT&T), or what we used to call Ma Bell, which started out being an all-American company, outsourced five hundred customer service jobs to India in 2003, in addition to another 3,000 jobs it outsourced before that date.

Dell Computers employs 3,000 Indians in Bangalore and Hyderabad, India. Sprint cut 21,000 American jobs in 2001 through 2003 and sent those jobs to third world countries. American Flyer, the makers of the little red wagon we all pulled as kids, out-sourced to China. Maytag in Pennsylvania shut its plant while displacing 1,500 workers, and set up shop in Mexico.

The additional savings from outsourcing and moving manufacturing companies are not passed on to customers nor do they get taxed; the bonuses for the CEOs are getting larger, however; I still lay a huge amount of blame on the American union bosses and government regulations as well as tax loop-holes that my flat tax will eliminate if I am elected president.

Is the American Dream Gone?

If the best days of America's working middle class fade in the rearview mirror, to be replaced by emerging foreign countries, you have to ask yourself who in America will have the money to purchase goods or services at any price, when America's middle class slides out the door? It means the American dream drops from achievable for the vast majority in the past, to a simple pipe dream in the present. Granted third-world countries have existed like this for hundreds even thousands of years; but this could never happen in America the land of the free that every country in the world envied. Or could it? Let us you and I refuse to allow this to happen. Let us start electing patriots and stop electing puppets who spend the most money dancing for us on the television screen to get our vote.

Do you agree that if we do not get tough leadership in the Oval Office and rid ourselves of the politics as usual in Congress that breeds corruption, the only thing we can hope for is total anarchy in the streets of these foreign countries, who oppress their people to a sub-human class, far beneath the lowest class in America; which may somehow give new status to the USA's poor. Who knows? Let's push the start button and make change happen.

Giving people something that is taken from another is not the answer because it destroys ambition. Just look at what is taking place in Greece. Greece ran out of people and other countries to take from and the people who were the receivers did not like that and are rioting in the streets.

Reagan Year Thinking

Researched from: the website: theconservativepost.com who cleverly points out along with my conception: What we must get back to in America is the thinking that occurred during the Reagan years. When President Reagan entered office in 1981, he faced a much worse set of economic problems than Obama faced in 2009. Three worsening recessions starting in 1969 were about to culminate in the worst of all in 1981 and 1982.

Unemployment was soaring into double digits at a peak of 10.8 percent At the same time America suffered roaring double-digit inflation, with the consumer price index (CPI) registering at 11.3 percent in 1979 and 13.5 percent in 1980 (twenty percent in two years).

The Washington establishment at the time argued that this inflation was now endemic to the American economy, and could not be stopped, at least not without an enormous economic collapse.

All of the above was accompanied by double-digit interest rates, with the prime rate peaking at an incredible 21.5 percent in 1980. The poverty rate began to climb in 1978, eventually growing by an astounding thirty three percent, from 11.4 percent. A fall in real median family income that began in 1978 snowballed to a decline of almost ten percent by 1982. In addition, from 1968 to 1982, the Dow Jones industrial average lost seventy percent of its real value, reflecting an overall collapse of stocks.

President Reagan campaigned on a well-articulated four-point economic program to reverse this slow-motion collapse of the American economy:

1. Cut tax rates to restore incentives for economic growth, which was implemented first with a reduction in the top income tax rate of seventy percent down to fifty percent, and then a twenty five percent across-the- board reduction in income tax rates for everyone. The 1986 tax reform then reduced tax rates further, leaving just two rates, twenty eight percent and fifteen percent. This you will note is similar to what I have suggested will be implemented in my outline under "Tax Code".

2. Spending reductions, including a $31 billion cut in spending in 1981, close to five percent of the federal budget then, or the equivalent of about $175 billion in spending cuts for the year today; in constant dollars, non-defense discretionary spending declined by 14.4 percent from 1981 to 1982 and by 16.8 percent from 1981 to 1983.

3. Moreover, in constant dollars, this non-defense discretionary spending never returned to its 1981 level for the rest of Reagan's two terms! Even with the Reagan defense buildup called Star Wars, which won the Cold War without firing a shot. You will note that the Star Wars project will be restarted as I have pointed out in my platform if elected president later.

   Total federal spending declined from a high of 23.5 percent of gross domestic product (GDP) in 1983 to 21.3 percent in 1988 to 21.2 percent in 1989. That is a real reduction in the size of government relative to the economy of ten percent.

4. Anti-inflation monetary policy restraining money supply growth, (stopping the Fed's printing press) compared with demand, to maintain a stronger, more stable dollar value is the answer.

5. Deregulation, (getting government out of the private lives of Americans) which saved consumers an estimated $100 billion per year in lower prices. Reagan's first Executive Order, in fact, eliminated price controls on oil. Natural gas production soared and was aided by a strong dollar so the price of oil declined by more than 50 percent.

These economic policies amounted to the most successful economic experiment in world history.

The Reagan recovery started in official records in November 1982, and lasted ninety-two months without a recession until July 1990, when the tax increases of the 1990 budget deal killed it. This set a new record for the longest peacetime expansion ever.

During this seven-year recovery, the economy grew by almost one-third, the equivalent of adding the entire economy of West Germany, the third-largest in the world at the time, to the U.S. economy.

In 1984 alone, real economic growth boomed by 6.8 percent the highest in fifty years. Nearly twenty million new jobs were created during the recovery, increasing U.S. civilian employment by almost twenty percent. Unemployment fell to 5.3 percent by 1989.

The shocking rise in inflation during the Nixon and Carter years was reversed. Astoundingly, inflation from 1980 was reduced by more than half by1982, to 6.2 percent.

It was cut in half again for 1983, to 3.2 percent, never to be heard from again until recently. The contractual tight-money policies needed to kill this inflation inexorably created the steep recession of 1981 to 1982, which is why Reagan did not suffer politically catastrophic blame for that recession.

Real per-capita disposable income increased by eighteen percent from1982 to 1989, meaning the American standard of living increased by almost twenty percent in just seven years. Meaning more people can afford to buy products. The poverty rate declined every year from 1984 to 1989, dropping by one-sixth from its peak. The stock market more than tripled in value from 1980 to 1990, a larger increase than in any previous decade.

In the book The End of Prosperity by supply-side guru Art Laffer and Wall Street Journal chief financial writer Steve Moore, the authors point out that this Reagan recovery grew into a twenty-five-year boom, with just slight interruptions by shallow, short recessions in 1990 and 2001. They wrote: "We call this period, 1982 to 2007, the twenty-five year boom, the greatest period of wealth creation in the history of the planet. In 1980, the net worth, assets minus liabilities of all U.S. households and business, was $25 trillion in today's dollars. By 2007, net worth was just shy of $57 trillion. Adjusting for inflation, more wealth was created in America in the twenty-five year boom than in the previous two hundred years."

What Is So Striking About Obamanomics as Compared to Reaganomics

My comments as well this website theacru.org website very astutely pointed out that what is so striking about Obamanomics, is how it so doggedly pursues the opposite of every one of the planks of Reaganomics.

Instead of reducing tax rates, Obama is committed to raising the top tax rates of virtually every major federal tax of the job creators. As already enacted into current law, in 2013 the top two income tax rates will rise by nearly twenty percent counting as well Obama's proposed deduction phase-outs. Everyone who understands taxes and is in business knows that all expenses including taxes get passed along to the consumer.

The capital gains tax rate will soar by nearly sixty percent, counting the new Obamacare taxes going into effect that year. The total tax rate on corporate dividends would increase by nearly three times. Obama's administration has lulled the public to sleep by stating that the corporations should pay their fair share. Well excuse me, that payment burden will always be passed back to the consumer. We have to wake up to see this for what it is, the Obama administration can be better describes as the guy behind the curtain in the Wizard of Oz who when discovered simply closes the curtain and states: "pay no attention to the man behind the curtain".

The man behind that curtain will increase Medicare payroll tax by sixty- two percent for the nation's job creators and investors. The death tax rate would go back up to fifty-five percent. In Obama's 2012 budget and in his recent national budget speech, he proposes still more tax increases. Do you recall on page 30 of Obama's book "Dreams for My Father" where Obama advocated dramatically increasing taxation on the rich even up to the one hundred percent level, arguing that there is no limit to taxation if the benefits derived from public services by society measure up to the cost in taxation which they have to pay.

Instead of coming into office with spending cuts, Obama's first act was a nearly $1 trillion stimulus bill. As if to say he could care less where the money would come from. In his first two years in office he has already increased federal spending by twenty-eight percent, and his 2012 budget proposes to increase federal spending by another fifty-seven percent by 2021.

His monetary policy is just the opposite Regan's as well. Instead of restraining the money supply to match money demand for a stable dollar, slaying an historic inflation, we have, as referred to earlier, QE1 and QE2 and a steadily collapsing dollar which are arguably creating a historic re-inflation.

And instead of deregulation we have across-the-board re-regulation, from health care to finance to energy, and elsewhere; new agencies are created on the backs of taxpayers and borrowed money to check activities of other federal agencies.

While Reagan used to say that his energy policy was to "un-leash the private sector, Obama's energy policy can be described as precisely the opposite, to leash the private sector in servitude to Obama's central planning, which embraces and dictates green energy; such as government subsidies for private-sector green energy projects, special tax incentives for green energy projects and low-interest government-backed loans for green energy projects however a fourth area of control is where the government has a mandate. This is where it can simply issue regulations and do market transformation. This is referring to authority the Department of Energy has under the Energy Policy and Conservation Act of 1975 as amended by the Energy Policy and Conservation Act of 2005. That law gives the DOE the power to set efficiency standards for energy-consuming products. This is not to mention the cap and trade tax that Obama is supporting that will destroy jobs right along with the destruction of companies.

As a result, while the Reagan recovery averaged 7.1 percent economic growth over the first seven quarters, the Obama recovery has produced less than half that at 2.8 percent, with huge spending and with the last quarter at a dismal 1.8 percent.

After seven quarters of the Reagan recovery, unemployment had fallen 3.3 percentage points from its peak to 7.5 percent, with only eighteen percent unemployed long-term for twenty-seven weeks or more. After seven quarters of the Obama recovery, unemployment had fallen only 1.3 percentage points from its peak, with a postwar record forty-five percent long-term unemployed. Unemployment rose to nine percent and above in 2011.

Previously the average recession since World War II lasted ten months, with the longest at sixteen months. Yet today, forty months after the last recession started, unemployment is still nine percent plus, with America suffering the longest period of unemployment that high since the Great Depression.

According to the Forums.catholic.com website, America should be enjoying the second year of a roaring economic recovery by now, especially since, historically, the worse the down-turn is, the stronger the recovery. Not true in the Obama administration.

Yet while in the Reagan recovery the economy soared past the previous GDP peak after six months, in the Obama recovery that hasn't happened for three years. In 2010 the U.S. Census Bureau reported that the total number of Americans in poverty in 2009 was the highest in the fifty-one years that the bureau has been recording the data. By the way, adding workers to the tax-funded bureau were jobs Obama bragged about creating. Spawning once again his total disregard as to where the money is coming from that he is redistributing.

Moreover, the Reagan recovery was achieved while taming a historic inflation, for a period that continued for more than twenty-five years. By contrast, the less-than-half-hearted Obama recovery seems to be recreating inflation, with the latest Producer Price Index data showing double-digit inflation again, and the latest consumer price index (CPI) growing already half as much.

The Worst Recovery Since the Great Depression

This websitehttp://theconservativepost.com/WordPress/?p=3380 and Economist John Lott have rightly talked about the Reagan verses Obama economic, for the last couple of years, Obama keeps claiming that the recession from the Great Depression created the worst economy. But this is not correct. This we are suffering today is the worst 'recovery' since the Great Depression.

However, the Reagan recovery took off once the tax rate cuts were fully phased in. Similarly, the full results of Obama-nomics will not be in until his historic, comprehensive tax rate increases of 2013 become effective, which only adds fuel to the already raging fire.

While the Reagan Recovery kicked off an historic twenty-five year economic boom, will the opposite policies from the Obama-nomics, once fully phased in, kick off twenty-five-years of economic stagnation and collapse of the economy, unless reversed?

Progressivism Helped Create Problem

Progressive, good or bad, my thoughts as well as I liked how the website jeremiahproject.com described it.

Progressive is one of those words that certainly sound like it should be a good thing, right? I mean, who does not want progress? The issue, however, is this: what are we progressing toward in progressivism? What was the connection between progressivism and socialism? What are some of the critical connections between progressivism and what is going on in our country today? Are there attempts to destroy the Constitution?

Living Constitution

I appreciate speaking of it from research one research website ChooseAmericanow.com:

The term living Constitution comes from the progressives. From the beginning the progressives wanted government to take on whatever role and scope that they saw times demanded.

Progressives detested the bedrock principles of American government and free enterprise. Progressives detested the Declaration of Independence, which enshrines the protection of individual natural rights (like property) as the unchangeable purpose of government; refer back to Obama's book "Dreams for My Father" to page 29 Obama advocated the communal ownership of land and the forced confiscation of privately controlled land, as part of a forced development plan. Certainly Obama fits the definition of progressivism.

Progressives detest the Constitution, which places permanent limits on the scope of government and is structured in a way that makes the extension of national power beyond its original purpose very difficult for them.

Practicing progressivism was all about moving beyond the principles of our founders, which the progressives refer to as progress. This is why the progressives were the first generation of Americans to openly denounce our founding documents.

Woodrow Wilson, for example who was a progressive, that I researched and by websites like http://volusia912.org/html/progressive_assault.html and http://www.glennbeck.com/content/articles/article/198/23936/ once warned that 'if you want to understand the real Declaration of Independence, do not repeat the preface" – i.e. that part of the Declaration that talks about securing individual natural rights, as the only legitimate purpose of government. In other words progressives see the government having the right to become involved in every portion of your daily life and that it knows best. Not at all as the founders declared, which was that government's duty is for the protection of America, Americans and their property.

And Theodore Roosevelt was certainly at the core of progressivism. When using the federal government to take over private businesses during the 1902 coal strike, Roosevelt is reported to have remarked, "To hell with the Constitution when people want coal!" This remark may be of questionable authenticity, but it is a fair representation of how Roosevelt viewed these matters.

Disregard the Constitution

The research is good in several websites on these issues but glennbeck.com pulls it together nicely. Progressives want to disregard the Constitution in order to enlarge vastly the scope of government. As a practical matter, how was this to be done?

It happened in a variety of ways, but principal among them was a fundamental change in the American presidency. Under the system of our founders, government was to have sufficient strength and energy to accomplish its ends, but those ends were strictly limited by the Constitution.

The principal way in which the Constitution keeps the government within its boundaries is through the separation of powers. The Federalists were originally those forces in favor of the ratification of the U.S. Constitution and were typified by a desire to establish a strong central government. As readers of The Federalist and of Thomas Jefferson know, the point of separation of powers is to keep any one set of hands from wielding all of the power in national government.

The progressives, especially Woodrow Wilson, hated the separation of powers for this reason: It made government inefficient in his eyes and made it difficult, if not impossible, to expand the power of government so that it could take on all of the new tasks that progressives had in mind. So they looked to the presidency as a way of getting around this obstacle.

From glenbeck.com he talked about The Progressive Assault on the American Constitution by Ronald J. Pestritto, Ph.D. Under the original system, the president seemed to be merely the leader of a single branch, or part of the government, and thus could not provide leadership of the government as a whole. In his book Constitutional Government, Wilson urged that "leadership and control must be lodged somewhere." Wilson pointed out, that the president was the only person who could claim to speak for the people as a whole, and thus Wilson believed the president should rise above the separation of powers—to consider himself not merely as chief of a single branch of government, but as the popular leader of the whole of national politics.

Wilson even contrasted the constitutional aspect of the presidency, its constitutionally defined role as chief of one of the three co-equal branches of government to the political function of the president, where he could use his connection to public opinion as a tool for moving all of the branches of government in the direction called for by the president, only it was disguised by stating that it was to be called for by the people.

It was in this way that Wilson believed the original intention of the separation of powers system could be circumvented, and the enhanced presidency could be a means of energizing the kind of active national government that the progressive agenda required, such as appointing people without the knowledge of Congress or approval to oversee and make political decisions concerning American lives. Does the Obama administration begin to come into view?

Socialism and Progressives

The Glen Beck website http://www.glennbeck.com/content/articles/article/198/23936/

On this issue I found knowledgeable: Since the Progressives had such a limitless view of state power, and since they wanted to downplay the founders' emphasis on individual rights, it is only natural to ask if they subscribed to socialism. There are several things to consider in answering this question.

First, when considering the relationship of progressivism to socialism, we must be clear that we are talking about the similarity in the philosophy of government; we are not suggesting that America's progressives were the kind of moral monsters that we see in the history of some socialist or fascist regimes al-though the case can be made that their racial views, particularly those of Woodrow Wilson, were indeed morally reprehensible.

Second, we must also bear in mind that there was an actual socialist movement during the earlier progressive era, and prominent progressives such as Wilson and Theodore Roosevelt were critics of it. In fact, Wilson and Roosevelt both ran against a socialist candidate in the 1912 election, Eugene Debs.

The progressives were ambivalent about the socialist movement of their day not so much because they disagreed with it in principle, but because the

American socialist movement was a movement of the lower classes. The beginning progressives were elitists; they looked down their noses at the socialists, considering them a kind of rabble.

Keeping these points in mind, it is nonetheless the case that the progressive conception of government closely coincided with the socialist conception.

Both progressivism and socialism champion the prerogatives of the state over the prerogatives of the individual.

Woodrow Wilson, Socialism and Democracy

Wilson himself made this connection very plain in a revealing essay he wrote in 1887 called Socialism and Democracy. Wilson begins this essay by defining socialism, explaining that it stands for unfettered state power, which trumps any notion of individual rights. It proposes that all idea of a limitation of public authority by individual rights be put out of view, Wilson wrote, and that no line can be drawn between private and public affairs that the State may not cross at will. Think about that for a second, no line can be drawn between private and public affairs that the state may not cross at will. This means no part of your life can be sacred and only under your care and your decision powers. Every day we are becoming more and more wards of the state. Ward of the state is a term that usually refers to children without parents who are under age eighteen.

After laying out this definition of socialism, Wilson explains that he finds nothing wrong with it in principle, since it was merely the logical extension of genuine democratic theory. It gives all power to the people, in their collective capacity, to carry out their will through the exercise of elected governmental power, unlimited by any undemocratic idea such as individual rights. What he failed to point out is that giving this amount of power to elected officials is a breeding ground for corruption.

In fundamental theory socialism and democracy are almost if not quite one and the same. They both rest at bottom upon the absolute right of the community through elected officials to determine its own destiny and that of its members. Limits of wisdom (meaning controlling the ideology and level of academia in public schools to ensure continued control over society) and convenience (government regulation into every part of American life), to the public control (serfdom revisited seemed acceptable in his view), Wilson finalizes that there may be limits of principle, but upon my strict analysis, there are none.

Roosevelt and Individual Rights

As this website http://www.glennbeck.com/content/articles/article/198/23936/ so aptly put it: Roosevelt argued as well for a new conception of government, where individual natural rights would no longer serve as a principled boundary that the state was prohibited from crossing. Again (wards of the state attitude).

He called it his New Nationalism program for the state to take an active role in effecting economic equality by way of superintending the use of private property. Did Obama read this before writing Dreams of My Father? You decide when referencing page 29 of Obama's book.

Roosevelt seems to have said that private property rights, which had been serving as a brake on the more aggressive progressive policy proposals, were to be respected. In other words, your land was not your land if the government so decides.

Roosevelt is said to have argued only insofar as the government's approval of the property's social usefulness. Roosevelt wrote: "We grudge no man a fortune in civil life if it is honorably obtained and well used." So this could mean that if the government determines It would be better served by the community then the man has no right to the property. This is what is being advocated in today's progressive arena. What is yours is only yours if we say so.

Roosevelt's writings mention that we should permit it to be gained only so long as the gaining represents benefit to the community.

This implies a policy of a far more active governmental interference with social and economic conditions in this country than we have yet had, but Roosevelt says," I think we have got to face the fact that such an increase in governmental control is now necessary."

We don't want these behind-the-curtain folks, running our country. Just keep in mind the Wizard of Oz when you listen to them on television; for this is the type of loony thinking being used as commonplace in today's government. The government knows best for the little people and their property, even dead people, ie; the return of the proposed fifty five percent death tax

There are important and suspicious connections between America's earlier progressive-era leaders and the leaders creating crisis we are facing today, and it is useful to consider these connections on two levels.

The first connection is at a general level, and that concerns our abandonment of our Constitution. The present crisis did not appear out of nowhere, and did not simply begin with the election of Barack Obama, although it did shift into high gear.

Politicians of both parties spent the better part of the twentieth century disregarding the Constitution, as they looked to have government step up to solve every conceivable human problem. Thus it ought to be no surprise that the Constitution's limits on government aren't even part of the conversation today, as our politicians debate the new interventions and regulations in our economy and society that seem to come daily by way of further expanding government.

The state of things today would have greatly pleased America's original progressives. Those progressives believed that the role of government should be determined not by our Constitution, but by whatever the needs determined by the elected officials for the current day to be. This is why they sought to eradicate the Constitution from our political discourse; today, that goal seems to have been realized. This is one of the strongest messages I can send to you the voting public; vote for the patriot not the puppet.

Non-elected Bureaucratic Agencies

The second connection between the earlier progressive era and our situation today has to do with policy. The progressives knew that our original system of government was not designed to handle all of the new tasks it had in mind for it. So they envisioned sidestepping the voting public as well as Congress by creating a vast set of bureaucratic agencies.

They argued that Congress should enact very broad and intentionally vague laws for supervising more and more facets of the American lives, economy and society as a whole, and then delegate to the bureaucratic agencies, paid for on the backs of the taxpayer, the power and discretion to enact specific policies governing people, product and property without the knowledge and consent of the people. I suggest that to get a feel for vague law which I referred to earlier, that you review this website: ricochet.com. Laws today are so sloppily written that many people truly don't know if they have run afoul of the law until after a judge or jury decides that they have.

Both Woodrow Wilson and Theodore Roosevelt Conceived of Government in This Way.

The New Deal certainly went a long way toward implementing this progressive vision, and what we have seen in our own situation with the Troubled Asset

Relief Program (TARP) and the various other interventions at the cost of the taxpayer are simply greater steps toward the progressive plan.

Our Congress has simply said to the treasury agencies: here is a trillion dollars; here is all the legal authority you need, now go out and determine what is in the public interest, then spend and regulate accordingly. That is the progressive vision of government, in a nutshell.

Daily we are reminded we have choices about most of the things in our lives but we refuse to pay attention to them before they are taken. How sad it is that we have lost our way so completely, that we put everything in the hands of our elected officials. It would seem as though we have given up and just accept whoever rises to the top of the two-party system. We complain and grumble from time to time but we lack the substance that our forefathers had to make changes, or as I refer to many times, to push that start button.

We need to regain our direction and purpose which we were given by heritage. We were born and raised to become adults in the greatest country on the planet and yet what got Americans here is slipping through our fingers like the sands in an hourglass.

Each American is a descendant of immigrants who came to this country to make a new life and to escape oppression. Yet will allow oppression back into our lives without a fight. Our immigrant forefathers endured the odds, hostilities, nature, and the perils of disease but in each case, they not only survived, they prospered. That greatness is buried deep within every American and it must be released once more in order for America to survive. I want to awaken that sleeping giant in all of the voting public and ask you to stop voting for the guy who can amass the most money who dances to any tune to get elected. I don't see patriot when I see Obama I see a puppet that has puppet masters who pay his way, and have a hidden agenda and it does not include our Constitutional rights.

I see no greatness in the candidates for 2012 and must ask for your support as your patriotic candidate, which you are being introduced to since you have allowed me into your living room with this book. Not only will I defeat the puppets for the billionaires with your support I will do it with a zero budget. This will be a step toward our return to our heritage.

Can you imagine when this method takes off that average patriotic business people, the Joes and Sues of America who are you and me and the people next door that we begin to trust and vote for, by default the special interest groups and lobbyists will become extinct?

Chapter 7

2012 Presidency

I don't see any of the front runners for the 2012 race as being willing or capable of doing all that is necessary to salvage our great country. This is the main reason I have placed my name David Tippie in the hat, as a write-in candidate for president in 2012; because I am a United States of America loving patriot who will run on those patriotic values which I have placed in print so as not to be misinterpreted or misstated by my opponents or media, I won't spend millions of dollars on television ads, I come to you in this book with the hope that you are a patriot just like me who will do everything within your power to help me get elected. I won't just represent you, I am you and I am the beginning of the patriot movement, not business-as-usual politics.

We have too much of the politics as usual in Washington and in Congress and we need the change that I am writing about, not change as in wait until I am elected, then I'll tell you what change means, as in Obama's case.

Everyone has stated that you must spend millions of dollars to get the American people to vote for you, because the face on television is simply how Americans vote. I know differently because I know the intelligence that exists in our voting population you will not be fooled or flimflammed any longer.

That is where I want the first change. I want you to see me as the patriot that I am, which is just like you, who loves this country and believes that this country deserves that and needs it so desperately right now and not just a puppet for billionaires. So invite me to your functions, get people to read this book; push that start button somehow.

I can do all things through Christ who strengthens me. (Philippians 4:13) But I do not turn the other cheek to my enemy; my savior will forgive me for protecting my family, which are my fellow Americans.

David Tippie's Platform Details

Please review and keep in mind, when reading all that I have talked about, as well as the following that I want your thoughts, approval-or-dissent, on what I have presented. Americans who come together are the most powerful force on earth; leading to the famous statement: United we stand, divided we fall.

Better Than Medicare and Medicaid

Although health is not an entitlement, because it is up to you to choose that lifestyle that will dictate your health. You should be able to elect natural prevention or pharmaceutical medicine. Each state and city can make decisions about medical pharmaceutical healthcare that could follow these examples.

Hospitals for Each County

I have a plan that will eliminate government-funded Medicare, Medicaid and the outlandish health care system Obama and his team has enacted. This system still provides assistance without destroying work ethic. It restores pride in people who once thought everything was due to them through entitlement programs they did not have to work and pay for. Like illegal aliens for example, it is not politically correct to ask them if they are illegal aliens and then not treat them in hospitals, so they wind up costing the taxpayer. Some of my ideas are listed further on; first I must touch on religion, because like not asking if an illegal alien is an illegal alien, religious political correctness can hinder progress as well.

Religion

I believe that you should be allowed to practice your religion, as long as it is not a form of government. If you believe your religion should be how you are governed over and above ours, you will be escorted out of our country. Islam for example has become a new protected class in our society, due to the left wingers who are forcing political correctness, as well as the institutions of our society who are bending over backwards to accommodate them so as to show their intent is not to show prejudice; it is more of Islamophobia rather than respect or disrespect. I have defined political correctness as being the object of widespread ridicule, usually a powerful weapon used skillfully in today's world. Used as a tool rather than a specific set of political positions. This is nonsense because we are justified in criticizing hazardous or reckless behavior, no matter what religion, race, color or creed has been associated with it. Facts should not be suppressed to keep from offending but yet it is commonplace today. The truth should not be suppressed because it might cause harm or embarrassment or hurt someone's feelings. Today we only need a political activist to tell Americans something is out of line, for every media to start tiptoeing around the word, issue or subject. This is hog wash and anti- American. You come to our country; you live with our value system and laws; End of story.

Islam was created by a man who grew up in a pagan culture 600 years after Jesus Christ walked the earth fulfilled Jewish prophecy and set in motion the Christian church age that is loved, admired and respected around the world. All love thy neighbor as we love ourselves.

However the minority radical Islam preaches the killing of Jews and Christians and most definitely seeks world conquest by force. Anyone who thinks a radical Islamic culture wants to live in harmony with a non-Islamic culture (infidels) is flat-out ill-informed.

Under the radical Islamic concept of Al-Takkeya, it is legitimate for Muslims to lie, cheat, murder, deceive and otherwise violate non-Muslims.

According to Takkeya, radical Muslims are sanctioned to communicate with fake sincerity. In reality, they may have just the opposite agenda in their hearts. It is clear that radical Islam permits lying at anytime and anywhere to promote the cause of radical Islam.

To debate whether Islam is a religion is moot! The reason I believe, as well as others, that radical Islam is a way of governing, is how they themselves view their religion. There are millions of Muslims in the world who are peaceful, law- abiding citizens; however there are also the radicals who must be removed before they cause harm. You can review an Islamic form of governing, sharia law here, you decide how relevant it is: http://en.wikipedia.org/wiki/Sharia

If we let radicals go un-checked, this country could fall to radical Islam's governance, such as sharia law for example. Then the radicals, just like in some European countries, will slowly take over. Under my administration if you immigrate to America you will pass a polygraph test stating you do not wish any harm to come to America or Americans. Since polygraph testing has been proven to not be absolute, any action which you create or join, which is determined to harm America, at that point you will be treated as a Radical

Radicals here now or who slip through the entry process will be tracked down and will be deported even if they are citizens of America. If crimes are committed or planned and discovered, the perpetrators and those who assisted will be tried for treason in a military court, even if they are citizen from birth or have become American citizens, and be held liable for any punishment, including death. If they are deported they are never to be allowed back into the United States.

Instant visas to enter our country will be a thing of the past.

Obama, with an Islamic father and stepfather has praised the extraordinary contributions of the Muslim-American community, and how they have been woven into the fabric of our nation, in a seamless fashion, which is mentioned here: http://www.rense.com/general88/mus11.htm

My research on all these Islamic issues is with newswithviews.com website, and usatoday.com The declaration of Muslims have woven into the fabric of our nation may have seemed a bit premature while 2009 surfaced, with Muslim honor killings in many states in the United States of America. Reported by various news outlets and police allege the latest honor killing was that of Noor Almaleki, 20, who died November second after she and her boyfriend's mother were run over in a Peoria, Arizona parking lot. Honor killings by Muslims average five thousand a year in Islamic countries and now with nine million Muslims in the USA, does the rise in honor killings coincide with Islamic immigrants?

The practice of so-called honor killings are perfectly legal in the Middle East via sharia law, which allows fathers or sons to kill wives, daughters and sisters for what they call disgracing the family for such things as wearing western style jeans or being too Westernized. You can review some of this information on many websites such as: http://www.rense.com/general88/mus11.htm

Also a website to review the Fort Dix Muslims http://www.aina.org/articles/mi21ca.jsp

Obama's pronouncement that Muslims are weaving into the fabric of our American culture appears drastically unrealistic considering the Fort Dix Six Muslims who planned to shoot as many U.S. Army soldiers as possible. In Michigan, Muslims engaged in a shootout with FBI agents, as the Muslims attempted to bring sharia law and a new Islamic order to the Wolverine state.

Additionally, states like Colorado created new laws to stop Islamic female genital mutilations.

Media Matters http://mediamatters.org/mmtv/200810140003 reported that "It certainly is a fact that not all Muslims are terrorists but it seems to be fact that all terrorists are Muslims".

Now I don't know how factual that is but I do remember Bobby Kennedy being shot to death in 1968? Who was Sirhan Sirhan, the assassin? Where did he come from? The origins of the Muslims assassins trace back to just before the First Crusade around 1080. The First Crusade was a pretty hostile action against Muslims.

I do remember the assassin John Allen Muhammad, executed for his crimes, snipered a dozen people from the trunk of his car in the Washington, DC area several years ago.

Then there is the U.S. Army officer Nidal Hasan, who killed thirteen and wounded twenty-eight in a shooting spree in 2009. He is awaiting military trial. Another Muslim was an army sergeant Hasan Akbar who threw a grenade into a tent of American army officers at the beginning of the Iraq war.

As your president I will start a mission that will subscribe to reporting suspicious activity of your fellow soldiers and fellow citizens, no matter what faith they happen to be when you see it, and that will no doubt be helping to protect America and Americans, which is the oath soldiers take and the one I shall take.

The stark fact remains that many Muslims in America have not woven 'seamlessly' into the American way of life. Some refuse to learn English, enclave in places like Detroit and build mosques that lend money and support for jihad. The FBI closed down four mosques in the New York area as a result of money laundering to al-Qaeda.

Which brings the burning question: Can Muslims Make Good Americans?

An unknown writer sent this question to a friend who had worked in Saudi Arabia for twenty years, and it is fair to read it through and decide for yourself. The following is his reply to the above question, Can Muslims make good Americans:

"Theologically? No, because Muslim allegiance is to Allah, the moon god of Arabia. Religiously? No, because no other religion is accepted by his Allah except Islam. Scripturally? No, because his allegiance is to the five pillars of Islam and the Quran (Koran). Geographically? No, because his allegiance is to Mecca, to which he turns in prayer five times a day. Socially? No, because his allegiance to Islam forbids him to make friends with Christians or Jews. Politically? No, because he must submit to the mullahs (spiritual leaders) who teach annihilation of Israel and the destruction of infidels, or unbelievers. America is seen as the-great Satan."

Under my watch as your president, I will make it clear that if you have disdain for America and Americans, you will not only be required to leave, you will be forced to leave.

Family values and Christianity along with the word "God" will return from our heritage and will not try to co-exist quietly any longer, just to remain (see my earlier definition of these two words) "Politically Correct" just to satisfy those who make a living getting interviewed about someone's perceived political incorrectness.

An Un-born Child

An un-born child is a human non-the-less that has a right to become a living breathing productive person. Un-expected pregnancies do not create trash to discard. I have a personal friend who has baked this into my brain, by just being himself. His mother told him she made every attempt to abort him, because she did not want a baby (at that time assistance for abortion was difficult to find). He is one of the finest men I know. Whatever is necessary to prevent abortions will be pursued if I am your president.

Schools Need to Return to Christian Values and Be Allowed To Express Them

Family values and prayer will return to our schools and honor will be bestowed on good grades and not on how well you can hit, bounce, kick, throw or catch a ball as is the case today.

Tenure for teachers will disappear and be replaced by those individuals who can and will teach our students to excel to their highest goals. Those teachers who choose not to do so will be terminated. Not as in Arnold Schwarzenegger's terminator-just fired. If I had not made that distinction I could envision some far left extremist making the wrong interpretation.

Constitution and Christianity

We are a Christian nation and we will not hide in the shadows any longer trying to be politically correct. If a belief in a God isn't baked into our Constitution in words, it is because in the days of our founders, that belief in God was an integral component of the culture, and woven into the very fabric of the people.

God was not an ingredient in the baking of the Constitution; the Constitution was baked as a result of that belief.

Specific Platform Issues

Each issue is important and must have experts in each of those prospective fields to analyze them for their merit and agree or give their objections, as well as their remedy.

1. Political: It seems that the thoughts of most Americans are consumed with the thought that someone else is responsible for them and constantly look to others for answers and try to find a likely person to blame for all transgressions that they suffer. It seems as though a spell has been cast over America and many walk in the fog of that ignorance, believing that government is always the answer to their problems.

It is time to regain our senses and deliver ourselves from those transgressions. If I am elected president, government will be limited in your everyday life. Americans are free to make good choices or bad choices and to live with either one without a bail-out attitude, and that goes for business as well; bailouts will cease to exist and free enterprise will once again determine success or failure.

2. Economist's: Review an immediate answer for the short term and then deliver a plan for the long term to reduce and eventually eliminate Social Security from government handling which will be privatized and not affect those on the program or those at a minimum age of fifty.

Medicare and Medicaid and government insurance will be replaced by private insurance that is allowed to compete across state lines and the county hospitals referred to later in item number 3. The programs will be paid for and governed by the local government and patient insurance companies, explained in item number-3.

For the short term, 500,000 below-poverty-level Americans would be offered a chance to earn an $80,000 401k for their retirement with personal contributions. The plan would consist of the following: Everyone at poverty-level or below, and at age sixty-five or older not receiving social security, or those with medical conditions preventing them from ever working again would be offered assisted living and the assisted living would be awarded the 401k money for four years of care.

At the four-year mark an additional appropriations plan for that group would be established only if it could be pre-paid within the means of local government, with minor assistance from the federal level as a last resort.

Everyone else at or below the poverty level who is capable of working would be entitled to the program provided they receive training for job placement; utilizing the training programs that are now offered.

After graduating they must continuously hold that job. They must contribute a minimum of twenty five dollars per week to the 401-k starting within one year of graduating from their training.

There will be no government funded living facilities or living subsidies for anything including food subsidies, farm subsidies or any other. Section-8 housing would be eliminated.

The funds to pay for this program will be provided from debate in Congress but must be within the means of current taxation, or as to what might be cut that is funded now, which would pay for this fund.

Social Security will not be affected by Americans fifty or older. Elected politicians will be entitled to the public dole until they die, in or out of office, not the special treatment they have now where Social Security was not a concern for them. If you have been paying Social Security taxes for fifty years and it should happen to be cut off because our country is broke, due to the spending from those career politicians, then they simply don't collect, period. So consider me as your candidate for president.

Social Security payments from millions of Americans were supposed to be safely tucked away in an interest bearing account for decades, until it was their time to retire. That was the deal they agreed to pay into. Now you find that it was the old bait and switch routine.

The career politicians decided to raid the account and give the Social Security money over to those who they said were more entitled to your money (the general slush fund that purchased the bridges to nowhere projects and the thousands of others) which in return got them votes, thus bankrupting the system and turning Social Security into a Ponzi scheme that would have made Bernie Madoff proud.

Fear Guilt and Racism

Now, in order for Social Security to be good for anyone in the age range to receive it, it must be moved farther out from age sixty-five toward the seventy-year mark for those younger than fifty. Using the system as it is now. Social Security as well as many other issues, is deadly serious and it is a joke to hear any of this played out in the media because all reporting on any subject boils down to fear, guilt and racism.

The news media personalities are entertainers who are paid to keep your attention, are not necessarily informed. But they get paid a lot of money because of advertisers. Millions of dollars a year they are paid to work you over with their media rhetoric and get you juiced up with the big three that stir the greatest emotions, which are, fear, guilt, and racism, fear guilt and racism, which is the far-left method of election or re-election.

So please don't make your decisions based on these folks and get ready for Obama's use of the race card to get re-elected, because remember he already has a billion dollars to campaign on. Which reminds me, look up his major contributor will you? Who is that you might ask? George Soros, I would say.

I would ask you to consider that if a person who works his entire life and pays into the Social Security system that a patriotic political belief should be that this may be this person's sole source of income. Social Security in this instance will be their very livelihood at retirement. They labored to pay into Social Security all of their life and to say it is some sort of mass generosity by the government is a criminal way of thinking in my view.

So when you hear the liberal left-wing news media spouting off that Republicans want to take that away, consider the source please. We conservatives are not going to let Social Security fail no matter what. This has nothing to do with entitlement mentality which I have outlined in this book, you paid for Social Security.

Removing Social Security would be the same as a bait and switch scheme, tricking you into buying into the S.S. scheme all of your life and when you grow old enough to collect it then the left-wingers say republicans say you are trying to milk the tax-payer if you try to collect it. We are a family in our country, meaning Americans who love our country. And I will not stand for illegal aliens to tap into it which is only one small reason why I am going to deport every one of them.

There is no middle ground between people who think Social Security is a government handout and reality. To keep our integrity as Americans, we should and will honor Social Security benefits and we will keep our end of the deal for the seniors who have paid for it all of their lives.

Career incompetent politicians spent American Social Security and tax-payer money so recklessly behind the backs of Americans and just kept on spending, even after they ran out of taxpayer money with borrowed money.

The reason was that they developed their own credit card and got other countries to be their creditors on the backs of a guarantee from the American people, which was theft by government that Americans were not made aware of.

After all, career politicians see the American people as the little peo-ple, who do not require being told about political decisions. Now the politi-cians are coming to the American taxpayers, after they have borrowed so much money on their credit card that it will surely destroy America and say that they need more money to pay for just the interest on the debt they have accumulated behind our backs and that they intend to continue their spending habits and creating new government agencies until Armaged-don.

Insofar as Social Security is concerned, the first thing the politicians say is that old people are greedy if they do not let you take their Social Security away from them to spend on the pet projects.

I say we are going to cut all right, but not Social Security. We are going to cut the hundreds of un-elected bureaucratic government agencies paid for on the backs of the taxpayers that are not directly given a mandate by our Constitution and return to physical responsibility. Redundant and wasteful gov-ernment bureaucracies are nothing but tax burdens. Taxes are not user fees and they are involuntary, so you're paying regardless of what you receive and regardless of whether they are worth it.

We are going to cut the lifelong dole to the career politicians and insist that they survive on the same programs set out for the average little people retirees, simply return to being a patriot because you represent patriots. This way we can rest assured politicians will not destroy it like they did when they threw the Social Security funds in with the federal slush funds. It did not con-cern them then.

The reason we can eliminate federally supported Medicare and Medicaid is that medical pharmaceutical health care, just like politics will become local once more and open to free enterprise.

3. Hospital: All insurances that are now forced to be carried, by county hospitals and doctors which are legal-and-liability Insurance will be

eliminated, which will play a part in not having federally supported Medicare and Medicaid.

No attorney representing any case related to hospitals or staff would be entitled to any of a jury-decided settlement claim, within a ceiling and the state and county would pay the prosecution and defense attorney fee and attorneys would bid on that representation, low bid to win.

Any physician causing death to a patient would not be allowed to practice further, provided guilt of negligence was proven and the court issued a judgment.

The next step would be down from the pre-determined death benefit monetary reward received by any family for other complications caused by doctors or staff at those hospitals.

No doctor may practice after he has been found guilty of causing two lesser improperly performed procedures where guilt was found and a judgment was awarded to the patient or family.

No doctor or hospital would be required to purchase insurance of any kind as stated earlier and any judgment awarded to any patient would be paid through the county-appropriated fund for the hospitals. That fund will be defined and paid for by each county with sales and state tax as well. The amount of free enterprise instilled in these hospital settings will be phenomenal, which will include the purchase of medication across American boundaries which will seriously reduce the cost of prescriptions and treatment. So it is not simply a change in the name of the bureaucracy and this will set up extremely lowered costs for everything. Insurance companies will be able to cross state lines further reducing the cost to the population that would not be eligible for originally set up Medicare or Medicaid that is canceled. If any of you have been visited by your provider for Medicare and Medicaid and saw what it was billing the government for, you will have no problem understanding that any regular insurance company beats these prices considerably plus there is less chance for fraudulent billing.

Any county not having a hospital will automatically pay into the fund for the hospitals surrounding that county in adjacent counties for their elderly population who would have had Medicare and Medicaid.

Hospital Staffing:

Medical experts: Continued from item three above. Medical professors and/or experts will formulate flat–fee based hospitals.

Hospitals will be controlled by the county in which they are located so the voting public will have its say and nothing remotely viewed as socialism can get started. These hospitals will pay the scale to the staff according to free enterprise and their experience (and doctors or staff will never develop tenure) so any bad performance will net termination and not protection due to tenure which would attract the best talent who can also teach, which would inspire promotion from within. Starting from the medical chief of staff and going down.

The chief of staff title would receive a yearly salary that would equal the industry standard per year, provided every member of the staff, (under him) treated every patient properly and in a timely manner with minimal to no fatal mistakes; and that the hospital environment was kept clean and free from illness or disease-causing pathogens. More people die from disease received from a hospital environment itself than of the disease they came for treatment of. You can see something about this here: http://emedicine.medscape.com/article/967022- over-view. Perhaps someone is familiar with Methicillin-resistant Staphy- lococcus aureus, or (MRSA)?

So this problem will by default disappear.

There would be a monetary penalty for dereliction of duty, up to and including termination of any staff member, including the chief of staff.

An environment of productivity would be rewarded and dereliction would be penalized. The county would collect the cash payments for treatment and collect payments from the insurance companies of the patients not of retirement age. Retirees must be residents of that county or of a county that is paying the county they are receiving treatment in. This could generate an environment of profitability for the county.

Since I will have deported illegal aliens no illegal aliens will receive free treatment; in fact the hospital will be required to report them to the proper authority for deportation should they come to the hospital.

The hospital would purchase any needed prescription drugs at the very best price wholesale, including purchasing from across borders if needed for best price. They will also keep stock on hand and the drug would be free to the retiree, not the patient having insurance for treatment only and the hospital would be penalized for excessive treatment or violating drug dispensing rules.

This would create an atmosphere of not over-prescribing medication or over-prescribing testing methods or un-required treatment of any type, but certainly would have it available.

The county would oversee the efficiency of the chief of staff and would hold the chief of staff and all staff members accountable, for such things as causing death through dereliction or to have been suspected of dispensing drugs illegally or any other offense that they are now protected from lawsuit for and are not required to hold insurance in defense. The county would investigate any suspect dealings the hospital was connected to or suspected of and would remove any person or persons creating or contributing to conflicting activity.

This would place those county politicians who were not diligent in their handling of taxpayer monies at risk of being voted out of office. They would also need to be diligent in the collection of cash and insurance money as well as the contributions from surrounding counties that had no hospital of their own. The state-elected officials would determine the fee amount paid by the counties who did not have hospitals so that no hospital would be flooded with non-contributing county patients; all would be issued cards for entry. However with proper insurance no card would be necessary.

This would bring back the old statement that all politics is local and if the voting public saw any activity it did not like, it could certainly replace its politicians. These politicians will appoint the qualified board to oversee and the public will be advised to bring complaints to the board. This pubic intervention will transform the hospital of today, which is basically watching its own hen house so to speak, into a clean, producing health environment, to be trusted.

There-would-be-no-need-for-federal-government-health-assisted programs all will be eliminated.

4. Accountants: A team of accountants will be assembled to examine people and companies who outsource jobs at a rate of zero to ten percent outside the United States. These people and companies will all be taxed as indicated here-in with the reference to "Tax Code."

All other companies who outsource more than ten percent will not be allowed to the same tax code and will have an increase.

Any company outsourcing more than ten percent showing no taxable income will pay a flat fee of twenty-five percent of its gross.

A family unit consisting of one male eighteen or older who is his own sole provider and does not live with any other person will pay no income tax up to $30,000 per year provided he (or she) has not fathered or mothered a child or children.

A women or man who has had a child or children out of wedlock will pay no income taxes up to $30,000 per year and will be required to set up a weekly pay, five percent of what they earn into a 401k account inaccessible to anyone except the child, and only then when the child reaches eighteen years of age and he is using it for university tuition; or when he reaches the age of sixty-five.

5. Military Experts: Americans have a military that is so down-sized, spread so thin, and ill-supplied and ill-trained that soldiers are sent into battle without enough proper mechanical devices such as armed drones, lead unmanned vehicles for surveillance, and body armor. Soldiers are expected to perform tasks they have not been trained to carry out. Some of that can be researched here: http://www.globalsecurity. org/military/library/report/call/call_95-11_ctc1-01.htm

America has the most advanced robotic technology on earth and yet we have not produced lead vehicles to provide reconnaissance on the ground or air that can guarantee safe passage for the troops that follow. Yet America announces the ability to retrieve rocks from faraway planets.

I am in favor of militarizing the Mexican border and will begin that task with the removal of all troops from all foreign countries. You might say militarizing the American border with Mexico and deporting illegal aliens, as well as those who hate America, is job one.

I am in favor of improving our defense systems to Regan-era Star Wars status. Our technology will once again aspire to be that of the greatest superpower on earth, able to retaliate with the push of a button and from many miles above the earth or from a ship.

I am in favor of turning off the money faucet to all foreign countries regarding their defense. They will certainly understand that we must heal our country first, to become strong once more. The world needs America to be the strongest nation on the planet. Not weak, petty and broken.

6. Social Economic Professors and Majors will be assembled: To discover and initiate ways to answer the-Hate that has been brewing between cultures in the United States which makes a breeding ground possible for outsiders who wish all Americans harm. Outsiders can take advantage of the disparity and play one against the other through all methods, including monetary.

It is time to reinstate prayer and the Pledge of Allegiance in our schools, as well as with the following:

To rebuild a society that is strong at our core again, with morals, scruples, and values that all may choose to adopt but not be dictated to. We must once again pay attention to our surroundings and be diligent about reporting hatred and criminal activity just as I will ask our soldiers to do in protecting our country. When you see something suspicious there is no penalty if you do not report it; but please be a patriot and do report it.

Also the Federal Communications Commission (FCC) will no longer be the dictator of American morality, it will be downsized or eliminated; nor will the FDA be the limiter to our health-choices to the favor of drug companies, which it firmly represents today. The FDA will be downsized and returned to supporting the people and not the drug companies.

If smut is present, then Americans will advise their families accordingly and take morality back into the home and around the dinner table.

If a family chooses to take natural substances and not to take synthetic substances, no elected or appointed bureaucrats will limit their choices. The fat police will cease to exist. The responsibility for a family's morals and health begins with each parent; and when the parents are unwilling to take aggressive action with their child who breaks the law, aggressive legal action will be levied against them, which will build an environment of greater family intervention and provide a way to limit legal intervention.

7. Scientists/Political Experts will be Assembled: Americans will correct the biggest injustice ever created in the world.

America has been led by minority billionaire families, not only in our country but abroad to this point. That world billionaire brotherhood has created and presented strange bedfellows, which has not surprisingly provided opportunity for the same privileged few.

This shrewd group realizes that a nation in debt can be controlled and convinced that to pay off debt; we must surrender our assets and our sovereignty to foreign entities. This would reduce America to third-world status and make it possible for the billionaire-induced, new world order to be implemented that is planned, which in turn builds a dependent socialistic society that is easily controlled by the now hidden from view billionaire puppet masters. That includes many of the world's wealthiest people, top political leaders, and corporate elite, as well as members of the so-called Black Nobility of Europe, dominated by the British Crown whose goal is to create a one world (fascist) government, stripped of nationalistic and regional boundaries, that is obedient to its agenda. May I throw out only one name? George Soros! You can investigate the rest.

The reason America is still tied to oil-based fuels is money and deals made behind closed doors that provide this narrow elitist group opportunity. When hydrogen cars were first built in the United States they were destroyed by the elitist group, because the cars use would have devalued oil.

Americans are going to re-enter their garages and produce hydrogen-assist units for their existing cars and car manufactures will begin to produce hydrogen and electric cars.

Some can learn to build their own solar panels and even sell energy back to the power company instead of purchasing from it.

The concern of greenhouse gases is not a matter of concern (even if it did prove scientifically correct, which it does not) because the politics behind it all, are all about money and without the greenhouse gas disguised threat to society, it's absence would interfere with the production of that money for the elitist group; Al Gore would certainly be cut. Over ninety seven percent of all greenhouse gases are natural (just for fun-one would be cow-methane) and there is nothing we can do about them. For example, India's population of one billion people produces more carbon dioxide just by breathing than is produced by all the coal-burning power plants in the United States.

Cap and Trade Are Off the Table

Cap and trade are off the table in my administration however, free enterprise is back on the table. This problem is fixed with solutions such as hydrogen and electric cars, as well as natural gas propelled automobiles and other alternative energy such as solar panels some can make in their own home garage that will allow you to sell un-used electricity back to the electric companies. Then the rogue countries that mean America harm will suffer in the face of the dying oil-based market economy. Since they can't eat their oil, when the bottom drops out of that market, they will need the United States ever more.

Oil will be seen in the future as an outrage by every American and they will punish themselves for allowing such rape to our country (high prices from foreign countries) and rape to the planet, from exhaust, to have continued for so long. Because it builds the bank accounts of the few, politicians got their share to keep the auto-propulsion monopoly on track.

The problem has to be approached from the short term to help manage for the long term. The first order of the day will be a fifty million dollar reward for the person or company who can develop a device that can be adapted to cars and trucks we all own today that will extend the gas mileage to a minimum of fifty miles per gallon for the biggest gas-guzzler and up from there, for the smaller vehicles. This technology developed by an individual or company will be tooled and manufactured with the only grant allowed by my administration from the federal government fund and only for inside the U.S. borders by Americans.

This fund will not create a deficit; it will be made possible by cutting programs and federal bureaucracies. We will return to our home garages to invent the newest technologies or capitalize on the old that we are famous for creating. This will not only help to build our economy but it will create jobs through our American genius, which we have allowed to sleep.

8. Top Educators, Teachers and Professors will be assembled: Academics will once again be America's prime objective and we will stop promoting complacency because of tenure. Sports will take a back seat to academics in our schools.

Tenure will be eliminated as mentioned earlier and top educators will be the most respected and cherished of our country once more and will be rewarded for their skills.

Preferred sports-playing students are the wrong focus. Low academic performance is a much more generalized and endemic problem related chiefly to a teacher's lack of performance but also by parent's failure to teach children to love learning by example, through reading and talking. Families should consider a grand center focus on education and less for the favorite team.

Promoting students ahead of their academic level, because of the way they play a game is over; no sport will ever over-shadow learning abilities. I will shine the light on the student achievers and suggest events for commending those student achievers that will over shadow the sports arenas and incentivize academics in the schools.

The Immortal Mr. Wizard Attitude

The immortal Mr. Wizard attitude will return to our home garages across this wonderful country once again. Our country will be so proud of our student achievers that they will be the focus for most all events that we want to be part of, even for programs that we choose to view on television. Watching and being part of America and Americans who come alive once again will be the envy of the world. I think of the program called Are You Smarter than a Fifth Grader when I think of promoting academics.

The teachers and professors of the United States of America will return to being the respected group they once were due to the abolishment of tenure and Americans wanting to pay handsomely for brilliance to teach their children will insure we get the best professionals who can and will be fired for under performance or adopting anti-American philosophies, which many have been known to do these days. William Charles "Bill Ayers" comes to mind here. Freedom of speech does not include the right to distort the minds of vulnerable children who are forced to listen in class rooms. The agenda for which the teacher is being paid to do is not to teach distorted American values that would be a breach of the teacher's contract. The teacher is bound by contract to teach sound American values.

Some might even say that removing tenure and adapting free enterprise symbolisms of rewarding performance while penalizing failure is a socialist act. The socialist enfaces being after praising teachers, you warn them that their necks are on the block and that by the way, if you prove not to be a true American patriot who believes in the American way of life and you believe in something else, such as Marxism, communism or socialism, etc, then your days will be numbered, because you will be fired. My explanation is, you can call it Mickey Mouse if you want but our contract with teachers mean they will not be able to desecrate our country through teaching distorted beliefs to our children. In fact a teacher could be asked to leave our country and go to where that belief system will fit those beliefs inferred terrorist act.

The impersonators who may hold these positions now due to tenure are finished with the degradation of our students and our country.

9. Persons: with organizational education and movement planning skills that have the ability to use the Internet and other media to raise awareness for the organization are needed to press our agenda forward to Election Day 2012. You can contact me through my web for comments at www.LiveLonger123. com

10. Productivity: hard work and commitment will be rewarded regardless of your culture or ethnicity or skin color just as long as you are an American citizen who loves his country.

Racial Issues and Racism

You small minded individuals who make your living by forcing the racial agenda will be ridiculed, as you should be, instead of praised as you are by the left-wing media due to its desire to be politically correct. I have previously pointed out the definition of political correctness.

As your president of our United States, should you determine to elect me, I will bring the presidency out of hiding with courage on these issues and ask people to grow up and move away from the past that should have nothing to do with our future American family, which recognizes not color.

Studying the rearview mirror will cause you to collide with the future in failure and not to achieve success in the future with un-foreseen opportunity that you could only see while looking through the windshield of life, and not studying the past, in the rearview mirror of life.

Criminal activity, scams and free rides will not be tolerated, from anywhere and especially from government officials all the way down to companies and individuals; the illegalities will not go unpunished. Remember the operable word in illegal-alien is the word illegal.

Just using one career politician's name that emphasizes political illegal activity would be, Charles Rangel, because there are many others, however the light punishment which he received is not going to fly in my administration. Rangel received a standing ovation from his fellow members when he admitted before them he had broken the law, but that it was politics involved.

Remember the computer analogy that nothing happens until you push the start button. We have to push that start button and begin firing these sick people and replacing them with true American patriots who love this county and would not let anyone destroy it. Let's make it a point not to vote for the billionaire puppets that have practiced that political smile on television. Let's make a free organization for you and me to express our views to the American public so everything is out in the open. Florida has a very well liked brand new senator by the name of Allan West who once answered a television interviewer's question of what he thought of Obama's speech on jobs, Thursday September-8, 2011 and Mr. West stated, "We do not need another speech, and we need something in writing." End Mr. West. This book is putting my platform in writing for all to see and to hold me accountable for in the future. This means you will get someone in office who will not break the laws of our Constitution.

While I am president any politician discovered breaking the law while serving the American people is going to be punished. An example of someone who broke the law is, Senator John Ensign (R-Nev), who announced April 21, 2011 that he would be resigning from the Senate effective immediately. Ensign has been under investigation by the Senate Ethics Committee following an admitted affair with a member of his staff. The Senate Ethics Committee is governed by the politicians and I see that as the fox guarding the hen house theory again. I will have a completely independent group, like a jury used in a courtroom trial, to undertake these types of actions.

Ensign's parents gave the woman in question and her husband $96,000 in what Ensign called an ordinary gift prior to the affair becoming public knowledge. This would be something the independent jury would consider before recommending punishment, just like a jury trial. Nothing would be withheld from my independent jury that may be withheld from a regular jury.

The senator also arranged for a lobbying job for the woman's husband in violation of Senate ethics rules.

This, as well as many other bribery acts will be punished to the fullest extent of the law in my administration. New hope and integrity will be instilled in Americans starting in 2012, because Americans are beginning to realize that when you elect the privileged, you generally get unethical privileged people, who do not have Americas best interests at heart.

It is time we take seriously the non-politicians who are true American patri-ots that love this country and stop putting our belief in and our votes behind the insider of the political beltway, who plays the politically correct card all the while he is hood-winking the public. These men and women do not represent the people and this misrepresentation has gotten America in the mess we are in today!

Trump had the guts to say what the timid Republican in name only (RINOs) refuse to say, but he is only using buzz words to get attention in my view; not that he is not a wonderful American mind you, because he is and he is a great entrepreneur as well. Look at his past where he has been courting the left as well as the right, to simply make the deal and make money, which is not a bad idea to make money, when running for president other thoughts help.

Being just another billionaire who is in search of a new way to further exploit himself (it's called name branding) and makes even more money. So Trump using Obama's birth certificate to launch himself, was brilliant and I think makes him a champion.

Obama's birth certificate issue is disgusting enough by itself; but Obama has broken the law so many times (which I will be outlining later), it over- shadows the probability of the scam of his birth certificate.

Could Obama's birth certificate be a big scam on the American people? I will examine this as best I can and you decide. What may go down as the biggest scam on the American people in history is the legitimacy of Obama; setting aside for a moment his monumental mistakes as well as the laws he has broken, touched on later that may have accomplished the total destruction of the United States of America; they are the blatant illegal acts that have gone unpunished by his fellow congressmen and congresswomen, which I intend to discuss in just a bit.

But when I look at Obama's certificate of live birth, (not birth certificate as all Americans must have) a few things that are suspect that jump out at me from the page.

For one, the race of Obama's father's was listed as "African." At the time, the choices for race (even if someone was from Africa would have been Negro), The choices would have been "White, Asian or Negro." That he was identified as "African" is adopting the more politically correct terminology we use today and not at all used back then; leading to the belief that it could be a fabrication.

It is also troubling that he is called Barack Hussein Obama (the second), using the double "II" to signify second, instead of "Jr."

People back then just did not do that which leads to the fabrication thought process again; also I wonder why the certificate lists Obama's address as being that of his grandparents, instead of his parents, which was in the university housing. These all should have created an issue with Congress that should have been resolved legally. The document presented by Obama appears to be homemade.

A certification of live birth is not a legal document and is explained on this State of Hawaii (DHHL) Department of Hawaiian Home Lands website: "In order to process your application, DHHL utilizes information that is found only on the original Certificate of Live Birth, which is either black or green. This is a more complete record of your birth than the Certification of Live Birth (a computer-generated printout). Submitting the original Certificate of Live Birth will save you time and money since the computer-generated Certification requires additional verification by DHHL".

Hawaii's official birth certificate is the certificate of live birth that was different from the certification of live birth. Changing the "e" to "ion" makes all the difference in the world with these two words.

Anyone can swear and sign the form to the registrar in Hawaii that he was a citizen of Hawaii and within the previous year gave birth. The individual gives the date and time of the birth and a document record is dully entered.

Perhaps someone can inform me as to whether you even need to show the baby! Does not look like it from my statute read.

Even if Obama was born in Hawaii, it still does not mean he meets the Constitutional requirement of (natural born citizen) because his father was a Kenyan. Further, why has Obama not released his college transcripts from Occidental College or Columbia?

Obama's life story, from his humble roots to his rise to Harvard Law School to his passion as a community organizer in Chicago was at the center of his presidential campaign.

But one chapter of the tale remains a blank and that is his education at Columbia College, a place he rarely speaks about and where few people seem to remember him.

The Obama campaign refused to release his college transcript, despite an academic career that led him to Harvard Law School and later to a lecturing position at the University of Chicago.

The shroud surrounding his experience at Columbia contrasted with that of other major party nominees, all of whom have eventually released information about their college performance or saw it leaked to the public.

Obama and Bill Ayres

Factcheck.org is a project of the Annenberg Public Policy Center of the Annenberg School for Communication at the University of Pennsylvania, and is funded primarily by the Annenberg Foundation. The Foundation gave Obama and Bill Ayres $110 million to spend on improving education. But Obama and Ayres actually spent the $110 million teaching Chicago kids to vote for his (Obama's) sponsor, Mayor Daley.

The Annenberg Foundation did a follow-up study that proved Obama and Ayres did not improve educational test scores by any amount.

In later years as Obama became the president and then employing radical Bill Ayres created a firestorm, and suspiciously Annenberg's Factcheck.org says that Ayres and Obama did not know each other back then, contradicting their own published facts.

The actual printed facts that prove they knew about Ayres and Obama, even though stating they did not was: It was known that Bill Ayres founded the Chicago Annenberg Challenge (CAC) and hired Obama to be its president for five years, all documented by the Corporate Minutes of the CAC that University of Illinois Prof. William Ayres donated to the archives section of the University of Illinois Library at its Chicago campus. This is the first website that popped up when I Google this: http://ngoldfarb.wordpress.com/2009/05/15/ state-of-Hawaii-says-Obama's-birth-certificate-not-valid but there are several.

Obama supporters are always quoting Factcheck.org as the truth in all things disputed by the center and right politicians.

I see the Annenberg Foundation as playing both sides of the fence, democrat and republican. I think it disserves the old cliché, follow the money.

The controversy regarding the birth certification of Obama while certainly packed with drama and when proven may be a huge scam on the American people; that should not drown out Osama's larger contributions to the destruction of America.

Obama Illegalities, Outside of His Birth Certificate

Impeachment is not the only method that could have been used to remove Obama; civil tort laws could have been used too. Not considering the tort laws had there been enough politicians who were for America at the time, --which there were not--so impeachment could have been in order. Not the least of which is Obama's misuse of the War Powers act. But you review that on your own.

However there is also the tort act for a civil action. In the United States, the federal government has sovereign immunity and may not be sued by citizens unless it has waived its immunity or consented to suit

The United States has waived sovereign immunity to a limited extent, mainly through the Federal Tort Claims Act (FTCA), which I refer to as tort laws on occasion; this waives the immunity if there is a tortious act of a federal employee who causes damage. Also there is the Tucker Act of 1887, the United States waived its sovereign immunity as to certain kinds of claims arising out of contracts to which the federal government is a party, such as Obama's contract with America when he took the oath of office.

I see how Obama's path to destroying America with an agenda that is contrary to Americas wishes, as being in violation of the federal claims acts and I see removal of this sitting president-as being possible and certainly prosecutable. I think most true left-wing liberals would not be in favor of impeaching Obama for any reason.

Perhaps some of the folks who are more moderate would join in for this type of cause, but hardcore progressive, socialist liberals hate America, just as I believe that Obama does from reading his words in his books to his actions.

But are there plenty of Obama illegal actions against the sovereignty of America to satisfy a claim using the FTCA? In my opinion: You bet there are.

Impeachment through tort is certainly possible, but removal is the objective even if it is in the election of 2012.

Whoever had prior knowledge of the high crimes and misdemeanors can be prosecuted as well. President Clinton was impeached on four much lesser charges, in comparison with some of the Obama offenses.

Some of the impeachment and or tort act offenses are:

1. On September 24th 2009, Barack Hussein Obama assumed the office of chairman of the United Nations Security Council. He was the first U.S. president to have accepted this responsibility because of what could arguably be a Constitutional prohibition against doing so. To wit:

Section 9 of the Constitution says that;" No Title of Nobility shall be granted by the United States: and no Person holding any Office of Profit or Trust under them, shall, without the consent of the Congress, accept any present, Emolument, Office, or Title, of any kind whatever, from any King, Prince, or foreign State."

How the courts could see the UN as being King, Prince or foreign state, remains to be seen but further explained as to how they might is in the next item, accepting the Nobel Prize.

2. Accepting the Nobel Prize without authorization by Congress was considered illegal and with Congress on his side, approval would have been easy to gain I would have assumed. But it would have made him look like less than an absolute monarchy, so he chose to trample the Constitution again, in my view and I agree with these representatives: Rep. Ginny Brown-Waite, Rep. Cliff Stearns, and Rep. Ron Paul who say "no, that he could not accept it" and have sent a letter to the president asking him to request congressional consent, which they expected would be speedily given because his side (at the time) was in the majority of both houses of government. They point to the example of President Theodore Roosevelt, who created a committee, including the chief justice, to hold Roosevelt's Nobel Peace Prize money in trust until he left office. After leaving office, Roosevelt asked for congressional consent to disburse the money to particular charities.

Article I, § 9, Clause 8, of the Constitution states that "no Person holding any Office of Profit or Trust under them, shall, without the Consent of the Congress, accept of any present, Emolument, Office, or Title, of any kind whatever, from any King, Prince, or foreign State."

When Roosevelt won the Peace Prize, there was apparently no controlling statute. Today there is: 5 USC § 7342 titled (Receipt and disposition of foreign gifts and decorations) which sets out the conditions under which foreign gifts can be accepted without a separate action of Congress. The statute applies to an employee, which includes the president and the vice president.

A foreign government includes any agent or representative of any such (foreign) unit or such organization, while acting as such." Since the Nobel Peace Prize committee is, as the Representatives note, appointed by the Norwegian Storting (Norwegian Parliament its legislature), it would seem to be within the scope of the statute.

A gift is a tangible or intangible present (other than a decoration). A decoration includes a medal, badge, insignia, emblem, or award. These definitions could also pertain to the acceptance of chairman of the United Nations Security Council.

You can read multiple contributions to these theories on this website http://www.volokh.com

3. Firing the CEO of GM, or, as being seen to be the same thing, Obama asking him to step down. The president has no authority to do so. He is the president of the United States, not of the GM board of directors, but the details would be left up to attorneys.

What happened to jobs in America is full of controversy but to a logical thinker quite possibly Obama having given Chrysler a thirty-day window to complete a proposed partnership with Italian automaker Fiat SpA, and offered up to $6 billion to the companies if Chrysler could negotiate a deal before time runs out, could have some connection with the same laws broken with the GM debacle.

4. Obama has overseen the effective takeover by government of banks, the largest insurance company (AIG), and General Motors GM and Chrysler's exit from America, representing the bulk of the U.S. auto industry, thus depriving bondholders, share-holders, and others of their property.

5. Taking GM in violation of all bankruptcy law. This constitutes seizure of a vast amount of private property and turning it over to political cronies (i.e. the United Auto Workers, UAW). It is not unknown of Obama accepting large donations from the big unions. Based on the reports of the House Oversight Subcommittee on Regulatory Affairs, Stimulus Oversight, and Government Spending, it's pretty clear that treasury officials lied to Congress about the degree of administration control over the auto companies, and therefore president Obama lied to the American people.

6. Forcing citizens of this country to buy health insurance is also a violation of the constitution. :www.wnd.com reported four Michigan residents who object to the government forcing them to purchase health-care

insurance and pay for abortions have joined in a federal lawsuit from many states challenging the constitutionality of the health-care reform bill President Obama signed into law. We are guaranteed Liberty by the Constitution.

Thomas Jefferson once stated: "When injustice becomes law, resistance become duty." What kind of leader would use the Internal Revenue Service (IRS) to send citizens to jail and seize their property if they choose not to buy government healthcare in 2014? This is the same president that does not require non-citizens to prove their citizenship to receive free medical care. One only need visit Arizona on internet or in person to become bombarded with details of government illegalities insofar as illegal aliens. If you did not read the health care law, well that is fine because house speaker Pelosi said; we have to pass the health-care bill before we read it.

7. The issue of illegal immigration and the utter failure of the Obama Administration to protect and defend (as he must pledge when taking the oath of office) is probably the most blatant issue of abdication of responsibility, but even more than Obamacare, Cap and Tax, TARP, etc. is illegal immigration. Mexican president Calderon stated in a state-of-the-nation speech: Where there is a Mexican, there is Mexico. Most believe he meant there are no borders and he sees nothing wrong with Mexican illegal entry into the US, which most conservatives can see as an act of war. Because the immigrants send home about $20 billion a year and because the yearly migration of more than 400,000 people relieve Mexico of masses of the poor, Mexican government has little incentive to support stricter measures making it harder for Mexicans to cross the border. The taxpayers in California alone must come up with twenty five million dollars for one hospital due to illegals using the emergency room for their free healthcare.

The other issues I spoke of are economically damaging certainly, but the border issues in Arizona, California, New Mexico and Texas, especially in Arizona, put American Citizens in direct mortal danger; while Obama has consorted with the president of Mexico at the expense of the American people.

In years past, this nation would have considered this an act of aggression and would have confronted the Mexican government with its responsibility to patrol its own borders and take care of its people and if Mexico did not, the United States would consider it a deliberate act of war.

Sadly we have digressed to warning our American citizens that they do not have the right of life, liberty, property and the pursuit of happiness anywhere within seventy miles of the Mexican border where U.S. government has posted signs warning Americans that they are entering dangerous territory, which is seen by many as the government admitting it is derelict in its duty to defend and protect America and Americans.

This is an armed invasion by the Mexican drug cartel and should be treated as such. To ignore this, to sweep it under the rug as this administration has done, is indeed an impeachable offense and at the very least, illegal and should be tried under the tort laws.

Mr. Eric Holders suit against the state of Arizona while the overall complaint of the White House against Arizona's immigration bill was its alleged potential for racial profiling; the lawsuit filed against Arizona by the federal government did not attempt to make the case that the law was discriminatory. Arizona was being sued for taking measures to secure its borders which the government refuses to do, is in direct conflict with the Constitution. In taking his oath of office in January of 2009, Mr. Obama swore to uphold the U.S Constitution. He has done nothing of the sort.

8. Also under the smoke screen of Obama's hidden agenda we must consider the alleged obstructionism as reported by Fox news and particularly Megyn Kelly of Fox News, who has reported that the Department of Justice has a policy not to prosecute blacks in voter intimidation cases when the target of intimidation was white. This is one reason that I say enough is enough with this political correctness jargon.

The genesis of Fox News claim-- is a Kelly interview with J. Christian Adams, a former DOJ attorney who recently resigned in protest over the department's handling of a New Black Panther Party (NBPP) case from the 2008 election.

9. The Constitution mandates that the president of the United States must be a United States "natural born" Citizen – Article II, Section I.

However, Mr. Barry Soetoro, (the name Barack Hussein Obama used when he was in Indonesia) does not fit that bill.

Barack Hussein Obama, Jr. or as the certificate of birth said (II instead of Jr.) was elected president of the United States on November 4, 2008. Prior to that, he was the junior United States senator from Illinois (2005-2008) and eight years as an Illinois state senator with virtually non-voting record from (1996-2004).

Obama says he was born in Hawaii on August 4, 1961, to a white mother from Kansas (Anna Dunham) and a Black Muslim father from Kenya (Barack Hussein Obama, Sr.). The couple had met when they were students at the University of Hawaii. When they married, Anna was unaware that her new husband was still legally married to a woman in Kenya, whom he had wed in1954, and with whom he had fathered four children.

Do candidates for office disqualify themselves if they seek office under a birth name different from a name by adoption, having not provided election officers prima facie evidence of legal name changes, or neglecting to legally change names? That is for tort civil laws to investigate.

10. Obama lied to the American people when he said we could keep our private insurance, knowing full well that his legislation would inevitably drive private insurers out of business. Or worse still, he did not read the thousand or so page bill he jammed down the throats of Americans. It proves to be one of the (I's) either illegal or idiot.

11. Gerald Walpin, inspector general of the Corporation for National and Community Service investigated Kevin Johnson, a friend of the president, for misuse of funds from an AmeriCorps grant, whereupon Obama vindictively fired Walpin to cover for Johnson. A subsequent investigation vindicated Walpin's judgment in the matter.

When this story broke early in 2009, it was said that by firing Walpin, Obama not only broke a federal law, he broke a federal law that he wrote or cosponsored while he was in the Senate; proving that he was not completely missing in action while in the Senate, none-the-less a law breaker.

He and a couple of other senators wrote and passed this law in response to the way George W. Bush fired seven United States attorneys in December 2006. The law established clear-cut procedures that were necessary to fire federal employees.

Obama violated his own procedures when he fired Walpin

12. Continuing to enforce his unconstitutional moratorium on off-shore drilling after it was ruled unconstitutional by a federal court. That he has finally lifted the ban does not reverse his breaking of the law from the beginning.

13. As reported on various news organizations, Barack Hussein Obama is actively pursuing cap-and-trade legislation. Instead of taxing the very air we breathe, it would instead, in a manner of speaking, tax the air we exhale and give the government unprecedented control over the economy and American businesses. By implementing an arbitrary and

restrictive cap on the production of carbon dioxide (seventeen percent by 2020, compared with 2005 levels), and then forcing high CO2 producers to buy carbon credits from zero or low CO2 producers this bill will alter and distort the current cost structure of the markets destroy business and cost jobs and not actually change the amount of CO2 put into the atmosphere at all. In essence this is a massive wealth- transfer scheme from efficient energy producers to inefficient producers, and energy users everywhere will pay for this multi-billion-dollar sleight of hand.

14. The effect of the debt Obama is accumulating will ultimately mean hyper-inflation, a continuous crippling of our economy and, quite possibly, personal hardship-on-a-scale that has not been experienced even in the Great Depression; it seems as if Obama is intentionally trying to destroy the country. The suffocating debt Obama is accumulating is due to bipartisan collusion and no matter whether a politicians shingle says, republican or democrat if either of them votes to increase debt or increase spending in general, you need to throw the bums out. Obama meanwhile, plays the innocent bystander who strolls up to a crash he caused and simply asks for more money and says if you do not give it to me I will say it is your fault. A personal note to Mr. Obama; Americans are not stupid, you will soon see.

This massive and rising debt is placing America and Americans at risk of losing liberty, property and sovereignty, which is in direct violation of our Constitution. The Fourteenth Amendment (Amendment XIV) to the United States Constitution was adopted on July 9, 1868 as one of the Reconstruction Amendments; it prohibits government from depriving persons of life, liberty, or property without certain steps being taken to ensure fairness. Please someone tell me if you think the out of control spending has been fair to you and your children?

15. Washington, DC—Fox News exposed this criminal activity and has continued to uncover a serious theft of public funds. It all began with a massive spam e-mail from the White House authored by Barack Obama's (political advisor) of whom I can't help myself in referring to as, his propaganda minister, David Axelrod. Obama was campaigning for support of his socialist health program and one of the spam e-mails was captured.

Fox News reporter, Major Garrett asked about the spam e-mail messages sent out by Axelrod to campaign for Obamacare at a White House news briefing. Garret was treated like a skunk at a picnic over his persistent questioning and now we know why.

The problem was and is that taxpayer funds were diverted from use in legitimate government functions to a political campaign pushing the hostile takeover of the health care and insurance industries in America. That was theft pure and simple.

Side-note: Many talk of the Shadow Government on the constitution.org website: A key question about the Shadow Government is how does it make decisions and carry them out. Where is the center? Some think it lies in a few major financial institutions. Others think that it lays in the intelligence apparatus. Still others think that it has no permanent center, but operates by consensus, with shifting factions that confer through various mechanisms. Some think that those mechanisms are reflected in public associations such as the Council on Foreign Relations (CFR), the Tri- lateral Commission, the Bilderbergers, the Federal Reserve, the World Bank, or the International Monetary Fund. It appears although I have not been able to find the actual investigation that in1963 was the year establishment media sector of the Shadow Government was given effective control over computerized voting in the United States, through its National Election Service, as part of a deal in which they went along with the cover-up of the Kennedy assassination through the Warren Commission. While campaign money continues to buy influence over elected officials, if the funds were not sufficient, the Shadow Government had other options. It put officials in compromising situations, and then used its evidence to black- mail them into compliance. Failing that, it could easily select the winner of any election, and suppress the support that third-party candidates might attain.

When a candidate or an elected official seems arrogant it could be to the detriment of an opponent. The real decisions from that arrogant candidate or elected official may be made not by that public figure, but by faceless persons operating in secret.

Short note: Lets you and I start electing American loving patriots, who are willing to protect their county with their very lives. My request is "vote for me. Won't you?

16. Accusing private individuals and the U.S. Chamber of Commerce of receiving foreign funding for campaign purposes and then presenting no facts to support the claim short of the propaganda czar Axelrod jumping the attention away from the crime, by asking the question, Is there any proof that the republicans do not take foreign money?" As if to say; it is not illegal if someone else has done it. In the same instance, the Democratic Party has taken twice as much and it refuses to reveal the facts about the donors.

17. The Sestak bribe to leave the race to protect the democratic incumbent is undeniable and in direct violation of our Constitution. The Law: Crimes and Criminal Procedure 18 USC Section 600 Promise of employment or other benefit for political activity.

Whoever, directly or indirectly, promises any employment, position, compensation, contract, appointment, or other benefit, provided for or, made possible in whole or in part, by any act of Congress, or any special consideration in obtaining any such benefit to any person as consideration, favor, or reward for any political activity or, for the support of, or opposition to, any candidate or any political party in connection with any general, or special election to any political office, or in connection with any primary election or political convention or caucus held to select candidates for any political office, shall be fined under this title or imprisoned not more than one year, or both and a felon cannot be president. Why Obama was not prosecuted on that specifically, let alone all the others—is beyond comprehension.

Also is lying to the American people grounds for impeachment? This is by no means the beginning or end of the lies from Obama, but it certainly is worthy of mention.

Release of the Lockerbie Bomber

Correspondence obtained by The Sunday Times researched from the website lakewood246.com/news reveals the Obama administration considered compassionate release of the Lockerbie bomber more palatable than locking up Abdel Baset al-Megrahi in a prison.

The intervention, which has angered U.S. relatives of those who died in the attack, was made by Richard LeBaron, deputy head of the U.S. embassy in London, a week before Megrahi was freed, on grounds that he had terminal cancer..

The document, acquired threatens to undermine Obama's claim that all Americans were surprised, disappointed and angry to learn of Megrahi's release.

Scottish ministers viewed the level of U.S. resistance to compassionate release as half-hearted and a sign it would be accepted.

The United States has tried to keep the letter secret; refusing to give permission to the Scottish authorities to publish it on the grounds it would prevent future frank and open communications with other governments.

In the letter, sent to Scottish First Minister Alex Salmond and justice officials Mr LeBaron wrote that the United States wanted Megrahi to remain imprisoned in view of the nature of the crime.

The note added: Nevertheless, if Scottish authorities come to the conclusion that Megrahi must be released from Scottish custody, the U.S. position is that conditional release on compassionate grounds would be a far preferable alternative to prisoner transfer, which we strongly oppose.

This clearly is not considering the families of the dead Americans.

Mr LeBaron added that freeing the bomber and making him live in Scotland would mitigate a number of the strong concerns we have expressed with regard to Megrahi's release.

The U.S administration lobbied the Scottish government more strongly against sending Megrahi home, under a prisoner transfer agreement signed by the British and Libyan governments, in a deal now known to have been linked to a pound stg. 550 million oil contract for British Petroleum. There is plenty of information out there on this, just Google it for yourself.

This is the type of weakness that I despise from Obama. He continually shows little courage to stand up for America's interests. Apparently, the White House doesn't care much for what the American people want. You do not need to simply take his actions as proof of his disdain for America, review his written work, some I have outlined in this book.

How are these puppet heads able to collaborate in the destruction of America? The answer: by providing entitlements to Americans to garner their votes.

Jewish Hatred Supporting Obama

We all know by now about Obama's African nativist shady heritage and his shady citizenship and his America hating statements in his book Dreams of My Father, plus his Israel hating attitude as presented by his snubbing of Benjamin Netanyahu in the White house and all his negative actions toward Israel played out in the media thus far and all this he shares with his long time Pastor Jeremiah Wright. However, Obama has more anti-Israel supporters, who are giving him lots of money. He feels he can smooth talk the American Jews to vote for him again just like he did the last election because of his charisma and charm.

As Obama took steps toward the United States Senate he found a very powerful sugar daddy that would help fund his political rise: George Soros. The billionaire who caused the destructtion of the English pound and hedge fund titan began supporting Obama very early. Politicians are a befit to a legendary speculative investor who is always looking for opportunities. Obama coveted support from George Soros and Soros responded along with many of Soro's family members and probably the Soros ring of wealthy donors. Soros even found a loophole that allowed him and assorted family members to exceed regular limits on campaign contributions.

Soros is also a fierce foe of Israel, for years funding groups that have worked against Israel. He is also a man who has flexed his political muscle as a major funder of Democrat candidates and a slew of so-called 527 groups that are active in pushing their agendas which include a reliance on international institutions, defeat of Republicans, Bush-bashing, Israel-bashing and so on. He has also openly proclaimed his desire to break the bonds between America and Israel and has written of his desire to erode political support for Israel.

Soros also called for concessions to Hamas the terror group that has killed many innocent people and that has called for the destruction of Israel. When this came to light, some leading Democrats personally denounced Soros; Obama had a spokesman issue this rather bland statement: "Mr. Soros is entitled to his opinions," a campaign spokeswoman, Jen Psaki, said. "But on this issue Soros and Senator Obama disagree.

Sound familiar?

It is similar to the response the Soros campaign has given regarding Obama's close relationship with Pastor Jeremiah Wright.

Remember the uproar when Congressman Ron Paul refused to return a $500 donation from Don Black of Stormfront? Apparently there are far too many naive white liberals who think blacks are incapable of racism or hatred. It is astounding to me that any Jewish American would support Obama, given his actions.

Some Citizens Just Live In America

There are a great many people who simply live in America who want more, without earning it. They believe the government owes them. Those entitlement residents of America find fault with America because they do not get enough entitlements.

They blame the government for their problems. At this point in our cultural history, enough people have been misinformed and misled that they are prepared to sell America to whomever offers them, personally, the most advantages. To these people I suggest visiting any one of the-third-world countries to see if this is the life you expect given to you. Because this is the direction that our country is fast headed toward becoming.

I suspect, if you visited any of these countries your answer would be no, you don't want to live there, or else you would be there, but your entitlement attitude and your vote for the politician who promises the most, is what generates the power of the powers that be today, who are turning our country into that third-world country and if they succeed, you would not choose to live.

Illegals are part of the problem we face today and my presidential stance for illegals is deportation as I mention throughout this book. Illegal means just that.

Although immigrants have been finding employment, the poor job-market conditions have pushed average wages down. It might be that ... immigrants were more accepting of lower wages and reduced hours because many, especially unauthorized immigrants, are not eligible for unemployment benefits and would not be a cost burden on the employer. Are illegal immigrants' reducing employment opportunities for native-born Americans? And are immigrants pushing down wage levels?

Economists say that more immigrants in the labor force mean tougher times for native-born workers at the bottom end of the labor market, who are younger or less-skilled.

Our educational system is developing a very large population of less- educated young people ... who have relatively little experience with work.

Some illegal immigrants leave the US during recessionary times as jobs in construction and other industries they normally seek-dry up. So it is not America where their heart is, it was simply a way to send money to their chosen home.

There are 11–to some say as many as 20 million illegal aliens living in the US. With elections around the corner, and the immigration reform debate heating up fueled by everything from Arizona's controversial immigration law to the 14th Amendment's birthright citizenship clause, it will no doubt be discussed by others besides me.

Immigration laws exist for a very good reason: Excessive levels of immigration can have a profoundly negative impact on the receiving society. There is no aspect of American life, jobs, wages, education, health care, taxes, and environment, to name a few that are not affected by immigration.

Just California alone has a tax burden for one hospital of 25-million dollars. This is a tax burden for the American citizen to pay for illegals using the emergency room at hospitals for their free healthcare. Employers pay illegals under the table low wages and avoid tax and the taxpayer funds everything else.

Mexico's President Felipe Calderón addressed a joint session of Congress: He said, "I am convinced that comprehensive immigration reform is crucial to securing our common border. However Calderon stated, I strongly disagree in recently adopted law in Arizona."

Calderon said he doesn't like our right to keep and bear arms. Perhaps if Mexico honored the second amendment philosophy of the right to defend themselves, then the people of Mexico wouldn't be held hostage by the drug cartels. He blamed America for the violence in Mexico. He blamed America for illegal guns going south to Mexico and he blamed America for illegal immigration and for drugs going north to America. Well, I have a solution for him: Americans should just seal the border frontier and deport all illegals; that is David Tippie's plan.

Mexican president Calderon loves Mexicans to come to America illegally because they send money back to Mexico, which helps his economy.

We can no longer avoid it, we have avoided the problem for as long as we can and just when we felt we couldn't avoid it any longer we were told that, indeed, somewhere between 12 and 20 million people had somehow snuck into America unnoticed and now, we must legalize them. Is this the message we want to send to those thinking about illegally crossing the borders?

Mexico is struggling with internal and external corruption as well as a devastating war against the Mexican drug cartels that are overrunning the Mexican government and the country in general. Mexico is a serious problem and threat for America. It could be turning into the Afghanistan/Pakistan of the Western hemisphere. At the very least, it will make the Columbia Drug Cartel wars of the eighties look not all that bad; maybe because Columbia was not so close to American borders. The important thing to realize about the illegal immigration issue is that people coming across the Mexican border are not all Mexicans; terrorists enter just as easily.

Do any of you see that Illegal immigration is destined to be a major controversy in the 2012 election? You now have my stand.

Chapter 8

White Americans voted for the first black president

Some whites may have voted to relieve something burden-some or pain-ful implanted in them from those who make a living keeping the past in the present, (which I refer to a racist mongers), as though the white should feel responsible for the past. No one likes a racist monger except maybe another racist monger. No one will stand for someone being denigrated because of their race, religion, nationality or gender. In a country where all men are created equal, it will not be tolerated. Under the First Amendment to the United States Constitution, everyone has a right to an opinion and the right to voice that opinion but that does not give them the right to denigrate someone who does not look the same as you or practice the same religion. Unless that religion is your law which you see supersedes American law; then I will deport you; to where that is not important, you choose.

Rehashing the past through the education in schools about past trauma placed on the black ancestors who were held in slavery, may be a reason whites vote for Obama, because some may have had pity for those black ancestors and has somehow transferred that pity into today's blacks, for those past miseries of the black ancestors.

That rehashing is aided with the help of racists mongers who use that white pity for those in the past to transferred that pity to today's blacks, who are now, according to the racist mongers, supposed to be seen as treated as miserably as was their ancestors and who are now requiring entitlements for those past ancestral miseries.

Whites that voted for a black might have been seeking a way to indulge in a sense of spiritual purging or cleansing, which will never be accepted as atonement by the racist mongers who make their living on the vileness of it all, by their efforts to kept it alive in the media.

Some white Americans may have felt guilty for the known existence of that past revulsion toward the Negro race in our past which they were taught in schools, and may have shown their disdain by agreeing to such things as housing subsidies, food-stamps and other programs, which unknowingly to them, helped to enslave the blacks of today, similar to the way their ancestors were enslaved by removing their will to achieve and replacing it with the entitlement attitude.

To compensate for their disdain for the past treatment of the black ancestors, some whites may have happily voted for a remote black male who virtually never held a real job or ran a business, who was nothing more than a community organizer, elected first to the office of a senator with a record of not voting on issues and then to the office of president of the United States.

It is a shame our first black president could not have been someone like Colin Powell, who at one time was the most respected human being alive, irrespective of color.

It may be true that some black Americans voted for Obama out of a purely racial ideology, to simply be against the white race. That would be sad and could be one way evil doers from around the world who hate America may be able to penetrate families as well as it has shown to be able to. These same blacks may vote for Obama again and again for the same reasons, spurred on because of racist mongers preaching hatred. Each individual citizen must help deal with this, by reporting evil wherever you see it.

We should never forget people like the Reverend Jeremiah Alvesta Wright, Jr. pastor of Emeritus of Trinity United Church of Christ where Obama spent years and what he spewed out of his mouth on Sundays; his attitude and vileness words were shocking and a wakeup call to everyone, that evil exists among us, more than we had come to believe.

The black and Hispanic minority did not elect the new president; white people combined with their vote is what elected the new president. The youth vote, the women's vote and the vote from all those in America who cherish government program dependency went to the candidate who appealed to their sense of want, entitlement, and self-justification.

This dependent voting bloc of people have never understood the glory of pride in one's self through self-achievement, which is rewarding in and of itself; plus-the-money-you-make by accomplishing your goals when government gets out of your way and life excels far above entitlements.

This voting bloc seems to look for someone else to provide for them. They learn that taking from the haves is better than working, and this produces a dependent society. That is when the haves who are taken from, begin to see that working for something is penalized, so they too become part of the have not society. There is a snowball effect that creates a shrinking population of haves that are providing for the have nots and that spells certain disaster.

This attitude is contagious, especially when learned around the dinner table and from peers and then carried into adulthood. If one gets freebies, then those they associate with will want the same freebies.

The Media Has Become Entertainment Propaganda Artists

The American media is almost wholly propagandistic. The media having become mostly entertainment, with the few exceptions of breaking news however, with the news organizations as a whole, we are circumstantially coerced into being exposed to the same personalities daily, who get more in tune with the glorification of themselves than the news, making news today is obviously a free enterprise business of entertainment, advertisement, and sales. As such, it can be bought. Shall I mention the name again of George Soros as an example of buying the press? Media definitely sold out to the anti-American movement.

2008 Election: What Change Took Place in America That Helped Bring About Disaster?

The 2008 election was not the beginning of change; it was the result of a half- century of progressivism and communism that took over our schools decades earlier.

Having long controlled the educational system, progressive liberal's destroyed all American history by providing strict rules for the books chosen for our children to study, which conceals the truth of where America came from and how America came about thus destroying American family values.

In a planned attack over the years, with the proper timing, an entire population was created which has little or no understanding of what America is and what being an American really means. This less than-majority population is most vulnerable to deception; which I believe Obama refers to as "change".

These deceived residents of America and I refer to them simply as residents because they lack patriotism for their country and have for too long ignored the signs of decay, not the least of which began with the removal of prayer and the Pledge of Allegiance from our schools and the removal of the word Christmas, having been replaced with the words "seasons greeting" and the abolishment of the nativity scene as well as developing a strong sense of entitlement among others.

Americans have been obedient to their political masters who gave them entitlements to get elected and stay in office; these Americans stood by allowing the courts and politicians to corrupt themselves for decades. One more Supreme Court appointment by Obama and the Second Amendment is out the door.

All acts of control over society should be from an elected official, who has a specific term limit and that includes the Supreme Court justices. There should be no such thing as a lifetime appointment, nor should there be tenure, to keep you safe in a job in which you may not be producing.

The American legal system can often serve the anti-American cause of progressivism for a specific reason and that is ultimate control over the population and for some, the destruction of America. Most who have a conservative demeanor will have deduced this from the beginning of my book up to now. But in view of some not conceiving this I state the following:

Americans can no longer tell who, or what, is telling the truth in regards to the government or the legal system. The majority who voted for this elite group of politicians in government or persons in our justice system who jointly push all the rest of America around oppressing rights & liberty, even freedoms while these few individuals in control of our lives, seem to live above the law, and can do whatever they want.

To weaken the system even further: Eric Holder is part of the destruction of America's trust we saw by his insistence at trying terrorists in American courts. Holder used the results such as the Casey Anthony trail as being his explanation as to why he would chose to try terrorists in the U.S. court system rather than military court? Nothing could be more ludicrous, military court is for trying terrorists.

What Happened to Honor?

Unlike the Founding Fathers who wrote and signed the Constitution, none on the left, as well as few on the right, including the conservative Republicans, have been willing to risk their political futures or their fortunes to keep their sacred honor.

Now we have a president who, through past actions and papers and books he has written, allegedly demonstrates that he feels a disdain for white people as well as America as well as Christianity supporting fact being that he sat in front of a vile despicable hate monger like Reverend Wright for years. He demonstrates disdain for the American Constitution as is apparent by his blatant actions to date, some of his actions challenged by states in court; some others I have touched on in this book.

It seems that his wording openly declares these positions in his if you care to read his book. One statement comes to mind about religion from his book, "Dreams From My Father" something like this; if the situation gets bad, I am going to side with them Muslims. And from his book, Dreams From My Father something like this: Of course, not all my conversations in immigrant communities follow this easy pattern. In the wake of 9/11, my meetings with Arab and Pakistani Americans, for example, have a more urgent quality—then further on. They have been reminded that the history of immigration in this country has a dark underbelly— but you should review all in his book for yourself to make any judgment.

America and Americans are Eroding

A small number of the residence in America, again who care very little of our country hence the reason I use the word resident and not American are so selfish and infantile and so slavish that they are the people that identify with Obama's anger. Need I mention Jeremiah Wright again for example, spewing his hatred? What about those who make their living exploiting racism in America? A good start would be the Reverend Al Sharpton and the Reverend Jessie Jackson, as well as others. They are not improving their culture they are contributing to the escalation of crime in the poverty level of their race. Crime has taken over the ghettoes and the religion of the past, has been replaced by socialism and Marxism.

This element supports Obama's alleged paths toward destruction. He calls it "change," but is it change that aggrandizes hate?

Can anyone remember the visceral attack that Obama launched against the police who arrested Henry Louis Gates, one of Obama's black friends, where Obama admitted he knew nothing of the facts in the case against his friend?

Obama's words were about the police in Cambridge, Massachusetts who he said, acted stupidly in arresting a prominent black Harvard professor Henry Louis Gates after a confrontation at the man's home.

The one acknowledgement by the true God loving America-loving patriots are that Obama loves being popular and it has certainly made him that. Obama does not typically veer too far off into his resentments for white America on camera, lest a remnant of patriots rise up against him.

A good indicator of this tactic was Obama's admitting that he knew nothing of the circumstances before he spoke out against the whites who arrested his black Harvard professor friend.

It is too bad loud incorrect racist voices receive favorable treatment in our liberal bias media today such as Obama with the rush to judgment in the Boston burglary episode. Is an off-color remark just a remark or does it reveal the true racist feelings from within? Jumping to wrong conclusions or labeling is not a sign of leadership; it is simply revealing your true inner self and your weakness.

Accounts regarding the confrontation between Gates and the police differ, it does not matter that it was outside his own home, the police would not have known that, but Gates was arrested by the responding officer, Cambridge Police Sgt. James Crowley, and charged with disorderly conduct. On July 21, the charges against Gates were dropped. The arrest generated a national debate about whether or not it represented an example of racial profiling by police.

If anyone is stopped on the highway or God forbid told to stop doing something in a neighborhood and you do not respond to the command of the police, you will be charged with disorderly conduct and jailed. Whether you are released from jail sooner or later will be up to the police department, suggesting that Gate's release sooner meant to me that he began to calm down and obey the commands from the police. That he was released did not excuse his behavior that got him arrested in the first place. Had he obliged the commands from the police officer at the beginning, he may never have been arrested in the first place.

After all, the reason we do not run red lights or speed on the highway is out of fear of being caught, translated by law-abiding citizens as having respect for the law and the law officers, which Gate's obviously did not have. Henry Louis

"Skip" Gates, Jr., (born September 16, 1950) is an American literary critic, educator, scholar, writer, editor, and public intellectual. He was the first African American to receive the Andrew W. Mellon Foundation Fellowship. He has received numerous honorary degrees and awards for his teaching, research, and development of academic institutions to study black culture. How is it with the amount of respect he obviously receives that he was not willing to give respect where it was called for? Not that Gates is a progressive socialist, but failure to offer respect while demanding it—does fit the progressive elitist.

Progressive Communist Liberals

Forms of socialism dominated much of the world for the first half of the twentieth century and slowly made its way into American governance. It took a half-century for progressive communist liberals to achieve this turnabout they now have in America through what is termed progressivism.

The future damage is incalculable unless we take drastic actions now. What are those actions? Start electing America-loving patriots and not money-hungry career politicians who are controlled by the special-interest groups like those supporting Obama's candidacy, as well as the millionaire and billionaire puppet masters behind the scenes who also support Obama's candidacy.

Elect patriots who mean it when they say: I am sad that I only have one life to give for my country. The following problems will never be quickly reversed or undone but will be attended to:

Corrupt American politicians must be replaced by patriots

The government-appointed bureaucrat agencies and problems that must be solved quickly, such as:

- The American borders
- The illegal aliens
- The entitlement programs
- The American banking system
- The Federal Reserve
- The American educational system

- The American Supreme Court legal system

- The American liberal media bias

As well as guaranteeing the American sovereignty by becoming debt free which will place America firmly on the road of accomplishing all of the above because these troubles were long in the making and they will not be undone overnight, However-as-many as I can undertake simultaneously, I will undertake them as your president.

They cannot be simply removed or quickly reversed but as with a computer, nothing happens until you push the start-button and I intend to be a massive Start-Button champion when elected president. Oh yes, and you do not have to guess at what my change is all about, I have it printed right in this book for you to hold my feet to the fire with, because I work for you, not the other way around, the way it should be: government of the people by the people and for the people. I am just like you, not someone to look down my nose at you (calling you little people), which as average Americans, we seem to have become used to by now; words from our masters who we have been voting into office. Here is an angle: Stop letting the cause of bad government be your bad choice when voting.

The media and those who have purchased the media have produced the population that elected a possible illegal candidate, who certainly seems to have broken laws while in office.

Part of the movement of white progressive liberals who helped put Obama in office were the communists with their Oedipal Complex, (the Oedipal Complex is a term coined by Sigmund Freud who explained present day neuroses partially on the basis of wish fulfillment). Oedipal Complex, which is murderous impetus thought toward free enterprise and the American Constitution. These communists have almost achieved their goals, which is collapsing America from within. If you do not understand this or, need more research than I have presented thus far then read: The Destruction of America, by David Yeagley which is available at: http://www.badeagle.com/2008/11/04/obama-the-destruction-of-America —-and—- Obama & Progressives Planed Destruction of America http://www.usacarry.com/forums/politics/11742-obama-progressives-planned-destruction-america.html

It would seem that dismantling America would dismantle their machinery. Why would they agree to dismantle their machinery?

On the contrary, they will defend it with all their power and lying words and sleight of hand wonders. They seek ultimate control. When you create insurmountable debt you can seize assets and then achieve the ultimate goal, eliminate sovereignty, which I have explained in this book.

Welfare or entitlement is to constantly reward those who refuse to work. When you pay people not to work that is exactly what they will do. Why does the left always frighten the old people when spending cuts are needed? The left says that Social Security checks and pensions are at risk but never mention the welfare money that goes down the rat hole every day. The free money that enslaves people should be the first thing chopped in the budget. No able-bodied person should be on welfare. We must greatly limit this safety net that is now a web of turmoil around the necks of those who are chronically dependent.

Speaking to those residents of America who expect entitlements, do you really see those in Africa for example, receiving entitlements, or, do you see any of them with a better form of life? I am willing to reach out to you to teach you that a better way of life is in self-achievement and reward.

You have to wake up before it is too late and see what your true rewards from government are going to be, by backing these progressive democracy fakers who may wear a democrat or republican hat who have one common goal with their lies to you and that is total control; total control over all Americans, who are not part of the ultimate wealthy elite. The new world order is what some refer to the controlling Elite' that I explained earlier.

Is America ready for a purely principled candidate to be elected as president or into Congress, when the political tide is the seductiveness of collectivism? Collectivism is described as the principles or system of ownership, and control of the means of production and distribution, which translates to the elite ownership of the people collectively, usually under the supervision of a government.

A true patriot is outside of this beltway and believes in staying a course for a more Constitutional form of government. When one only thinks what is right for one's self, voting for someone who puts the country first could be challenging and this would mean that we could never hope to change the culture within the people elected.

It Takes a Change In Mindset

We all have a belief system that consists of paradigms that control how we interpret the world. However, once we look at the results of what our past voting record has netted our country, which was choosing only the candidate that pandered to our desires, who did not place the country first, then perhaps we can use a different kind of collectivism. By that I refer to a majority vote that can change what is so obviously broken in our country, corrupt politics and politicians.

Until we can change the thought process of a person who does not think about what is right for the country, but only what is right for them, then the culture behind every election will not change and we can never hope to change that culture within the people elected. Please give this considerable thought. Helping that thought process along would be to research Argentina.

Argentina We Should Not Follow

In the early 20th   century Argentina was one of the richest countries in the world and the United States challenged Argentina for the position of the world's second-most powerful economy. Like the United States Argentina had abundant agriculture with vast farmland and accessible ports. Argentina's level of Industrialization was higher than many European countries; railroads, automobiles, and telephones.

In 1916, Argentina elected a new president, Hipolito Irigoyen from a new party called "The Radicals" under the banner of "Fundamental Change", which appealed to the middle class. Among the newly elected Argentine president Irigoyen's changes were: mandatory pension insurance, mandatory health insurance, and support for low-income housing construction to stimulate the economy. Put simply the state assumed economic control and began assessing new payroll taxes to fund its endeavors.

With an increasing flow of tax funds into the government entitlement programs, which were growing as well as the size, and scope of government, the government became overwhelmed. Before long government outlays surpassed the value of all taxpayers' contributions. At that point back in history, Argentina was just like America is today with all of the union entitlements as well as all of the other enormous government growth and added scope as well as government entitlement programs that are about to crash.

You might say the final nail in the coffin for Argentine economy came with the election of Juan Peron with his wife Eva, with their populist rhetoric of taxing the nations rich.

Under Peron government bureaucracies exploded through massive programs of social spending and encouraging the growth of the labor unions. The handouts attracted the farm workers to unionize leading to large reductions in beef and wheat production.

Inflation and higher and higher taxes forced on business created hyper-inflation in 1989; the final stage of the process characterized the "industrial protectionism, redistribution of income based on increased union wages and a growing intervention from government in the economy.

Please visualize the Federal Reserve when reading this next piece.

The Argentinean government's practice of printing money to pay off its public debts had crushed the economy. Inflation hit three thousand percent, food riots were rampant, stores were looted and the country descended into chaos. By 1994, Argentina's public pensions, the equivalent of Social Security had imploded. Twenty six percent payroll tax was not even near enough so value added tax and personal income taxes rose and an added tax of the wealthy creeped even higher, which had been increasing steadily as determined by the government. All these government interventions and taxes crushed the private sector. When Argentina's government defaulted on bonds, it raided pension funds and the economy was worse than the American great depression. Now a hundred years after it was the richest economy in the world, it is a poverty-stricken country that never left the depression it created.

Populist Plans for America

The American Democratic Party's populist plans for the U.S. cannot possibly work, because government bankrupts everything it touches.

Democrats and republicans see things differently because of differences in the way each are predisposed to interpret the world. I am asking both the left and the right to step out of that terminal death box which all have confined themselves to and fairly determine what course our country is on now, which you the American voting public may have contributed to by your vote.

Your vote should be viewed by you, as the direction that will bring safety, financial security, life, liberty and the free pursuit of happiness without government intervention for you and your family and not just to meet your immediate desires. Your vote should be for your entire American family, all patriot Americans which I have referred to often in this book are your brothers and sisters. That is if you are "NOT" just a resident of America, which I have also explained. Hopefully you are genuinely a patriot, red, white and blue-blooded American, our future is in your hands, when you vote.

The democrat leaders today are guilty of more than stupidity; they are enslaving future generations to poverty and misery. If you are a democrat I am asking you to visualize Argentina happening in America and pitch in with us with your vote against your democrat politicians who are racing toward our destruction. Let us stop the train of madness.

If your answer in the privacy of your own home is yes, that you are a red, white and blue-blooded American patriot, then consider not voting for the candidate who promises you the moon and any of your desires at the taxpayers' expense. Remind yourself what effect it would have on America long-term. Then consider voting for the true patriots who love this country, and who are not spending millions of dollars spreading lies on television to get your vote, to wind up giving you more of the same. My platform is in this book so you can hold my feet to the fire and it cannot be misquoted by media, you have it in your hand.

Paradigms do exist and must be weighted; for example: Some transactions, like selling a paper clip, have short-term implications, and may have only simple paradigms. Some transactions have long-term implications for both buyer and seller, like a life insurance policy, which creates a different set of paradigms.

If we are getting what we want today from government through entitlements and welfare programs, what are the long-term complications? -If you fail to consider the long-term, this attitude increases the problems. -You won't get them once the country is broke anyway. Why not take the advantage now to stop the madness to save your country that will by default, provide you with greater opportunity. -Looking at the long-term effect is how the American patriot who loves his country would look at it.

If these ideas sound like you could join in, then your focus and your attitude play a large part in solving your paradigms. Your focus is the screen that you use to choose what you will pay attention to and to notice from all of the possibilities in your environment that you may not have ever focused on before.

Your attitude is how you interpret what you focus on and this is where I would ask that you place your country first and disallow past thoughts based on your culture and life's experiences and to consider yourself as part of the American family: The giant American family that I always refer to is a family that sees themselves as having no color, race, or creed that has a belief in God and a love for country. Then make your voting decision as though it would be life or death for that family.

Do I fear anything when it comes to saving my country? The answer is absolutely not. My enemies will learn without their respect to quickly to fear me and America, and because no one or no country will get the opportunity to destroy America or Americans because American security is first. Security will be on the top burner as resonated by my intentions for the military the restarting of Star Wars and our American borders earlier mentioned. All of our soldiers will become highly trained teams that demonstrated such honor in the death of Ben Laden, but if somehow the enemy does harm Americans any-where, that enemy will be destroyed and so will anyone trying to assist them. And we not undertake nation rebuilding or building.

The true patriot leader must speak about recovery from this disaster as I have and not so much the major surgery necessary to keep this country from falling over the cliff; recovery can only exist with the help of patriotic voting Americans.

My platform speaks about some of my major surgery that will eliminate redundant government bureaucracy paid for by the tax-payer, but in turn will create the atmosphere for everyone to create jobs that count. Jobs where the dollars you earn and spend did not come from the taxpayer are true jobs, and job creators will mean you and me America.

Americans are the brightest entrepreneurs in the world and we will once again return to our roots. Be brave America, get on board with me, stand up strong with me and become a team player right alongside me; I am for you and will represent you to insure that America's best days are in our near future.

On our American ship, remember there are only Americans. There is no such thing as White Americans, African Americans, Asian Americans, Latin Americans or Middle East Americans, there are only Americans as I have been describing them and we are a family, we don't allow the imposters to come on board with true red white and blue-blooded Americans.

If you see yourself as just a resident of America by referring to yourself as to one of these names just mentioned in the place of simply being a true red, white and blue-blooded American, then leave before you are asked to. If you love America and Americans then you should be for our family and I am asking you to be for me, who is an American patriot that wants to become your presi-dent without being beholden to billionaires. I love each and every one of my patriotic American family; you are part of my family. Help me stop our country's demise please! I should not need to spend millions on television for your vote.

Obama came into power because of suppressing facts, the promise of entitlements and by not revealing what change he was speaking of, as well as receiving ninety nine percent of the minority vote and going over the top white votes. To help that ninety nine percent minority vote toward Obama were the results of hate, fear and racist mongers with their hidden agenda for national negligence of their own minorities, so as to keep those racist mongers in the news, this makes the environment culpable to continue making money on the backs of those same minorities they scream are being mistreated. Please see this fellow Americans; these racist mongers do not need or want you to be elevated in your life, which would stop their money machine. If you were to see and seize opportunity that you had never focused on and reject dependency, their money machine would fizzle out and become seen for the sickness that it really is. Consider it now, before you place your magical hand on the pen that will mark your ballet come 2012 Election Day.

Progressivism slowly implemented in our school system for the past one hundred years started paying off even more when the race card began to surface. Ignorance would light the pathway for the future of the socialist, Marxist and progressives. By producing through the educational system an entitlement immaturity that would last throughout life, which is an attitude that sees others being responsible and not themselves, you could say progressive education is working.

Covertness of Covetousness from the Puppet Masters Control Obama

The hidden from view covertness of the Covetous attitude of the elitist puppet masters who control Obama's actions, is woven in message in his teleprompter when he speaks. To deconstruct this Obama labyrinth-like network of puppet masters, you could choose to start your research with this website: http://www.americanfreepress.net/html/behind_barack_obama_188.html

Victor Thorn on this website starts out by saying one must start at the top with global slash and burn speculator George Soros and his ties to the world's most powerful banking family, Journalist, historian and economic researcher William Engdahl and that began to set the stage at identifying Soros who is funding Obama.

Soros has been identified as a front man for the Rothschild banking group writes Thorn. "Understandably, neither he nor the Rothschilds want this information to be public. So please do your own research. Soros's connection to the ultra-secret international finance circles of the Rothschilds is not just an ordinary or accidental banking connection."

Finally, in a November 1, 1996 article, Engdahl writes, "From the very first days when Soros created his own investment fund in 1969, he owed his success to his relation to the Rothschild family banking network.

Soros, through his Open Society Institute, funnels approximately three hundred million dollars a year into various liberal venues, including the liberal influential MoveOn.org, which he owns.

According to veteran researcher Anton Chaitkin, Soros also is said to have hand-picked Barack Obama to challenge Hillary Clinton, even though Hillary would have been his choice over McCain (and ultimately defeat of GOP nominee John McCain). On September 5, 2008, Engdahl wrote, "Barack Obama came under special Soros sponsorship in the 2004 U.S. Senate race and raised $60,000 for his campaign. After attaining victory, Obama met personally with Soros, and then Obama attended a fundraiser at his home.

Obama's message was called "change," but without explaining what that change would be; now we begin to see what that was to be and it reminds me of what Paul Harvey, the sports journalist used to say:" Now for the rest of the story!"

Obama's use of the teleprompter and his lack of impromptu skills are true indications of the organization and planning of his backers, the puppeteers I call them, who have the destruction of our Republic and our Constitution at heart, not the adherence to, in mind. See above Soros report.

Being more aware of our Constitution would serve America better at the voting booth. When reviewing a candidate you would be more in tune with his platform inconsistencies to our Constitution. Do you think "We the People" should know and understand the Constitution that has been in the background and taken out of our public school academia for so long?

Please read from the London Review of Books, v. 10 no. 7, March 1988: During the year of the bicentennial of the U. S. Constitution, many celebrations were held throughout the United States, not only in Philadelphia where our Framers met from May to September in the summer of 1787, but in many American cities, large and small of today. The point of these celebrations was not just to recall a moment in the nation's past, but to educate the public about the meaning and value of the Constitution.

None of these events, however, served the educational purpose so well as two wholly unanticipated events: the Iran-Contra hearings and the Senate Judiciary Committee Hearings on President Reagan's nomination of Judge Robert Bork to the Supreme Court.

In both instances national telecasts provided Americans with a civic education. Those who listened now have a far greater understanding of the Constitution than they could have gained from a dozen or more bicentennial events; because the Constitution has systematically been removed from the teaching in our schools.

Judge Bork had a definite opinion about constitutional interpretation stressing the necessity, as he put it, in an American Enterprise Institute lecture in 1984, "to establish the proposition that would have the Framer's intentions with respect to freedoms are the sole legitimate premise from which constitutional analysis may proceed.

In 1982 he objected to the use of the equal protection clause of the 14th Amendment "to protect groups that were historically not intended to be protected by that clause," and he criticized the Supreme Court's efforts to extend the application of the equal protection clause, to women, arguing that it was originally intended only to apply to racial discrimination.

The Constitution is open to interpretation as to what the Framers meant, because the document does not wear its meaning on its face. But the Constitution should not be subjected to interpretation; however it is subjected to interpretation again and again in a majority-controlled democracy.

The series of commentaries, which the Constitution has generated, rival the voluminous studies on the Bible and the Talmud, as well as those on the most commented upon of all texts, the plays of William Shakespeare.

Although we might wonder how the Constitution means certain things in it, an equally intriguing and not unrelated question is: how is it that the Constitution can go on meaning and meaning and meaning, seemingly endlessly?

A highly and widely praised and regularly practiced feature of judicial review is to ask, what the Framers' intent might have been.

This would appear to be Judge Bork's view of the matter. Thus, in the Furman v. Georgia case, a decision before the Supreme Court in which the majority took the position that in all the states whose systems were under review, capital punishment was unconstitutional Justice Blackmun argued in dissent that while he himself believed that capital punishment serves no useful purpose and is not compatible with his philosophical convictions and is antagonistic to any sense of a reverence for life, it is evident from even a superficial reading of the text that as far as the Framers were concerned "capital punishment was not unconstitutional per se, under the Eighth Amendment."

How do we win when it comes to the Constitution? We put the Constitution (and original intent) first and I say that is the answer.

No matter what your belief system or someone else's is, we must follow the intent of the Framers in our republic or, the elected majority officials, who often do not represent the majority of the people will rule and interfere with our constitutional rights, in the democracy that is being forced down our throats; a democracy that will slaughter any chance we have at holding on to our charter and to our republic.

We must fight in every manner we can find power to do so any attempt made to replace that original intent; even if it may conflict with a belief, it still must be defended lest we fail at defending it in more personal instances where the outcome directly affects Americans.

Is the Federal Reserve Part of Our Problem? And Kennedy's EO-11110

Being a conservative Republican or quite possibly Independent, depending on how the Republican Party accepts my agenda as their candidate, it may be hard for you to understand my love and admiration for President John Fitzgerald Kennedy, who understood that the Federal Reserve notes being used as the legal currency before 1963 were contrary to our Constitution.

He signed "Executive Order 11110 to basically strip the Federal Reserve Bank of its power to loan money to the United States federal government at interest.

Kennedy declared that the privately owned Fed would soon be out of business or at least out of the U.S. currency printing business. I ask my readers to visualize Argentina when reading this portion. Kennedy's Executive Order 11110 has never been repealed, amended, or superseded by any subsequent order. In simple terms, it is still valid.

This order, returned to the federal government, specifically the Treasury Department, the constitutional power to create and issue currency-money without going through the privately owned Federal Reserve Bank, which is an un-elected body that has a large influence in our lives.

This order gave the Treasury Department the explicit authority to issue silver certificates against any silver, silver bullion or standard silver dollars in the treasury. This means that for every ounce of silver in the U.S. Treasury's vault, the government could introduce new money into circulation based on the silver bullion physically held there.

As a result, more than $4 billion in United States notes were brought into circulation in $2 and $5 denominations. Ten dollar and twenty dollar United States notes were never circulated but were being printed by the Treasury Department when Kennedy was assassinated. Those notes differed slightly from those issued by the Federal Reserve; one says "Federal Reserve Note" on the top issued by the Fed, while the other says "United States Note".

President Kennedy was assassinated on November 22, 1963 and the United States notes, which he had issued, were immediately taken out of circulation. This did not raise any red-flags.

Kennedy knew that if the silver-backed United States notes were widely circulated, they would have eliminated the demand for the existing Federal Reserve notes.

Virtually all of the nearly $14 plus trillion in federal debt has been created since 1963 on printed worthless paper.

If any subsequent president were to have the courage to enforce EO-11110, he would have almost immediately given the U.S. government the ability to repay its debt without going to the private Federal Reserve banks and being charged interest to create new "money". E O 11110 gave the United States the ability to once again create its own money backed by silver real value and actually worth something.

Some have speculated that the reason Kennedy was assassinated was to protect the Federal Reserve Bank. People need to understand that they would pay less income tax and the middle class and lower middle class would see more of their hard-earned money, as well as the wealthy job creators who simply pass their taxes back to the consumers who purchase their goods and services. So never forget you the consumer pay those taxes that some want to increase on the wealthy job creators.

After downsizing the federal government and creating our own money to stop the interest paid to the Fed, our standard of living could become debt free in the near future. All the bureaucracies created by government starting decades earlier and enhanced by the present administration caused the debt crisis because it was living outside of our means.

Government started taking out loans when tax revenues began to be over burdened by the constant government expansion and spending programs. Government began to create a credit card on the taxpayer's back, without his consent and take money from this centralized banking monopoly who in turn, borrowed money from foreign countries to lend to the American government with interest.

The majority of Americans need to be aware of this; we are in fact being lied to and as your president, I will follow president Kennedy's lead on this matter.

What can we do? How can we make changes in this country?

Our right to vote seems to be our only voice; however the coverage the media gives to candidates seems to be determined by who has the most money. The huge amounts of money thrown towards the media seem to result in who we select from to vote for. We only hear from those who have amassed large amounts of money, so our lack of research on our own, nets American voters what they deserve.

We even used to be appalled at the seizure of our private property; we are now lulled to sleep by politicians and we allow government intervention into our private lives.

The Federal Reserve is making a handful of old families wealthier in the world, mostly out of the United States and is controlling America's currency so the Fed can keep "we the people" in debt over our head, so that we are preoccupied with that debt to such an extent that we won't find out how they control Americans with that debt, which I believe is the Fed's mission.

Get rid of the Illegal Immigrants Tax Burden, the Fed Tax Burden Would Help Support a Balanced Budget

Why do we allow ourselves to feel like we are working to educate the children of the illegals, or to provide free heath care for illegals in emergency rooms across America or to allow them to draw Social Security? We will pick up the tab for the illegals as well as for those who got loans, which they could never afford to pay, considering their income (with the help and support of our corrupt politicians and bankers) sanctioned by the Fed.

These people who should not have gotten the home loans in the first place, had their bogus loans packaged and sold around the world to unsuspecting foreign entities who, at the time actually trusted America,.

These consumers who could not afford to pay for the house loans they were given unscrupulously, when asked to pay for those houses they decided to walk away from them. But before they started walking away from these loans, these faulty real estate loans had been packaged and peddled by Wall Street to many countries. The default on the home loans created a bailout era and still Wall Street profited from these bogus deals; and we the tax payers paid Wall Street again when we bailed the banks and others out, including the corrupt banks who started the ball rolling by authorizing the bogus loans in the first place, and who are still looking for more bailout money.

In some foreign countries the Federal Reserve is viewed as the most evil institution on the planet. They say: Americans, wake up to this monstrous ogre that sits in your midst this polluting entity has no more power than what you grant it.

The ogre feeds off of taxpayer efforts with the support of corrupt politicians. This offensive organization needs to be downsized and returned to being just another bank to be left to survive in a free enterprise, where you are allowed to prosper as well as allowed to fail. Help elect a non-billionaire patriot to the office of president, one who loves his country enough to risk everything for it and that patriot is David Tippie.

There will be a new sheriff in town, though I hate to quote the left winger, Nancy Pelosi on that; however I will be a sheriff as brave and as tough as Sheriff Joe Arpaio has displayed, if you vote for me. Your vote will be all in how you focus on the future of America and how you see the support for the welfare or entitlements will fail anyway; however when they fail with the full steam-ahead spending, you think your life is bad now with them, just think what your life will be when the entire country is bankrupt. You can get food and water now, but if everything shuts down, there would be mass starvation. You could take a different view and focus on reversing the trend we are now in and taking advantage of an environment that would create jobs in that new America that lived within it means. Of course the choice is up to you the voter.

Education Is in a Shambles!

We pay taxes to operate the public schools, which are woefully under-educating, our children. But you can't opt out of those taxes; even if you have the good sense to send your children to private schools you still must pay the same public school taxes. You can't opt out of them.

Nothing is changing for the better in our public school system. Where is the outrage? Why are we picking up the tab for the destruction of the minds of our children in public schools? When as parents we are clearly not getting what we need for our children, our school system is seventeenth in the world. You will get the choice to school your children privately when I am elected president and you can use the public school tax money that you won't have to pay, to pay for private schooling. I will at the same time do my best to privatize all of the public school system. First---by getting government out of the picture, by eliminating the U.S. Department of Education and returning the power to the states.

Why do people go to universities in America if they only graduate as sheep, going to their slaughter?

Sad isn't it. We have stood by while the politicians and unelected bureaucracies tell the press what to say, tell Americans what to say and do, what we can buy and not to buy, what we can eat, mandate that your child take vaccines and what medical treatment we must undergo, which some have tried to escape such as the treatment radiation and chemo who were arrested as seen here on the CBS website: http://www.cbsnews.com/stories/2009/07/06/health/main5135062.shtml

Crime Is Explained to be Related to Poverty but Responsibility Starts Somewhere:

Many lawmakers in Congress and in the states assume that the high level of crime in America must have its roots in material conditions; such as poor employment opportunities and a shortage of adequately funded social programs. When at the heart of the explosion of crime in America is the loss of the capacity of fathers and mothers to be responsible in caring for the children they bring into the world. This loss of love and guidance at the intimate levels of marriage and family has broad social consequences for children and for the wider community. The empirical evidence shows that too many young men and women from broken families tend to have a much weaker sense of connection with their neighborhood and are prone to exploit neighbors to satisfy their unmet needs or desires. This contributes to a loss of a sense of community and to the disintegration of neighborhoods into social chaos and violent crime.

The unfolding debate over welfare reform, for instance, has been shaped by the wide acceptance in recent years that children born into single-parent families are much more likely than children of intact families to fall into poverty and welfare dependence themselves in later years. Over the past thirty years, the rise in violent crime parallels the rise in families abandoned by fathers. High-crime neighborhoods are characterized by high concentrations of families abandoned by fathers.

Neighborhoods with a high degree of religious practice are not high-crime neighborhoods. Even in high-crime inner-city neighborhoods, well over ninety percent of children from safe, stable homes do not become delinquents. By contrast only ten percent of children from unsafe, unstable homes in these neighborhoods avoid crime.

The central proposition and the official thinking in Washington about crime are that poverty is the primary cause of crime. In its simplest form, this contention is absurd; if it were true, there would have been more crime in the past, when more people were poorer. And in poorer nations, the crime rates would be higher than in the United States. Entitlements and welfare creates more dependence and more crime. In fact unconditional welfare is a crime against the poor.

The word dependency contains a curious contradiction. In premodern times, dependency meant being part of a social unit (estate, family, empire) that was headed by someone else. Dependents (such as servants, retainers and peasants in a feudal estate, wives and children) were dependent in the sense that they had no legal status in society at large, and were represented by their master. But in retrospect the master was dependent on everyone else in the unit for his material existence.

The young, single mother is today the icon of dependency and yet it is not she who is dependent in any material sense, but it is the children she looks after. If she did not accept legal responsibility for the child, then she would not be entitled to welfare payments. But she raises her children, generally under incredibly difficult conditions, while the father and the state who are both seen as responsible for the support of the child, are riding free on her efforts, depending on her, in fact, to do what they will not.

In our beginning when there were only two classes of people the ultra-rich and the ultra-poor. The condition of dependency was perfectly respectable and covered the vast majority of people including vagabonds and foreigners, excluding only the top layer of the nobility.

In today's world however, to entice or force someone to become dependent through entitlements is nothing more than an attempt to lower their self-worth and socioeconomic stature, removing his desire to succeed compelling him to be poor and controllable all of his life and completely destroying his ability to pass anything helpful to his off-spring other than disrespect and a complete lack of drive, attention-span or self-worth. Is it any wonder those subjected to this are more prone to criminal activity?

We have produced a generation of children that do not want to do anything but talk and play games because their attention-span is addicted to short stimuli. If the scene lasts more than five seconds it's deemed too long. And these are the people who will be running our country someday if there is a country left for them to run.

It is high time for a second American Revolution in the form of an American "evolution" to gain a higher moral and ethical standard. I believe ethics to be our next evolutionary step in taking our country back, which includes improving our public schools or privatizing them to attract talented teachers who are paid for their ability and fired for their inability. If we do not take this opportunity, we may not survive.

We must stand together as patriots to get our country back from such evil doers (go back to my discussion of George Soros to get a sense of a small list) that control our lives today; it's not just one country they want control of, it is all of them. Remember the new world order propagandist want you to believe is nonexistent? It is a concealed internationally run system and it is actually illegal. Problem is today, there are not enough patriots who are willing to take action in the courts with against the corrupt congress, however with a strong president who actually loves our country can help to reverse these evils.

We are controlled like puppets in a manner that most of Americans don't even realize. The "big guys" never pay attention to these types of books enough to care what is revealed in them; no more than drug companies believe you pay attention to the side effects they tell you about when advertising a drug on television that you can't even purchase from them. It will take millions of American middle-class patriots, and remember what I classify an American as being, not based on anything other than your love for our country- to make this happen.

I don't mean people banding together and physically marching around the Federal Reserve building or political offices with banners and signs that demand change, although that certainly may take place; I mean we must do the opposite of what we have always done and stop voting for the privileged in our society who do not have Americas interests at heart. A free Internet based campaign, website and YouTube for each candidate to express their views is needed. Where there are no special interest groups or billionaire puppet masters paying for television adds that the candidate would then have to become beholden. Just free American patriots running for all offices in America. I can envision getting this kind of support to help me win the presidency. Word of mouth is the best advertising.

The definition of insanity is doing the same things over and over and expecting a different outcome. What I am saying is that we need to stop paying attention to, and electing the puppets who are spending their special interest group's money to tell you what you want to hear just to get elected. If you keep voting for the person who spends the most money and time on television what are you achieving?

We must find the true Americans like myself, who love this country and are willing to make the sacrifice for the changes we must have and a return to our Constitutional form of government-which we must have to survive.

I can think of one patriot to reverse the business as usual in Washington right now and that is David Tippie. You are reading my platform and it is not hope that something will change that you won't be informed about, as was the case when Obama promised hope and change without substance because you are reading it. Without your help, no one will ever hear about this change however. I am not a billionaire; you will have to help me push the start button, to save our wonderful, beautiful America.

More of the Federal Reserve from a Friend

I received something from a friend I shall only refer to as J, who posted something on a LinkedIn website group of mine who said: God bless you David. Your words announce your intentions, and your intentions give way to exciting others into action which Americans need to replace the apathy they have shown over the years you back down from nothing.

The posts are on the LinkedIn group called: "The Political Conservative Objective". Comments on this group reflect both facts and opinions. The facts are consistent with much of what I have read and researched throughout the years; though as I point out U.S. citizens have largely been kept in the dark from the seriously negative consequences that await them, in what I refer to in this book as the train wreck we are all headed for.

"J" says David you are right: many foreigners know more about this travesty of the Fed than do Americans. And most if not all in developed and developing countries have their own version of our Federal Reserve. It seems that inside the international banking industry all share the same agenda and practices with the Fed in America. However, the United States Federal Reserve is particularly heinous and powerful because the currency they control is the "world's reserve currency" virtually the foundation of the world's banking system (at least for now).

"J" continues, David know you are not the first to challenge the Fed, nor would you be the first presidential candidate to do so. Consider the forces at play, the power and money to silence common sense.

He further states to; consider also the ignorance and ambivalence of 200 million Americans who are oblivious to this economic train wreck. You talk about an "evolution" not a "revolution". "J" says, I cannot imagine a way to "evolve" or in any way gently correct this train wreck.

He says David think about it: the world's reserve currency, the U.S. dollar, and all other economies that are hinged to it are deliberately being railroaded into bankruptcy by the wealthiest, most powerful individuals and institutions in the history of man-kind.

I answered "J" this way: "J" the evolving I speak of is the termination of these puppet heads that represent the powerful puppeteers.

America's new dawn is coming and it is not delivered in the form of control by millionaires and billionaires, it is delivered by American loving patriots like David Tippie who want to ensure freedom and the pursuit of happiness to his American family. David Tippie wants to make certain his American family will stop being duped into thinking that the train that they are on, although it serves free lunches to some, will none the less be hurled over the pending cliff, if Americans do not start putting on the brakes with their vote.

Patriots are going to unite once again in brotherly and sisterly love, as a family of brave Americans who will stop the madness of destroying our country by those who are speeding the train toward the cliff with no bridge. We will accomplish it by every means within our power through our massive numbers.

The next train conductor or what I am calling the president, if it is David Tippie he will need engineers and conductors with his same passion, commitment and love of country as well as moral character, not the sub-human characters who surround the president today.

Revolt as in Revolution

Revolt as in revolution, if necessary, but we will return to our Founding Fathers morals, scruples, values and character which I refer to as honor. The honor of our Founding Fathers was good for the most part, except for the fact that they did not abolish slavery and they believed women should never exercise authority, that only white propertied men should vote, and that slavery was what the entire world was involved with at the time so how could they envision a future without it. However do we really believe they could have thought of everything in the future? Absolutely not.

I would like to introduce some of my views by opening them up to a fuller acknowledgment (notice I didn't say interpretation of our Founders) of the realities of which the Founders which we are descendants of, have lived. Comparing some of the fuller realities which we have lived through and learned from in our past and to those accomplished from that learning which we have achieved and to those we shall not return, so that our future as the American family means just that, which is: we all have the same unalienable rights that will not be surrendered, endowed by our creator with certain inalienable rights owed exclusively to God and cannot be enforced, regulated our impeded by civil government and we all shall defend them with our very lives, if need be. True Americans are all the same.

The world will once again see our strength from our perseverance and willingness to resolve our own problems and change status quo as an American family team that we will accomplish together where our enemies will fear our decent to their actions once more, which will by default reduce terrorism.

We will not bow to our enemies, nor will we be supporting the world's problems by pouring new bad U.S. borrowed money into them after previous bad borrowed money which we have already provided; money that we allow our elected puppets to stupidly borrow and to give away to foreign countries and that they need not tell us about. Does the word Federal Reserve pop into mind?

Many people have reminded me that we are a charitable nation and that is very true. But you don't as a family, go out and borrow money that you cannot afford, to pass out to people who are asking for money on the streets. Your family must come first.

I am sure these countries will forgive America for taking the time necessary to regain our strength and to stop borrowing money that our children and grandchildren will be forced to pay with assets and American sovereignty.

The public's lack of awareness could start anywhere, not just the Fed. The lack of public education on the Constitution and issues of our Constitution being ripped apart by the political Marxist communist thieves is also a good start. We elect these thieves to hold political office who often wind up on the news when caught in a criminal act, crimes caught are too numerous to mention, even when we hear of their illegal activity on the television we seem to have become oblivious to it and not outraged as we once were, because we are so ill-informed and lack the will to join with others until now, there is the Tea Party and individuals such as myself who write books.

Chapter 9

Educating through Progressive Communism

I will not stop trying to awaken those individuals who have allowed for so many years, the progressives to silently, slowly and methodically dumb down our school system and who can defend the un-defendable. The past governor of Florida Jeb Bush has my hat off to him due to his actions reforming that school system. He said we should benchmark ourselves to the world and not accept mediocrity when it comes to the education of our children. Jeb's results were: boosting charters, school vouchers, voluntary universal pre-school and teacher merit pay which increased student test scores by more than twenty percent in Florida in just over a decade proving that over the long haul you can move the needle toward progress on student achievement.

In the case of higher learning we must remove the cancer at the very core, which is to rid the school systems of tenure and eliminate those who do not subscribe to our American way of life liberty and the pursuit of happiness and who profess to be communist such as Bill Ayres who could not have been fired due to his tenure, teaching our young adults his views of America.

The kids become sports worshippers from grade school forward and view academics as nerdy, which make them, become controllable by the left-wing America haters and this helps to destroy America from the inside.

Although this is only touching the surface we must not leave out the fact that progressivism has won so to speak, in our educational system. Progressives have slowly made people think that a democracy was the same as our Constitutional republic.

America, Destroyed from Within

America will never be destroyed from the outside. If we falter (do not fight) and lose our freedoms, it will be because we destroyed ourselves from within. This was stated by Abraham Lincoln.

The dogmas of the past are inadequate to our stormy present; and we too often can say that someone's actions are not enough, so we say let's not bother to take any action with the action seekers, it is too big of a fight and they may not win, so why bother if results are not guaranteed.

Nothing could be further from the truth. When we stand together to make it happen, hope is not a plan, defeat of our proven enemy is the goal and due to our numbers, death will not even alter our end result.

You must put pettiness aside. Please help me take back our country; stand up and be counted and be strong with me. Put down the petty jealousies that divide Americans, there is no longer room for American impersonators. We are going to throw the bums out and take our country back.

If you are an African American or a Latin American or a European American or any other word before the word American then stay away from this movement; we only want our family of true America-loving red, white and blue-blooded American patriots who see each other as equal not as a certain color, period. Love our country and be willing to fight for it, or leave it.

You must put your pettiness aside and be a tough American again, just like our forefathers; I anticipate serious civil and social unrest and dissent from those responsible for violence when their entitlements are on the table as well as from the union bosses when your right to choose is restored in all states. When the progressive Marxist communists see that we are winning and they see no other way to destroy this country other than violence then expect their anger to control their actions.

But if we are joined together as a team, an American family, we are unbreakable, we can protect each other and we will win. Our country is worth our every sacrifice.

We are already seeing some violence in several states where union protesters are breaking windows and threatening any legislators who endorse fiscal responsibility. The only thing they're protesting is the loss of collective bargaining! Wait until they find out that their pensions are unfunded. Wait until the municipal bonds turn to junk, cities and states file bankruptcy and all public sectors experience massive layoffs. We have to be strong and to be standing together and ready.

Would you prefer to live in a third-world country?

The socialistic communistic progressives I refer to are not just the sneaky few un-Americans lurking behind the curtains of Washington DC; like the guy in the Wizard of Oz..

The secret brain-altered human created by progressives through entitlements represents at least forty percent of this country's voters. The brain-altered I speak of comprise a large segment of the fifty percent who don't pay any federal income tax and they like it that way. Hello out there to the brain altered folks we don't want to leave you behind, will you listen to reason?

So you see God-loving America-loving patriots, our job is to teach as well. Ask this entitlement group if the third-world status, Africa for example, which we are headed for at warp speed is the entitlement state in which they would prefer to exist in? That is where the train that we are on is headed for, if we don't change conductors fast.

Part of this vast number of voters is the forty four million food stamp recipients (that's one out of every two households and this entitlement-prone section of people do not want to see that end. Some of them represent the millions that got cheap loans through the failed government programs of Fannie & Freddie and they still think the government owes them more.

They represent the millions who want free health care and are convinced they're entitled to it and that the haves should furnish it to the have-nots. To do nothing, as we have been doing for years, will only make the problem worse, which is the divide between the haves and have-nots?

What has China Got to Do with the Fed?

The Federal Reserve and its quantitative easing (QE) of the dollar have ensured that the dollar will experience uber-inflation.

Our $14 trillion and rising debt continues to threaten our ability to borrow and we currently must borrow forty six percent of our budget; AND the interest on our debt alone, is approaching fifty percent of that budget.

It is unsustainable and irrevocable, which means we must pay it back either in dollars or with our assets and sovereignty.

Sovereignty is the quality of having supreme, independent authority over a geographic area, such as a territory or our United States of America. Losing sovereignty would mean some other country would own our country and we would be serfs.

What is worse, is when the International Monetary Fund (IMF), China, Russia, India, Brazil and the United Arab Emirates (UAE) succeed in replacing the dollar possibly with the euro as the world's reserve currency, referred to as the Special Drawing Right (SDR). This will instantly catapult our inflation by at least another twenty five percent and make borrowing even more difficult and costly. When the unfunded liabilities of Medicare, Medicaid, Social Security, and underfunded federal pensions dry up or when these programs cannot keep up with inflation rates at twenty five percent or higher, then, if that occurs, there will be violence.

So replacing the Medicare and Medicaid programs with the hospitals controlled locally is one answer, which I point out in my platform.

Does Greece come to mind when you think of anarchy in the streets when money dries up for the entitlement groups? We have to push that start button now, together as a family of Americans; we must work together on taking back and taking over our country, and you must stand with me strong and proud on this.

What Happened to the Jobs?

America increasingly manufactures or produces less; which means we have less to export and that it generally costs more than similar goods from other countries thanks to unions and mainly the union bosses, who are interested only in money and power and forcing every worker to pay union dues.

That's the primary cause of our trade deficit, which continues to expand with each year. Furthermore, most of our favorites trading partners are in worse economic shape than we are; and are increasingly less able to buy our goods. And since they are heavily invested in the U.S. dollar, when we falter so will they and so will their ability to import U.S. goods. Consequently, there will be fewer American jobs and less corporate and private income tax; which means less revenue to fund our government's debts, entitlement programs and public services. Do you agree and do you see this has to stop?

Those on the left say consider not leaving the owners out of this equation and they cite examples of the 1920s and 1930s, such as textile mills across the south becoming unionized. And they say it is not because the mill workers wanted to get rich—but because people wanted to be paid a living wage; have you ever met a rich mill worker they add?, They further stated, they needed other things basic to human dignity; as though any of this applied to the educated mass of workers today. They even recite some of the deplorable conditions they had to work under back then, such as not being allowed to take a bathroom break on the job, which many were denied if they got uppity. They will then remind Americans that all of those mills moved to Mexico and then overseas, leaving in their wake not a population of rich mill workers but broken promises, high poverty, and high unemployment.

How absolutely spot on they are about our labor force back then when no one could read or write because education was almost nonexistent back then. This meant the unions evolved to help the ignorant worker who had no defense from lack of education. But as we exceeded in education all the way up to through the 1950s as being number one in the world and the 1960s unions began to re-invent themselves as union bosses got the feel for power and corruption and began the destruction of companies through forced union labor because they used a portion of the union dues to lobby for their exclusive rights. This began to force companies to flee the United States to foreign countries where these companies could get cheaper labor.

The owners had chosen to become the owners of business in America because of free enterprise, not because of forced labor unions. Americans who invested their money and opened a business in America did so because of being a country where it is not illegal to make profit. Profit allowed them to continue to offer jobs. Money and power the left says were only on the shoulders of the company that made it off the backs of the workers and not the union bosses. Union bosses who could not care less if the company profited or not as long as they got the dues from the workers. Think about it, today education protects the American worker and free enterprise provides a job for the workers. The worker is no longer the uneducated vagabond that could not defend himself; he now can create businesses of his own or progress up the ladder in the company he works for by educating himself to become more productive for the company. Unions have simply out lived their usefulness to the educated American worker of today, who chooses not to pay union dues. What part of the Constitution supports forcing a worker to pay union dues if he so chooses not to?

People outside this country know about surviving with much less than we have, they know about sacrifice, which the current generation of Americans do not. We have grown accustomed to wasting more than most others live on. We are quick to anger, quick to blame, and quick to violence if we do not get our way.

We must put our petty jealousies aside and see the enemy in our midst. We must come together now in our collective strengths to amass a force strong enough to take on the enemy and save our beloved America.

Can You Envision Food Riots in America?

The man who predicted the 1987 stock market crash and the fall of the Soviet Union, Gerald Celente, wholeheartedly agrees with this analysis. He is now predicting revolution in America, food riots and tax rebellions, all within four years, while cautioning that putting food on the table will be a more pressing concern than buying Christmas gifts by 2012. Celente, the CEO of Trends Research Institute, is renowned for his accuracy in predicting future world and economic events and he is in lock-step with the things I have just pointed out, if we do not come together as a team quickly. That means right now, or our country is surely doomed!

If the train is not stopped and the conductor along with all of his helpers is not thrown off, we are going to start seeing huge areas of vacant real estate with squatters living on them.

It is going to be a picture the likes of which Americans have never seen. I must remind you of Argentina I mentioned earlier. It could come as a shock and with it there could be a lot of crime. And that crime would be a lot worse than it has ever been before, because in the Great Depression, people's minds weren't wrecked on all these modern drugs and over-the-counter drugs, or illegal drugs like Crystal-Meth or whatever it might be. So, you have a huge underclass of very desperate dependent people with their minds chemically blown beyond anybody's comprehension.

Celente adds that the price of not heeding his warnings will be far greater than the cost of preparing for the future now, by making those tough decisions.

If Americans keep making the same mistakes in voting for the billionaire puppets the government attitude cannot be changed then think about storable food and gold to make a start at getting prepared. But I will add to that: have plenty of ammunition for your guns, because of the people's desperation. If we are unwilling to come together as a team and change government then protecting your family will be paramount. But let Americans not forget, we can stop this train wreck together, if we act fast enough together as that American family.

Are you starting to see America? We cannot wait any longer, please recognize that the puppets speaking to you on television are controlled by the puppet master behind the screen; remember—The Wizard of Oz, ask who are they beholden to?

Now having said all of that, I am going to reiterate that there are more patriot Americans than them scenario, because of education we now are capable of seeing our past mistakes in our voting habits for those who promise the moon and where the money will come from for those gifts, which I have earlier mentioned; and what effect huge spending will have on our country.

A great majority of Americas are patriots who would die for their country, and about thirty percent who will look for a hand out until they parish and ten percent are those who want to see disaster; such as the elite of the world (need I mention the George Soros and the new world order) who make huge amounts of money betting on disasters around the world.

My research over the past years of how we are becoming increasingly under government control by the elitists is what has convinced me that I, or someone with the same courage should be at the helm of our America. We need a true patriot who can and will make lightening speed cuts in government bureaucracy and will eliminate the scourge to the point of simply protecting America and Americans, because that is what the Constitution states is government's purpose.

Anything and Everything is on the Table

I used words like fiery delivery from the president in the bully pulpit to insist on the cuts in government bureaucracy and spending from both the Senate and House, in my platform and to the truly knowledgeable patriot American, I believe understands what that means. It means anything and everything are on the table when considering cuts in government.

I am now, and will be searching for the true stand-up Americans, who can and will defend until death their families and their country; true patriots realize that America loving people like me should be at the bow of the ship, or, as I have stated, to be the conductor of the train.

We are up against the billionaires

Obama has already amassed a $1 billion campaign fund; and the republicans will spend at least half that or more to promote what will probably be a splintered platform and ticket. When I make it to the White House, with zero dollars against those billions because of your help, do I think all the legislators will flee to a neighboring country (like the Democrats from Wisconsin and Indiana) to avoid casting the difficult votes?

Well let me answer this way: we the people are back and we are taking back this country, not just David Tippie. David Tippie is going to have the support of the toughest, strongest patriotic Americans and those weak legislators will be fiscally brought back or, immediately removed from office by the Constitution and voice of the people; either way will be fine.

I do not need legislators to reverse many of the things that Obama and his people have put in place without legislative mandate. Remember that it was the progressives starting as far back as Woodrow Wilson that have increased the power of the president; so now it will work in the favor of America and not against it as has been the case so far. It will be my duty to get each of those weak legislators running for their political lives and I will do all I can without them.

One task of mine would be emulating JFK's chosen task to print money and fire the Fed's printing press.

How did the Fed originate? This has been reviewed somewhat but more than one hundred years ago there was a conspiracy to extend that banking system even farther, to slowly gain control of all assets, and resources as well as the reserves from the American people. Our government called it the Federal Reserve. Although JFK may have been assassinated because he began the process of elimination of the Fed, this will not slow my actions to accomplish that as president.

Where Do Our Soldiers Need to Be?

Obama has already amassed a $1 billion campaign fund; but it takes an unconscious, unthinking imbecile to deny or disregard the existence of conspiracies. Sadly, we are surrounded by many of such imbeciles, so I will rely on your help to keep me informed of plots against my life when you hear it.

As I have stated earlier, I would bring home every soldier we currently have stationed around the world and militarize the Mexican border then strategically place battalions across America to ensure American safety and the deportation of illegal aliens.

In the same mode I would stop foreign aid and tell the world we are going to clean up our ship at home before we will be able to think of supporting other nations with our borrowed money.

And you can bet that every government organization that I could shut down that is not constitutionally required would be shut down. I would find the quickest but most efficient way to induce a simple flat but graduated tax system so that everyone would be paying taxes (which I introduced in the beginning of my platform under Tax Code) and that would include everyone—importers and exporters as well.

As president, one of my major tasks will be to emulate President Ike Eisenhower and deport the eleven million plus illegal aliens, which our strategically placed battalions of soldiers would help deport. Can you say no more free lunches or entitlements for illegal aliens? That alone will be a big support to boosting our economy. Look out employers who hire these illegals.

I would solicit the brightest minds in America to help me with these tasks and yes, I would deal with the anarchy should any arise to protect Americans. Would you mind being one of my best and brightest? I will be searching for you.

LBJ and the New World Order

Do you remember the words, "I shall not seek and I will not accept the nomination of my party for another term as your president"? Lyndon Baines Johnson was told to get out of Dodge by those in the background who run the new world order. If you are a conspiracy theorist, you surely know what that is; and if you don't or you are a skeptic, deal with it however you want.

Friends have reminded me that when JFK threatened to reduce or remove many of the autonomous powers of the Federal Reserve; they did not like it.

I was further reminded to: give the Fed the benefit of the doubt and assume it would not resort to murder. We know there is very little that they wouldn't do to ensure their continued prosperity and it's control of the richest, most powerful entity in the world.

Some have said, David your cojones may be big, but the Bernankes of the world have all of ours squeezed firmly in their grasp.

Being originally from Texas, I answered with this: "Do you know why the Mafia never got a foothold in Texas? Let me answer that since I was brought up in Texas, you were taught manners, always to say yes Sir and yes Maam and always to respect your elders, to be courteous and give the right of way. But when you grew older, your teaching shifted some, which was that a coward is already dead. So when we could not get respect back from those to whom we offered it, we would attempt to walk away, and if they were even further disrespectful to the point of a threat to our family, or ourselves we put them on boot hill, utilizing the Second Amendment.

Since I am one of these courteous, likeable, kind Texans, I will have a swarm of folks just like myself, with me; and I do not mean to imply that Texas is the only place where these patriotic Americans are located, because they are everywhere. I and those other very tough folks with massive courage like myself who are impossible to intimidate will be by my side. So come on board, we have got a job to do; to save our country.

I am familiar with the possible reasons JFK was assassinated, as I mentioned in the beginning, which could be due to the Fed and JFK's EO-11110, explained earlier. Yes I agree that LBJ knew something and was not alone and that he was not the leader in the plotting; those behind the new world order are the leaders. Those are the ones who will make their presence known first to the president, if their person did not get elected. In Obama's case, he is their prize puppet for the puppet masters. I will do my best to run everybody connected out of Dodge and those who refuse to go will have company on boot hill if, or when, they threaten me. Have you decided if you will stand with me yet?

I hope the answer is yes. All American-loving patriots know that these guys play for keeps and that it will take courage, beyond what many are capable of. Again, I have the courage and will surround myself with those who share my courage.

Perhaps it comes down to a question of logistics:

Logistics that I spoke of earlier, which are the details of what events the socio-economic chain of events supported by Celente and so many others, will occur, which note there will be impoverished people who will live as squatters and shortages of food and as to where it will take place will be all across America and to what extent of severity will be determined by what patriotic movement to fight back is mounted to take back the reins of existing government.

Although words are important, if they lead to no action, what purpose shall they serve? If I can't motivate you by sharing my message and platform, then I too have failed. This task includes you, the everyday patriot, because without you we all fail and shall deserve our destiny with the new dictators of the world, who shall quickly surface when we lose our sovereignty. I don't think for one moment that you will sit idly by and watch our country sink into the third-world pit that is planned for it..

Chapter 10

What Is a Conditioned Response?

Today's society is unaware that it has been conditioned (brainwashed) to react with skepticism to such conspiracy theories, as the new world order by institutional and media influences. Most people have a built-in picture that short-circuits the mind's critical examination process when it comes to certain sensitive words and topics because of the programming from media sources that Americans are exposed to..

These pictures placed in our brains by the constant barrage from the media can be better explained, as a term for a conditioned type of response in the brain, which dead-ends a person's thinking because the brain has placed a certain picture in it to remind you quickly of your belief or disbelief in any particular subject. Your belief terminates debate or examination of the topic at hand when you relate to the quick picture reference you have stored. A good explanation of this is to listen to what is referred to as a fair and balanced debate on a boob tube news programs; where they get far left people who can spin fact to a meaningless pile of rubble they choose to discuss, who can explain the un-explainable and when all else fails, simply lie about the facts. Another example is the mention of the word conspiracy, which often solicits a certain picture response in the brain with many people because of how they have been programmed by the slick lefties.

What most people believe to be public opinion is in reality carefully crafted and scripted propaganda designed to illicit a desired behavioral response from the public. I ask my readers and yes, hopefully my supporters, to become aware of this conditioning and to review the skeptic who disagrees with what I have stated.

There are great examples of these word artists who seem to be able to explain the un-explainable, like the Guy named ED Schultz of the ED show on MSNBC, or the woman following him who is almost robotic in her negative rebuttals of anything even remotely conservative; her name is Rachael Maddow. Even in the far right-wing media in the attempt to be fair and balanced or what is referred to as politically correct, the news media slime up the facts on occasion with rhetoric from a far-left cretin guest, to name one such that comes to mind, would be Bob Beckel a Fox News contributor. I am suggesting that each American take back their own thinking process and their own deducing abilities.

Just consider what is stated from any media talking head and judge for yourself what is factual. Because if someone speaks like he has a corncob pipe in his mouth, as thought he is looking down his nose when he speaks, it should make you laugh at him, not respect his opinion over your own research.

Public opinion polls are really taken with the intent of gauging the public's acceptance of the new world order's planned programs. A strong showing in the polls tells them that the programming is taking effect, while a poor showing tells the NWO manipulators that they have to recast or re-tweak the programming, until the desired response is achieved.

Are you starting to see why George Soros owns most of the media in our country? George Soros' money ties to media outlets worldwide enable him to influence the most important audience of all: journalists and commentators. The NWO global conspirators manifest their agenda through the skilful manipulation of human emotions, especially racism and fear. Do you recall those in the Obama administration saying these words: "We don't want a good crisis to go un-exploited?"

Or how about when Obama was running in 2008 when he said to a listening audience: "and don't forget I am a black man."

NWO strategists create the problem by funding, assembling, and training an opposition group to stimulate turmoil in an established political power, which may be favoring legislation to their detriment. Can you think of one going on right now in our country, funded by them? Hopefully, Wisconsin comes to mind.

Do you think that chaos is created? The word chaos is a mathematical concept that explains that it is possible to get random results from normal equations. The main perception behind this idea is the underlying notions of small occurrences significantly affecting the outcomes of seemingly unrelated events. Union protests come to mind as they travel across country when summoned by the union bosses to carry out their predetermined agenda in a particular area.

Do you think that the union members are solely acting through their own objectives, by traveling across country to attend a peaceful rally, then to riot? Not on your life.

Jay Nordlinger from nationalreview.com put it like this: As I look at the union members swarm the Wisconsin capital, I have a familiar thought: A great advantage of the left is that they are organized and determined and have a lot of time; Paid time. The taxpayer is likely funding these days of protest, engaged in by the public-school teachers. They are using their sick leave, provided by the taxpayer, to go rallying.

Much in the same manner the National Organization for Women (NOW) creates opposing factions in a conflict that the new world order (NWO) themselves maneuvered into existence. In recent decades, so called opposition groups are usually identified in the media as freedom fighters or liberators.

Have you noticed that the name has not stuck with the Tea Party events? No matter how hard they try with their left-wing media puppets? With Tea Partiers, enough is enough; so say all patriots, as I mentioned earlier.

At the same time, the leader of the established political power where the conflict is being orchestrated is demonized and, right on cue, with something like being referred to as another Hitler (take your pick: Saddam Hussein, Milosevic, Muammar Muhammad al-Gaddafi the Libyan revolutionary, etc.).

The freedom fighters are the groups that the left-wing media does its best to associate with the Tea Partiers. Freedom fighters are not infrequently assembled from a local criminal element. Those associated with the puppet masters, such as the Reverend Jessie Jackson's group, are a good example.

Jessie-Jackson-and-AlSharpton-Ploys-that-Oppress-Blacks

The organization that the Reverend Jessie Jackson heads Rainbow PUSH is allegedly involved in criminal activity. Jackson's organization does not rely on donations for its operations, no indeed, the vast majority of its funding comes from government handouts; where else they get money from is for others to determine.

These handouts from the government is not the "leg up" program JFK started to help the black community to begin to help themselves rise above poverty and was supposed to motivate them to become better citizens to work harder and achieve for themselves sooner. This backfired into creating a dependent society. The words "leg up" got high-jacked by the racist mongers and are now being called, entitlements.

Why are there so few "Independent" candidates for political office anymore? Why are there just hand chosen puppets? Voting for (R) for Republican or a (D) for Democrat seems to be the only consideration that people will consider. I am a conservative and an independent if not chosen to be the republican nominee and feel a need to explain the following: People are in the habit of voting R or D and not on principles; if you have no idea what you are doing you simply start with the letter (R or D) and expand from there. Sacrifice from someone or group must be voluntary, such as giving to our favorite charity. No one votes to subtract money from his salary to give to a charity not of his choosing. If he can't get others to sacrifice for him he does not vote for any sacrifice that would include himself and he will choose to vote for something else, (extortion, slavery, robbery, etc.).

How do you vote for extortion? You vote to raise taxes on those who got serious in life and have made a success through their consistent hard work, which you had refused to do, so that you may continue to have your entitlements. How do you vote for slavery? You vote for those who continue with and expansion of the entitlement programs, which removes all sense of accomplishment, or achievement, which enslaves a person to something he or she does not have to work for. How do you commit robbery? You state publicly that you agree with someone's words or line of thought, when down deep inside you know that it is lies and wrong. A politician does it just to get a vote. Wrong as you know it is you still join with your fellow thieves under the camouflaged name of fairness, or justice and you try to convince complete societies to justify forced sacrifice from others for your gain; conflating a good' with a right.

Jackson's group is a participant of conflating a good with a right. His group is one of the recipients of this forced sacrifice in the form of handouts from the government doling out of taxpayer money to further remove self-achievement from Jackson's own black community; instigated by Jackson himself and many others, like the Reverend Al Sharpton. All make a living keeping racism from the past, on the front burner and by appearing on television to discuss the political correctness from others and spew their villainous rant which is the camouflage for their true intensions.

Mr. Jackson has faced investigations into the use of those, government hand-outs and was found to have used nearly four million dollars of that money for his own use. So his statement that he is only helping his black community is just a ploy to give himself a bountiful income on the backs of blacks. It seems that he does not want to have the racial divide bridged with peace and prosperity; that would not create wealth for him.

Simply because we cannot be the ultimate solution does not mean we can't be part of the solution; because by ourselves we are not powerful does not mean we are powerless. We can speak out and join in a group for the good of America and we can vote, with our country at heart and clear our conscious for our past poor judgments nothing is impossible. I am searching for the patriots who will stop putting right for themselves above what is right for their fellow Americans as a nation. Remember my definition of American patriot.

When you make the choice to become a candidate for president and to do so without becoming beholden to anyone or any special interest group and vow to beat those that do so, you must advertise to state your platform to the public as best you can and this book is my choice in accomplishing that and will only work if my readers who are voters, say it will first, then pitch in and help spread the word.

LBJ Had a Hand in Racism

There are huge amounts of information from the Lyndon Baines Johnson era you can access, but LBJ was merely an un-principled politician who used the civil rights issue when he realized the worth of the Black Vote. However Johnson himself claimed to be an idealist who dreamed of making America a Great Society and some believe he had hidden agenda. It was Johnson who put the presidential signature to the 1964 Civil Rights Act and the 1965 Voting Rights Act (a good thing). But it was also Johnson who used entitlement programs to enslave the blacks, to keep their vote. I have touched on the entitlement and government handouts and their destruction of ambition earlier.

The LBJ administration set out to depress the motivation of blacks by giving them handouts to deliberately reduce their desire to achieve for themselves.

This attitude of entitlement was latched onto as I have discussed earlier, by some blacks who started making their living from appearing on television and other media, grabbing onto and creating villains to speak about in the media so often that the media now turns to them as experts to determine what is to be viewed as a racist remark or, in my view, just as despicable, why is it for them to determine what is politically correct or incorrect?

Who was Niccolo Machiavelli?

Arming the enemy of the power that you propose to be your friend is in the spirit of true Machiavelli, who was a Florentine statesman and political philosopher of deceit, from 1469 to 1527. Machiavelli has been called the brilliant creator of modern political science by some, and a cynical beast by others; he is considered the originator of the idea of a political pragmatism that says "the end justifies the means."

This is the adapted philosophy by new world order (NOW) strategists who are equally involved in covertly arming and advising both sides of a conflict, which they themselves start. They advise the leader of the established power as well as their enemy.

Keep in mind that the NWO always profits from any armed conflict by loaning money, arming, and supplying all parties involved in a war. Money from both sides can also be used in true Machiavellian spirit. There are many evils in our society and I keep referring to George Soros when that word comes up, so let me revisit a time years ago when he broke the Bank of England by wagering against the British pound, pressuring it in such a way that England had to devalue its currency. This was Soro's first billion-dollar payday.

Various ploys over the years further enriched him. Then he made billions by wagering that the housing and mortgage markets would collapse in America, which was a multi-billion dollar payoff again.

What is the NWO?

International bankers, oil barons and pharmaceutical companies, as well as other major multinational corporations dominate the corporate portion of the NWO. The royal family of Britain, Queen Elizabeth II and the House of Windsor, who are descendants of the German arm of the Saxe-Coburg-Gotha family who changed the name to Windsor in 1914, are high-level players in the oligarchy which controls the upper strata of the NWO. The decision-making nerve centers of this effort are in London (especially the City of London), Basel Switzerland, and Brussels home of NATO headquarters.

The United Nations, along with all the agencies working under the UN umbrella, such as the World Health Organization (WHO) are full-time players in this scheme. Similarly, NATO is a military tool of the NWO.

The leaders of all major industrial countries such as the United States, Brittan, Germany, Italy, Australia, New Zealand, etc. (members of the G7/G8) are active and fully cooperative participants in that conspiracy; remember the word conspiracy if you recall is one of the conditioned responses in your brain; reviewed earlier.

In this century, the degree of control exerted by the NWO has advanced to the point that only certain hand-picked individuals are even eligible to become the prime minister or president or leaders of countries like Britain, Germany, or in certain instances, the United States. Where did the billion dollars come from that Obama has to use to run for re-election?

Bill Clinton and Bob Dole Were the Same

It didn't matter whether Bill Clinton or Bob Dole won the presidency in 1996; the results would have been the same. Both men were playing on the same team for the same ball club.

Anyone who isn't a team player is likely to be taken out: i.e. Kennedy, Ali Bhutto (Pakistan) and Aldo Moro (Italy). More recently, Admiral Borda and William Colby may have also been killed because they were either unwilling to go along with the conspiracy to destroy America, weren't cooperating in some capacity, or were attempting to expose or thwart the takeover agenda.

This is serious, and yes I do know my life could be in danger if elected president, but action must be taken against the powers that be or we are looking at living in third-world status. Who wants America, the greatest country on earth, to become a third-world country, to be easily managed and dictated to and to lose our sovereignty? I would rather die trying to save my country than live as a passive peasant controlled by a master because I chose to do nothing. I need you to stand up and be strong with me of course, without you I don't stand a chance.

However, no matter what your skin color, if you are a God-loving true America-loving patriot, then it is you that I represent and it is you that must step up to help me take our country out of the jaws of these America haters.

This fight will not be easy. We cannot win this war unless we have the support of patriots like you.

Republican, Democrat, Independent or Whatever

Just because someone hangs out his shingle that states that he is Republican, he should not automatically win the American patriot's vote. What we want to project is that every mother's son and daughters who are running for office--

will be held accountable--from this day forward. America-loving patriots will take back our republic that has been devalued and destroyed by the majority rule of a progressive socialistic democracy from the far-left.

I challenge everyone of any persuasion to defend in a practical, logical and fiscally responsible way, the merits of or justification for the labor unions; particularly those representing government employees; which existence can only be viewed as conflict of interest.

No one has risen to the challenge. What I continually get are emotional beliefs, nostalgic reminiscing, hypothetical scenarios, and something that blends a cultural tradition with a religious cult. We have moved far from our past where few were educated (that meant a person would be marginalized in the work place), as well as for his skin color. The same is not true today for our America. Work ethic and goals are up to the individual; government will not be your master if I am elected and don't bother giving me the media-rehearsed sob stories about race no matter what yours happens to be. If you are the best man or woman for the job no matter what your race you get the job in a free enterprise system. If you think you should get the job regardless of your qualifications because of your race, you will have to find another job. We are all family and we work and take care of our immediate family at home meaning each state, while our federal government does its only Constitutional job and that is to protect American property and Americans from our enemies and not to feed, clothe and house Americans, or for that matter, illegal aliens.

The unions are rapidly losing membership and credibility in the private sector due to work ethic, education and the union-skewed sense of fundamental rights. Various leaders throughout history have warned against organized labor and collective bargaining in the public sector. Danel Disalvo, from nationalaffairs.com brought this into the light when he wrote about Chris Christie who became New Jersey's governor and wasted no time in identifying the chief perpetrators of his state's fiscal catastrophe. Facing a nearly $11 billion budget gap, as well as voters being fed up with the sky-high taxes imposed on them to finance the state government's profligacy, Christie moved swiftly to take on the unions representing New Jersey's roughly 400,000 public employees.

Fundamental rights are not what unions are interested in defending. Even if the fundamental rights are difficult to define and even more difficult to list without fear of leaving something out, or worse yet, including things that are not true rights, but benefits or privileges granted by misguided governments. Even the attempt by George Mason and other Founding Fathers of the Constitution, to make a listing or as it is referred to Bill of Rights was limited to the worst abuses current at that time. Had they known that the twentieth century Supreme Court would tamper with those first fundamental rights against the citizens, perhaps they would have been more pointed as to how those fundamental rights could not be tampered with, possibly even pointing it out in our Constitution.

The Constitution should have two objectives, to enable and restrict governmental power that should be strictly for the defense of those fundamental rights and the defense of America; In short, the Constitution is a law governing the law making. The Constitution should not contain specific laws or statutes, but rather only the laws that govern and restrict the specific law-making process. The failure of the first Congress to ratify one of the proposed amendments, originally included in the Bill of Rights would have made the Bill of Rights binding upon the states as well as the federal government, thereby protecting our fundamental rights from future generations suffering from the Supreme Court deciding what those fundamental rights consist of. The Founders failed to see into the future the inevitable rise of influence based politicians in office too long; those who would rise to the temptation of buying votes with benefits and suppressing the rights of some in order to favor others.

Unions are truly a conflict of interest working against the American taxpayer by unionizing federal employees. The union bosses are the only ones to benefit; they want to force membership so they can collect the dues; it is all about money and power for the union bosses. I am for your choice, and that is the right-to-work state. Don't interfere with my fellow American patriots' choices; they can make good ones or bad ones, but it is up to them, not a government agency or some union boss.

Though I welcome anyone to convince me otherwise, I am one hundred percent in favor of defunding the labor unions. I feel this way regardless of whether or not it would destroy the political contributions for democrats. I do not believe it would destroy that party but I do believe it would significantly redefine it and its platform likely shifting it more to the right perhaps to favor more of human rights as opposed to simply union rights to collect dues.

We the people are not about to go away quietly! We choose our freedom, or death; but passive we will not remain.

Even though the people won in Wisconsin, which means there will be no more compulsory union dues for public employees, and which will benefit Wisconsin taxpayers, the teachers will also start to benefit our students and not just benefit themselves through unions. The bad teachers can now be replaced with those who have a passion for teaching and should be paid for their teaching abilities. I believe that type of teacher or professor should be some of the highest paid in the workforce. A fair liberal-minded person enquired of me: "It would indeed be interesting if a large group of highly skilled and passionate teachers could get the high pay they deserve without union representation. How would that happen?" My answer: "It is called free enterprise! Firms don't set wages and working conditions; that depends upon the productivity of labor and free enterprise." This is eloquently defined by Walter Block of lewrockwell.com as the extra amount of revenue brought in by adding one more person to the payroll. For example, if there were one thousand workers creating an item that sold for X dollars and then the one thousand and first employee came on board and the firm's sales rose to $X + $seven, then the marginal revenue productivity of the last person hired would be sever dollars per hour.

Wages can't (long be) higher than this amount, or the company will lose money on every worker it hires. For example, if compensation is ten dollars for a union wage and revenue taken in due to the efforts of the worker is seven dollars, then the firm loses three dollars every hour the man is on the shop floor. Does this give reason to understand why companies were leaving the United States at breakneck speed?

The victory in Wisconsin means a battle has been won, not the war. Michigan, Ohio, Indiana, and many other states across the country will be facing similar battles and we can only hope and pray that the Republican-elected officials have the same courage and stamina, as Governor Walker. If I am elected president, the help they need will have arrived.

I am satisfied that union bosses will not support me.

The small victories last November and now in Wisconsin however do not represent the end of the war. Neither does removing union funding from the Democratic Party result in the overall victory, nor would it represent all the changes that this country must undertake

Are you a Resident of America or an American?

I'm sure everyone sees in the news that thirty five percent of Americans' primary income is now a government handout. Do you remember the statement I made about the haves and the have-nots? Handouts or, what are now referred to as entitlements are self-promoting and destroy self-worth and self achievement. The attitude is why work, if you can get it for free? It only produces more who have that same mindset.

Even some of the haves who were helping to fund the have-nots, have begun to join the have-nots. This is the secret that those who are trying to destroy America from the inside, do not want you to know. If you are one of these people and are willing to wake up and become a true red, white and blue-blooded American patriot instead of being a person who is simply a resident of America, then I am your president and I intend to do all things to inspire the entrepreneur in you to achieve for yourself and your family. I want everyone to return to our American values with pride and honor that you can once again display around the dinner table. Right is never going to be made wrong, and wrong is never going to be made right.

These entitlement residents of America, a group that has traditionally voted for and promoted Democrats and who are wanting to throw every asset that America has away by handouts and starting agencies on the backs of taxpayer and so forth, need to be asked why? This group must be taught that this is sending America over a cliff, which serves the Democrat's purpose, to reduce this nation to third-world status that is more controllable. Then they can laugh at you while they strip you of every human right the Constitution afforded you and return you to serfdom that took revolution to escape. Please wake up before it is too late for everybody.

Instead of allowing the entitlement attitude to grow exponentially change those voting patterns to save our country. By mathematics your old voting record will create disaster. Minorities also have traditionally voted Democrat because they are the first to be placed on the taxpayer dole by Democrats. Their numbers also continue to grow while the percentage of non-minorities who are more conservative; these voters also continue to shrink due to entering the handout mentality.

We have got to educate more and I am proud to say that this black man has some answers and his name is James David Manning and he delivers the Manning Report on YouTube. If you can type this address into your computer address bar, you will get a sense of this man's love of country and passion to teach others: http://www.youtube.com/watch?v=-4oxch8af0l One of his many subjects is where he talks about why Americans Jews made a huge mistake voting for Obama; you can listen. I won't elaborate on it. He also speaks candidly about the black race and their time, which they themselves are destroying.

Also Mr. Manning explains very well what exists that must be altered to eliminate the shadow of racism, that does not actually exist but is being pushed onto society by race mongers who make a living creating that turmoil: http://www.youtube.com/watch?v=djm7FiysLOl&feature=related

We have to see the plot to destroy America from within, and to those American patriots who have been on this tilting scale such as Mr. Manning and the millions of Americans who can see the light of what is intended for America all to face one day, those who wish to climb aboard our train to retake America, we welcome you.

The train that you are now on, although it serves free lunch, is heading for the cliff.

Just as concerning to me is the number of elected republicans that often vote just as irresponsibly as their democratic counterparts. Far too often, both parties get behind (or just tolerate) ridiculous pieces of legislature. GSE atrocities like Fannie Mae and Freddie Mac are good example but on another level there is the minimum wage intervention.

What gives the elected officials right to mandate what you can and will pay your employee? I gave some statistics of the math that must work in order to pay an individual; government circumventing that math sends jobs overseas. A better way government can get involved with raising wages is to deport illegal aliens. I have a friend who is in the lawn care business and he is just barely surviving because some competition are hiring illegal aliens and paying them far under the minimum wage.

He told his four fellow workers that if he was going to be able to keep his company open he was going to have to pay them strictly commission for the jobs that they could land. Now this is only one small example of free enterprise at play trying to survive against all types of odds. He could have simply gone out of business, but he chose to keep it open and his workers thank him for it. Of course if elected I am going to eliminate the illegal alien part of the equation but free enterprise should go unencumbered and unassisted by government.

In so far as the biggies, Fannie & Freddie are concerned, it would be nice to blame these two entities and subsequent guaranteed securities of subprime loans and other toxic assets solely on the Democrats. But it just isn't so.

The self-absorbed Republican elitists are equally culpable in allowing these cancerous growths to evolve over the last two decades that ultimately have crippled the real estate industry and our economy. That came to a head in 2008 and inflamed our national debt by billions of dollars since, with the support of each president involved and the Fed.

If we throw the Federal Reserve into this mix: Republican administrations and Republican-majority congressional sessions have continually allowed the Fed to threaten our economic stability and national security, while devaluing the USD for a century now.

Far too many sins exist for Republicans to throw stones with such feigned innocence. If my fellow patriots are indeed willing to enter into a war with me and help me get elected then as your president, let us continue to be sure to choose our allies with both eyes open from now on; and let Americans be sure that our victories do not embolden or empower yet another puppetmaster's pawn that would countermand our ultimate objectives.

I gladly give my life for my country if it would save it from this pending doom. Patriots please stand solidly with me because righting the wrongs in our country can never be accomplished without each of you.

If you are in favor of bringing jobs back to America with me, you can't deny that organized labor is a huge supporter of the liberals and creates an anti-job atmosphere.

Labor unions have played a huge role in the destruction of American manufacturing and the automobile industry, etc. Has anyone been to Detroit lately? When the non-union wages for autoworkers were thirty dollars per hour as opposed to union-made vehicles at eighty dollars per wage hour, it does not take a rocket scientist to see how negative the impact was going to be on Detroit. By the 1990s, consumers found they no longer had to accept the sky-rocketing costs of American-built cars.

Why do you think that foreign car manufacturers locate their plants in right-to-work states?

It does not take a PhD to see the connection and how unions are part of what is killing this country. An airplane company is being sued in court for moving its plant out of a state where unions control the workforce to a state where there is a right to work. The Obama National Labor Relations Board through lawsuit told Boeing that the company must build a plant in Washington State not in South Carolina. South Carolina is a right-to-work state. The National Labor Relations Board sued the company saying Boeing shifted some of its787 Dreamliner productions to South Carolina; partly to retaliate against the International Association of Machinists and, Aerospace Workers for past strikes in Washington State.

The NLRB is seeking a court order that would require Boeing to maintain its second 787 assembly line in the Pacific Northwest, an International Association of Machinists and Aerospace Workers (union) (IAMAW) stronghold. If successful, that could stop Boeing from building the plane in North Charleston.

Right-to-work laws are statutes enforced in twenty-two U.S. states, mostly in the southern or western United States, allowed under provisions of the Taft-Hartley Act which prohibit agreements between trade unions and employers, making membership or payment of union dues or fees a condition of employment, either before or after hiring.

Many southern states have passed the Taft-Hartley Act, which may have contributed to their boom of new automotive plant construction by foreign auto manufacturers.

America is suffering from many symptoms and many ailments to focus only on one such ailment. Focusing only on labor unions would be short-sighted; consider the respected Donald Trump only focusing on the Obama birth certificate. There is much more to correcting the mistakes, whether they were intentional or accidental, and our problems in America must be corrected.

I want you to know every issue and how I stand with them all, which is the reason for this book. Not keeping you in the dark like the current president, who was elected on hope and change, which he did not explain, nor did he want to. We now see why. Simply defunding the Unions would not resolve this nation's problems with liberals but certainly is a step in the right direction.

George Soros pockets are very deep, and he is not the only sugar-daddy in the liberal's corner. Materially it is correct to say that defunding unions is in fact, reducing the funding for Democrats, who are the main representatives and allies of unions.

The progressive movement predates the American labor unions however; and it will not be silenced so easily. Are you tough enough to stand with me? You know our pledge to each other from the very beginning: United we stand divided we fall.

What Is Too Minor To Do?

Money and power have corrupted the lifelong politicians absolutely, but to say we need not do something so minor, as to defund unions because it is not the big answer to today's problems, would be counterproductive. We must not leave a stone unturned.

I keep reminding people that when you are on your computer, nothing happens until you push the start button. Any one thing may seem small given the massive amount of problems that exist, but the more issues that we can start to address at one time, the better off we will be.

I mention several of those dismantling issues in the base of my platform of this book.

Who Is the Sleeping Giant?

I see the sleeping giant as the American patriot and he is waking up. There is no such thing as guilt by association when it comes to Democrat or Republican, because they both stink. That is where the voter is going to take over. I personally feel that an Independent, such as myself, who wants to force the Constitution and republic back to the top of governance, so that no democracy majority can ever devalue it again, is a perfect platform, which should fit any political candidate who is chosen for any office in our future.

Honest and trustworthy patriots who love their country did not deliver America to where we are today; I don't care how far back you care to go. To a certain extent, greed and self-interest groups interfered with our country back then and do even more so today and they are called corrupt politicians; but that is going to come to a halt starting with David Tippie in the White House and every other able-bodied man and woman with the courage to stand with me will have been the power that put me there. I work for you, and that is what government should always do.

We are going to return to our republic and for those who have been lulled to sleep by the special interest groups that have you thinking that democracy is the same thing as a republic we are going to wake you up as well.

Many in our country think that only millionaires and billionaires should run for political office, because of petty jealousies that have been passed down from the lord and master through our serfdom mentality from our past.

Every one of these lords who runs for office has his or her hand out to lobbyists and special interest groups and that simply feeds the corruption that has existed for years due to our own ignorance and lack of will to do something about it.

Joe the plumber, who was talked down to by the anointed one (as Sean Hannity refers to Obama) would have made a one thousand percent better president than the political/activist group organizer that we now have who has never held a real job or ran a company and in my view has shown disdain for America.

For years, public sector unions have spent billions electing pro-union politicians who will vote favorably on wage and benefit packages for government employees. Although the majority of those are Democrats there are plenty of Republicans as well. This politics as usual, referred to as the good old-boy syndrome must stop and there has never been a better time than right now while the unions are scared to death that the sleeping giant will be awakened to their scams; Remember who the sleeping giant is: we the people.

Unions are a game of power at any cost, which unfortunately places these costs on already over-burdened taxpayers. After years of being told, "If we love the children, we have to pay" finally American taxpayers have had enough.

Insofar as unions go, a strong private sector economy and a very small constitutional government would relegate the public sector unions to the level of an insignificant annoyance.

The unconstitutional practice of predicating employment on mandatory union membership and participation has destroyed American industry. The states that have allowed these practices are dying specifically because of the demise of industry. I ask again, anyone been to Detroit lately?

As an American I have a right to work and support my family. I must have the right to decide for myself whether or not I will join a union. Freedom of assembly and association are supposed to be protected by the First Amendment. Unions have long hidden behind those freedoms to insulate themselves against criticism but if union members are not allowed to choose such association, it is not free association and it is not protected.

Collective bargaining is not a function of free association or assembly. Collective bargaining under duress is thuggery. Negotiations entered into by free parties; with willingness by all parties is the American way.

My position is to ensure choice and eliminate handouts period, and return to our American pride. This is why I ask everyone to read my book and if you agree with me, help me, at the very least get others to go to my website: http://www.LiveLonger123.com to purchase my book. Spreading the word cannot be accomplished without your help.

We need to be enforcing our immigration laws and also put a moratorium on immigration. Our Constitution says that if a person's parent owes allegiance to another country, his birth here does not make him an American citizen.

I know that Mexico has a law that states that if a Mexican citizen's parents give birth to their child in another country, that child is still a Mexican citizen.

To our Constitution we shall return and as I have stated, the eleven million or so illegal aliens here now, pack your bags, because I intend to do what President Ike Eisenhower did and that is deport every illegal alien.

Certificate of Live Birth or, Birth Certificate

You have the right to acquire a certificate of birth, which is different from a birth certificate. Hence the issue's with Obama. This is why I have never seen him as my president. That issue, as grand as it is, takes back seat to the destruction he has intentionally caused to our country, a country that I believe he hates. I know that he was not born before 1746 so he does not meet that criteria as natural-born citizen required becoming president, and he has never proven birth on U.S. soil. What he produced was a certificate of birth from Hawaii, not a birth certificate. Pretty simple stuff as covered earlier.

Fortunately I am not one of the sit around and do nothing but complain doomsday guys; returning America to a land of individualism and freedom with a Constitution and limited government does not require complete agreement on every thorny topic.

Reducing government involvement could be as small as each person peacefully talking to and persuading his neighbor without it becoming a matter of life and death, prosperity or poverty, freedom or parasitism, all or nothing approach. Just a simple talk with a neighbor can start the process. After all, a problem only exists because the right solution has not been applied to it. I promise that you will understand this statement from me, and how truly profound it is to me, as you read about me further on.

There are many problems we have to face and fix with a solution and Social Security happens to be one of them.

Social Security Scam on Americans

We are just now finding out that everything was a lie, as I have stated earlier: None of the Social Security surplus revenue has ever been saved and invested in treasury bonds or anything else, as was promised. All revenue, not needed to pay current benefits has been put into the general fund and used to pay for wars and other government programs, as well as the other (political) good old-boy programs, such as the bridges to nowhere, and found in places like the freezer of the politician in Louisiana; just a small reminder of corruption is all this is.

Every dollar of the $2.5 trillion, that was supposed to be in the trust fund, has been borrowed, embezzled or stolen by the government and spent for other purposes, including other nations and now mainly spent on interest from our borrowed money, which is increasing our debt.

Now what do we do? Simply because we are not the solution does not mean we can't be part of the solution. Simply because by ourselves we are not powerful -does not mean we are powerless when it comes to our joined numbers. The many things that I outline in this book for certain will be accomplished when I am elected president. We also have to deliver the guarantee that our citizenry paid for fifty plus years called Social Security.

We can't forget our school system either and we need to be pushing back against progressives in our public school system on the way to privatizing it entirely. This is one of the most important things freedom-loving individuals can do.

Governor Walker and his attempts to replace underperforming teachers who have tenure was a good start. Mandatory action would be replacing those teachers who are not performing with those who provide excellent teaching skills who get paid on merit, which in my view, means privatizing schools.

When you are fighting a serious outbreak of a virus, the first priority is to stop spreading it. It means challenging school boards on textbook selection, teachers on essay topics, and more. Every year, millions of schoolchildren become new unwitting inductees into the progressive camp.

Certainly we have to stop the hemorrhaging in our country, which means stop the spending. Of course the retirement age has to be raised for those just entering the job market and of course Medicare and Medicaid must be eliminated. I have offered my thoughts on local hospitals under county and state control, but that's not all; the federal government must be reduced to being solely the protector of our country and not its dictator, then the old statement that we have not heard in a long time must re-surface: Politics is local!

That means the governance of the people of each state shall return to the city, county and state. If you don't like what is going on in your city, county or state move to another one or, vote the bums out.

But federal government is about to be out of your personal and private lives, after the upcoming 2012 election when David Tippie is elected your president.

Restoring America to a (STRONG) and free country, one where the dominant ethos is respect for the individual's rights and free exercise of judgment, won't be easy. But despite the Pandora's Box of horrors imposed on citizens by Washington for the past three generations, the odds have never been better for a renaissance.

If we are to have a country that does more than seesaw between two power-hungry parties, while spiraling ever downward, then we must have a leader who is not afraid of the issues and not afraid of either party because of his fear of not getting re-elected. I intend to be that leader and candidate for president in 2012.

Other countries don't need a weak America, they need a strong America and they will forgive America when I stop the funding of others before we have our own house cleaned up and secured; by default our strength will make them stronger as well.

I think we have to make learning and understanding the Constitution of the United States of America a lifetime discipline, for both our school children and ourselves, to pursue understanding of the original intent of the Founding Fathers. It cannot be better interpreted by anyone other than those who created it, debated it, and ratified it; so we must discover what their intent was and continue to live by that meaning. We must not let elected people band together and change it, under the guise of democracy.

By definition, a republic is a political unit governed by a charter, while a democracy is a government that has the prevailing force of a majority. Republic and democracy are considered synonyms but they are no more alike than an apple or an orange and yet they are often used interchangeably.

Why do democrats support the voting rights by illegals? Think of the free-bees the illegal's get from democrats; this makes them prone to vote democrat.

(Michael Spence/The Patriot Journal) website: thepatriotjournal.com states "What else could it be? The Democrats in the Nevada legislature are obstructing Senate Bill 178. SB178, which in addition to making it a felony to threaten an illegal with revealing their immigration status in order to compel them to perform certain acts, also makes it mandatory for anyone registering to vote to show proof of citizenship."

Chapter 11

If We Don't Stand for Something, We Will Fall for Anything.

In these times we cannot afford to be either feckless or fey. We need the resolve of the bold and the brave; if you stand with me we will prevail. But if we don't stand together then just maybe we're getting just what we deserve for allowing the democracy to trump our republic. Too many Americans have for too long been complacent when it comes to that most important subject.

Academics or Sports?

I have observed that more emphasis is put on high school sports than academics and stated so throughout this book.

More high schools spend more money on football stadiums and basketball courts in the place of spending money on books. A lot of kids basically attend high school to play sports and teachers give them good grades because teachers want their high school to have a good football team, so allegedly the top football player at a high school can get a one hundred on a test where he missed more than half of the questions, just so he can go to college and play football.

This ideology came from somewhere and I think the blame starts with parents who themselves may take little pride in education for themselves or in the education of their children.

The sooner we fix the tenure problem that ensures a teacher a job, regardless of her performance, the sooner we can expect things like the Constitution to become relevant once again in our society. My research from the huffington- post.com and others tells me in the 1950s we were number one in education and today we are about fourteenth worldwide. We must have abrupt changes like the elimination of the federal Department of Education and many other redundant government agencies as well as other government wasteful spending such as, the average American working three months a year, without pay, for the federal government. If you are in a higher tax bracket, you could be spending up to half your life working for Uncle Sam.

And how is your money being spent? A recent report from The Heritage Foundation simply named three taxpayer funded government bureaucracies to make the point of wasteful spending:

- The Securities and Exchange Commission spent $3.9 million rearranging desks and offices at its Washington, DC headquarters

- The decision of many federal employees to fly first class and the refusal to fly coach costs taxpayers $146 million annually

- Washington will spend $2.6 million training Chinese prostitutes to drink more responsibly on the job (are you starting to see something wrong here?)

Then there is the Senator Tom Coburn's "wastebook" guide that I suggest all to become familiar with.

Do banks need to tell the truth? Think you could borrow money from a bank without saying what you were going to do with it? Well, banks borrowing from you don't feel the same need to say how the money is spent.

After receiving billions in bailout aid from taxpayers the USA's largest banks say they can't track exactly how they are spending it. Some won't even talk about it. "We're choosing not to disclose that," said Kevin Heine, spokes man for Bank of New York Mellon, which received $3 billion in bailouts.

Thomas Kelly, a spokesman for JP Morgan Chase, which received $25 billion in bailout money, said that while some of it was lent, some was not, and the bank won't say exactly how the money is being used. "We have not disclosed that to the public. We are declining to," said Kelly.

The Associated Press contacted twenty-one banks that received at least $1 billion in government money and asked four questions: How much has been spent? What was it spent on? How much is being held in savings? And what's the plan for the rest? None of the banks provided specific answers.

We are not providing dollar-in, dollar-out tracking," said Barry Koling, a spokesman for SunTrust Banks, which got $3.5 billion.

Some said they simply didn't know where it was going. "We manage our capital in its aggregate," said Regions Financial spokesman Tim Deighton, who said the bank is not tracking how it is spending the $3.5 billion it received as part of the bailout.

Troubled Asset Relief Program, or TARP

The answers highlight the secrecy surrounding the Troubled Asset Relief Program (TARP) which earmarked $700 billion to help rescue the financial industry, who themselves helped bring about the disaster in the first place. The Treasury Department has been using the money to buy stock in U.S. banks, hoping that the sudden in-flow of cash will get banks to start lending again.

Corrupt Private Sector and Un-elected Bureaucrats

Corrupt private sector buying off of government and unelected government-appointed bureaucrats is huge. Many people actually consider the unelected bureaucrats of the government-appointed FDA to be a subsidiary of the Monsanto Company.

It sounds impossible, but when you look at all the Monsanto executives who have gone through the revolving door between private industry and government oversight, a truly disturbing picture emerges that seems to show the foxes are guarding the henhouse; which is one of my favorite lines.

The FDA is packed by pro-business; pro-corporation advocates who often have massive conflicts of interest when it comes to protecting the health of the public over making money.

In fact, the revolving door between private industry and government oversight agencies, is so well established these days, it has become business as usual to read about scandal, conflicts of interest and blatant pro-industry bias, even when it flies in the face of science or the law.

Corrupt Agencies and Their People.

FDA Commissioner Margaret Hamburg, a former dental amalgam company executive, helped subvert a federal judge's order to label mercury fillings as a hazard to children and pregnant women.

The FDA's top medical-device regulator, Daniel Schultz, re-signed following internal dissent over his decisions that his critics said were too friendly to industry.

Janet Woodcock, the director of the FDA's Center for Drug Evaluation and Research, was accused of a massive conflict of interest stemming from an ethics complaint filed by Amphastar Pharmaceuticals Inc.

The agency's list of corruptions and collusions is now a mile long. And each piece of new legislation aimed to improve its function seems to do just the opposite, making the FDA even more dependent upon financial support by Big Pharma.

I wrote a book titled "Collapse of Drugs, due to wellness", in which I shine the light on much of this corruption and show you the monopoly that the drug companies have on our health care system, due to the collusion of government non-elected bureaucrats who take money from big drug companies, which makes the health care industry monopoly the most expensive in the world and produces the least amount of results of any country. This is why I suggest county-controlled hospitals to take the place of Medicare and Medicaid, as well as for the dispensing of drugs that I spoke of earlier.

A monopoly can never exist without the help and support of the government. David Tippie says, free enterprise will once again be allowed and that will reduce the need for government agency control when I am elected president. Free choice will return to the private sector; not just concerning unions but with all things including the return of your choice in how you want to treat and cure yourself, be it pharmaceutical or natural.

Obama Signed Legislation That Reduced Natural Health Choice

Right through the back door, while everyone was focused on the Gulf oil spill, Barack Obama gave his signature to legislation permitting the U.S. government agencies to further restrict supplements and alternative health treatments. While his legislation does not name CODEX it brings forth language that supports its ideology.

That means that the supplements you take and therapies you use to keep your body healthy, can now be made illegal by the Centers for Disease Control (CDC) and U.S. Department of Health and Human Services (HHS).

Obama quietly gave permission for this to take place; mirroring the Codex Alimentarius objectives, which is the United Nation's worldwide plan for food standards that the new world order politicians would like to take effect in the United States. The U.S. was placed firmly on the road to this via Executive Order 13544 of June 10, 2010.

The President's Executive Order creates yet additional new government controlled taxpayer funded agencies, as if we need more, which are the National Prevention, Health Promotion, and Public Health Council, a group of so-called experts that carry out whatever activities Obama deems appropriate.

Contact me; join me with your support in any and every way you can devise. My website is: http://www.Livelonger123.com

At 211 degrees water is very hot but at 212 degrees it boils, and that steam can power a locomotive. In life, that extra degree of effort can create profound results. Time is short and effort is hard to locate when great things need to be accomplished. Will you join my effort?

I am asking each of you to put on your thinking hat and to absorb what I have stated.

The Cloward-Piven Strategy is a Scheme

In an article by Kurt Nimmo website infowars.com, the Cloward-Piven Strategy is discussed, Many have reported that Obama studied the Cloward Piven Strategy, which is a scheme cooked up by academic Marxists referred to as the "new-left" a global elite to consolidate power and destroy all opposition. The plan calls for the destruction of capitalism in America by swelling the welfare rolls to the point of collapsing our economy and then implementing socialism by nationalizing many private institutions.

I believe that Americans know that we are watching this happen right before our eyes; stand with me, enough is enough.

Chapter 12

Who is David Tippie?

The most important things are those that I have touched on from the beginning. The following is to let all Americans see if someone who is just like yourself and who is running for president can meet with your approval. Let's proceed shall we?

HOW DAVID STARTED

I have been a medical and natural-to-the-body researcher for the past thirty-years. I opened my research and development institute, the Anti-Aging Clinic in 2001. I have developed the most advanced aging-younger techniques and products, which work synergistically with each other and which are slated to take unfair advantage over medical pharmaceutical competition when I open clinics across America.

I have developed what the baby boomers that control the majority of the purchasing power in our country are looking for; they are searching for age rejuvenation and wellness in a non-pharmaceutical, non-invasive approach that will smooth fine lines and wrinkles, improve overall health, balance hormones, and sculpt the body.

But why and how I started will take me back to my childhood, and I pledge to talk to you as I would a good friend while describing myself.

I am proud of my accomplishments and feel blessed to have started my chosen path in the manner that I have, because it provided incredible drive and a never-give-up attitude toward life. I have the same passion for my continued studies and research today as I have had from my beginning, which translates to my ability. I feel my ability is second to none for I was not immersed in sports as today's youth certainly are.

My education is ongoing and will continue for the balance of my life, not the least of which will be my presidency. I will continue to educate myself and others in not only what has been my passion in life, natural-to-the-body alternatives that originated from the distant past to my ever-evolving future, but also in our constitutional form of governance that I have been passionate about for over two decades.

It was not through traditional means of attending class and only being exposed to some professor's point of view, where those in attendance are yawning and wanting the class to be over, that I learned. What I learn from my past until today, even if it is another's viewpoint is just as important to me now as was learning the first detail for improving health or improving our government. If the person has a view that I disagree with, it further guides me toward the greater understanding; so critics to me are valued.

I received an email that had an opposing view on a particular subject and when I disagreed with that view, I was amazed to see the reply, which was that I did not have to be disrespectful. I remember receiving that email and thinking how funny people are who find that those who disagree with them are being disrespectful and that those who disagree are wrong, but those who agree are kind, respectful and right.

These are the folks that George Carlin, the comedian spoke of in one of his routines that went something like this: "People, who drive the same speed as they do themselves on the highway are the only people who drive correctly and those who are faster or slower are the nut jobs." I find that amusing. Of course there are varying views and who said you can't be wrong?

Science should always prevail in my business and so should our Constitution for our government. I know of only one perfect person, and he was nailed to a cross a long time ago. I have no hope of being perfect.

If I am to ask my reading audience to invite me back into their living room again and again with their reading interest for my writings or to vote for me to be their president, then I must help them discover who David Tippie was as a young boy, up to becoming the young man and then the very knowledgeable older young man of today.

I see chronological aging as a fact of life, but biological aging as lifestyle mistakes. At the time of writing this book, I was 64 years young.

David Tippie is still passionately educating himself and sharing with others. You can see me walking about in a video on the front page of my website; I am not a fat man selling a diet program; so if I take my own natural health advice, I hope you see that I will represent you in our White House with what I believe is right for America.

I use a metaphor time and again, "a fat lady can't sell a diet program" talking of those in the media presenting something but they themselves don't look like they should be expressing views on that particular subject, if you get my meaning.

In my book "Collapse of Drugs, due to wellness" I speak of a medical pharmaceutical sickness industry doctor, who was asked to give advice to someone on a TV program about losing weight who himself possibly should have taken his own advice. Well let me rephrase that; maybe he should not have taken his own advice, because his advice was deadly and consisted of mind altering drugs; possibly he should have taken someone else's advice in the wellness industry instead; since he looked as though he could occupy two chairs instead of the one he was sitting over; or dare I say, hanging over.

You have heard of the old saying: One man's trash is another man's treasure. Well if you think about it, when you did not know there was anything better in your life than what you had, or were exposed to, you simply valued what you had as priceless.

David Tippie the boy was fortunate enough to have two older brothers and one older sister. A brother Richard Tippie who is alive today and a brother Sonny or Bernard Jr., named after my father, who along with my father is deceased. My sister is Mary Ellen, the oldest of the siblings and very much alive. All siblings are different as in all families.

Being the youngest in a modest family, not wealthy by anyone's stretch of those standards, provided me with the incentives I needed to do better in life. This is why I am so positive that removing entitlements will rebuild American pride. Don't get me wrong, at the time I had no idea what wealthy or poor meant. I learned that to have anything in life meant you had to work for it.

Working consumed me because it was one form of learning, which is one of my greatest passions in life.

My father had many flaws, as do all humans; I have my faults right to this very day, but as I look back, were it not for those flaws in others and myself, I would not have the strengths that I possess today.

In some ways, it was because of those flaws that I look through the windshield of life today and not at the rear view mirror, in all that I approach, so that I miss no opportunity.

David the boy saw mentors everywhere where others who had more in life at the time could only see the mundane and faults. A critic was not seen as a critic, but viewed as a mentor or a teacher.

When I was seven years old, in my mind, I did not know there were certain things that a seven year old was not supposed to be able to do; after all, my older brothers and their friends could do them. I saw things that other people could do that I could not do as simply something I had not tried or had not practiced doing before.

For example I saw who I thought was the smartest boy I had ever met in my early youth. He went to the same school I attended; as I recall, he was in a higher grade, the same as one of my older brothers and I knew where he lived. One day, as I was walking home from school, I saw this boy mowing the grass in the yard of a house, which was not his so I approached him with this question: "Why are you mowing this grass?" It isn't your yard, I said. I was thinking to myself at the time, that after all, cutting the grass was one of the chores for my brothers and me at our home and here this boy was cutting someone else's grass.

The boy said: "This is how I am able to buy my clothes and shoes for school;" Still a little lost, I asked, "How is that?" He replied, "I cut the grass for several people and they pay me."

I was in awe of this boy. In my mind this boy was brilliant. I asked him how it came to be that he got the job mowing the grass for these people? He said that he knocked on the door and asked them if he could mow their grass. I asked how much money he made and he said that it depended on the yard. He said that when he first started, he didn't know how much to charge, so people paid him what the job was worth.

He said, I noticed that I got more from some than I did from others, for about the same yard size and after a while, I began to learn what I should get.

I said to the boy, you have this mower and it runs on gasoline; we have a mower at our house that you have to push and does not use gasoline. Do you think that people might let me mow with it?

He said he didn't even have a mower when he first started; he asked them if he could use their mower and most of the time, they said yes.

Amazed at what I had just learned, I thanked him and started walking home, but all the while that I was walking my mind was in a whirlwind of thought.

I began developing a plan; beginning with who I was going to approach about mowing their grass first. Miss Lilly (not her real name), our next-door neighbor was whom I decided would be the first person to ask; she seemed to be very old to me at the time and she lived alone. When she came to the door something came over me my heart was in my throat and I muttered something about mowing her grass. She said, "Bless your little heart; well yes you can mow my grass you little dear, and she added; David I am impressed."

I ran next door and got our push mower and about two and half to three hours later I knocked on the door once more, having finished mowing. When she came to the door, I said, through the sweat dripping off my face and body, I'm finished.

She said, "thank you so much you precious little dear" and handed me a lemonade, then she added, and sit here until you cool off and just sit the glass on the sill there when you are done you precious boy."

That was what I refer to, as my first hard lesson. Admittedly, one of many I would encounter, as the years went by. By hard I refer to a job I had chosen to undertake that netted little or no money.

Having failed miserably at making money with my first job, which is part of working that will bring you success in life; I went back to my friend and mentor, the next day. I told the boy what had happened and he understood, to my surprise. At my house, as a young boy, when you failed at something around older brothers, there was a lot of laughter and heckling and that sort of thing; not a lot of understanding like this young boy seemed to have for me.

He said, "I know what you mean about knocking on a stranger's door; it is very scary at first. But you just have to decide if what you have is all you want or need. In my house, if you want something you have to get it yourself; so I just make myself do it and it is getting easier and easier."

Bouncing back to my political platform for just a moment, do you see the similarities in this boy's statement and what my passion is today about teaching those who have little, that working for it is the real and just way to live your life? You become your own motivation with this attitude and the satisfaction you get from it becomes your driving force.

I said to the boy, "But what about the money; how do you ask for money?" He said; "I tell them I'll cut your grass for an amount I've pre-determined before I get to the door, say two dollars, and they will say yes or no."

God knows this is basic free enterprise

I took his advice and began to build a small business with the trial and error method throughout that summer. Toward the end of the summer I knocked on a door and a man came to the door.

I said Sir; I will cut your grass for two dollars. Are you going to use that push mower he said? Yes Sir.

He showed me his shop in the back of his house where he repaired lawn mowers. He said, If you are looking for work, I got a job for you in my shop. His shop faced an alleyway with another shop across the way. I exploded with joy, inside of course, concealing it from him.

He said: If you can come here every day after school for four hours and all day Saturday, I will pay you twelve dollars a week and during the summer months I will pay you forty dollars per week for-six eight-hour days.

I had a hard time making twelve dollars per week, every week; mowing grass all summer long and a big smile came over my face, as I shook his hand in agreement.

In Texas we were taught that a handshake was better than a written contract, which was part of my early basic understanding in life.

In the little over four years that I worked for the lawnmower man, that old man taught me everything about repairing lawn mowers and anything that had a small engine, for that matter.

After nearly a year I could troubleshoot, disassemble any mower and repair every problem. He taught me what billing was and how to order and bill for every mower part we used and what labor was applied to what, in the most simplistic form, which was a system of three file boxes containing what you received, what you charged, such as buying mower parts and what you spent, such as paying for parts or my salary.

I began to know everybody by name when they brought equipment in, not just lawn mowers because different equipment uses the little lawn mower-type engines to power them, as I mentioned.

When customers were talking to me, when the old man was not present it was like they were speaking to the old man who owned the shop, which was with respect.

Since he was not around much anyway, their respect gave me great joy and I would eventually learn why the old man was not around much.

I would record sales in a small receipt book and give a carbon copy to the customer; my copy went into the Received box. The Planed Out box was where I put my copy of the receipts from the vendors who I ordered the parts from and in the Out box there was the tablet to record the checks that I had written with invoice numbers.

Looking back, the old man seemed to want everything to go through my hands and so I did everything and I was glad to be given the authority.

He even taught me how to make the deposits to his bank down the street from the shop when I was paid in cash or check. As a boy, being given this amount of responsibility was like becoming an adult and in my eyes life could not get any better.

It never dawned on me why the old man was never there. I was actually doing everything most of time and didn't really think about it, because it had been a ritual for me to knock on the door of his house to get his wife to sign the checks for vendors and for my twelve or forty dollars, depending on the time of the year for each weeks salary. I prepared the envelopes and the hand written notes, serving as acknowledgement of what invoice I was paying when I was ready to mail the checks to the vendors.

One day when I knocked on the door, neither the old man nor his wife answered. The front door was not closed all the way, so I pushed it open and yelled both of their names. With no answer and seeing his car was in the drive way, I felt that he must be at home.

I slowly walked back through the house calling out his name and then I smelled something burning. I went to the kitchen and I saw a pot on the stove sitting over the open flames of a gas burner. Two eggs that were inside were burned to a black stinky mess in the bottom of the pan, where the water had boiled away.

I turned the fire off and went looking for the old man once more. I found him lying on his back in bed with his arm hanging off the side. Not far from his hand was a large empty vodka bottle. My education in alcohol had come many years earlier from my father, who drank every day as long as he lived.

I shook the old man a little and he stirred some, so I knew he was alive. My heart stopping pounding but no sounds came from him. I closed the door behind me and went back to the shop with no idea what to do.

The shop where I worked faced another shop across the alleyway. That shop had a lot of giant equipment and some important-looking people worked there, as well as people coming and going from that shop.

I saw the man that seemed to be the boss approaching me from across the alleyway and I can remember looking at him in the same way as I did the principal of my school or some other very important person.

The man wore a brown brimmed hat and a pressed light-brown shirt and pants that all matched. One of his legs was shorter than the other and the pant leg was cut to match the length of the short leg and when he walked he seemed to rise and fall; but the way he carried himself, you didn't see that as anything less than dignified.

When he got to me, he was my same height resting on the shorter leg. When he spoke to me, it was as though the principal of my school was speaking to me, only with the special frankness that always seemed to come from important people, frank but gentle.

He introduced himself as Marvin Smith and asked for my name. Even though I told him my name was David he called me Davie. He said, I have been watching you over here for the past few years Davie, and I want to know if you would come work for me?

As I reflect back on it now, the way I was feeling about the importance of the man, would be like the president of the United States approaching a very young man or boy and asking him to come and work for him. It was unthinkable.

I told him that I didn't know how I could; because I had given my word to the man I was currently working for.

He said he knew this man and his wife and that it would only be a very short while, until the man would be sent somewhere that would help him with his problem and the shop would close.

I instinctively knew what problem he was speaking of. I then told him in a shaky voice that I would like to work for him.

So I did; I began to scrub down the big equipment and sweep the floors and anything else Mr. Smith or any of the other men who worked in the shop asked me to do. I learned that it was a machine shop.

I was holding measuring tapes, calipers and micrometers and helping generally and learning the names of the equipment, even learning to weld as well as to learn what each machine could accomplish.

Mr. Smith seemed always to take the time to come over when I was cleaning a piece of equipment and stand down on his shorter leg to explain something about it. For example when I was working on a lathe, he told me what it was and what it could do, including that it could reproduce itself.

I was introduced to each piece of equipment in the shop in the same manner and slowly over the course of seven years, while working in an after-school work program and every weekend, as well as all summers; I became the youngest machinist in Austin, Texas.

It was the engineering brilliance from my mentors that helped me shape who I am today that came from this little machine shop in Austin, Texas.

When we would design build something to handle a particular need the customer had, Mr. Smith would say something like: Designing and building a piece of equipment to provide a special service is just like life Davie. You set out what you want and need to accomplish you study with the same passion that brought you to the task, which you use for every task and there is absolutely nothing you can't learn, build, repair or accomplish in life or in this machine shop.

He was aware of my home life and took every opportunity to relate to life and how one might look at life.

Mr. Smith would challenge me to find the error in something brought to the shop by a customer for repair. "What's wrong with this, Davie?" He would ask.

Use your head and determine what it is supposed to do and then correct whatever it is that's keeping it from doing its intended task or design something to take the place of the broken part that will make it provide the same task or better."

He would always say, "Remember, a problem is only something that has not yet had the correct solution applied.

Those moments and his words helped shape my life and I believe they apply not only to everyday life, but to government as well.

I earned his trust and respect over the years and became the go-to machinist who handled all the problem research and design-build projects, which is a much respected place in the profession. And my hat goes off to all in that industry, even today; and it will be those folks when reviewing my written work who no doubt, will see how teaching myself physiology or government as well as learning the ways in which to improve health or government was only second nature to a person who came from that honorable profession. If there is a problem, it merely requires the application of a solution.

My life as an adult not only started very early but my circumstances made it necessary for me to provide my own lodging at age sixteen as well and shortly after doing so, I had a friend in high school, named Joe Schnitco who found himself in similar life circumstances. We decided to share the rent of my apartment, which was very near our high school.

One day after we turned eighteen, after listening to the news about the Vietnam War I said to Joe, "Let's go be real men and join the Marines.: He was game so we got into my fifty five Chevy and drove from Austin to San Antonio to enlist in the Marine Corps.

We got there and took the required test. A Navy officer approached me and said: "Mr. Tippie, with a grade like this, why don't you join the Navy?" I thanked him and then I told him that Joe and I were joining the Marines on the buddy system and we were going to basic training together to go on our first mission together; was how we were advised by the recruiting officer.

He understood, and we went to have our physicals. After that we went back to the YMCA where the Marine Corps put us up. The next morning we went back to the office and Joe was given his orders while I was singled out by an officer, who privately said that they wanted me to stay over another day to give me another physical, and that Joe was to fly off to California that day.

I told him what I'd told the other officer about the buddy system, and he said that that was not a problem because I would simply arrive a little later than Joe. So I took the second physical and went back to the YMCA. The next morning, I went back to get my ship out orders to California and catch up with Joe.

I was again asked to take another physical and again told it would not hinder my buddy-system enlistment program, so I took the physical and again I stayed at the YMCA.

When I got to the office the next morning I was quickly told that I was rejected for enlistment. The recruiters strongly suggested that I visit with my doctor and advise him that I may have diabetes.

I could not have felt worse; my chest felt as though it had a knife stuck in it. My life seemed to sink into a dark hole. I did not know how to contact Joe and I was devastated. It had been my idea to join and now Joe was the only one to be accepted.

I went back to my apartment in Austin and certainly never went to a doctor. Truth be known, the way I was feeling, I would rather have died of something. Within a few days I received a phone call from my buddy Joe. I told him what had happened to me and we were both traumatized; we had no answers.

Several months later Joe's family contacted me; Joe had been shot through the heart jumping off a helicopter on his first tour in Vietnam.

No one who has experienced life in any form can relate to living with the knowledge that he was directly responsible for his best friend's death.

All my life, I have tried to live a life that I privately share with my buddy Joe. I never did go to the doctor after I left San Antonio that day, nor did I for years afterwards. Looking back, facing death would have been more pleasant than to face life with what I believed I was responsible for. The experience has shaped my life I believe for the better, because I knew Joe and I know he would have wanted it that way. No one ever knows what is in the cards for themselves and I am one who believes that things happen a certain way for a reason. I would like to believe one of those reasons was to become a conservative independent presidential candidate in 2012, due to these very troubling times.

It is going to take someone who is tough and will not compromise his integrity. Trickle on you economics do not work for the bulk of Americans (middle class), and we need to turn this thing back around in our favor! Our politicians are puppets, the lobbyist control government, and big banking will never give up on this goldmine they created for themselves until our country collapses in debt!

I am positive my life is similar to some American lives, as will sometimes happen in life, early marriage from high school and children would chart a new direction in life, including a new profession that would help me better provide for my family. I never looked to others for my responsibilities.

I left the machine shop and started at the ground floor of a large corporation called Brown & Root which in later years merged with a company called Halliburton, run by a man named Dick Cheney; this was long before the company became popular for receiving contracts from the government and alleged shady deals. I moved to Brown & Root because it paid much more than the machine shop and now with family, change was imminent with more responsibility. As always, my thirst for learning propelled me to the top. I went from being a welder to running organizations and then to starting and owning my own small companies.

Once again health landed on my radar screen when I was in my early thirties. I was like everyone else; I felt I was invincible, more because of what I was responsible for with Joe than anything else; death did not concern me, until a symptom occurred that alerted me to just how vulnerable we humans are.

No matter what you are doing or achieving, including gathering wealth, without health it doesn't matter much anymore. There are no U-haul trailers, at the graveside; you take nothing with you. What you accomplish while you are alive is the only thing that counts.

I was just like the majority of people in our country; I began blindly following everything the doctor told me to do; I took the prescription drugs he told me to try. He never said: This is exactly what you need; as I recall, he always said, "Try this and I was just like everyone else, fully expecting "this" to make me all better.

I would learn in later years, exactly why the doctor called his business a "practice." When he handed me a prescription for a drug, he would say. "Try this! That sounds like practicing to me; but that is for others to decide.

Let me take just a moment to explain something about the creditability of doctors. Make no mistake, I think that the majority of people who become medical sickness industry doctors are professionals that they become doctors with the highest of moral and ethical reasons; and that they provide the finest critical care that there is in the world.

In my opinion, where they seem to have strayed from the Hippocratic Oath, is in prescribing synthetic pharmaceutical drugs, of which they are trained to do I might add, because of the monopoly that the pharmaceutical industry has on our health care system, natural remedies are not offered.

Some doctors prescribe drugs with reluctance, because they probably would not prescribe the same drugs to their mothers that they would prescribe to their patients. Andrew Carnegie once said "No amount of ability is of the slightest avail without honor." And that is how I have lived my life; I know for a fact that my buddy Joe would be proud.

Having introduced you to that, so that you will know that I am not writing this book just to get elected, but anticipating that you see me as the person who you could trust to run our country, before you choose to vote for me, I want you to be comfortable with me.

Indeed I only want to level the playing field, so the billionaires will know that if I can get your support, no amount of their money which they spend on advertising is going to sway your vote for a patriot who is looking for the opportunity to serve his country and serve it proudly just like my buddy "Joe did".

But if I am elected you may have guessed that those in the wellness industry will be able to exist without constantly coming under siege from the drug cartel government profit protectors, that some refer to as the Food and Drug Administration (FDA), Center for Disease Control (CDC) and some others. Drugs ought to be your choice, as well as to choose natural treatments and substances if you wish. Americans must not be dictated to about anything.

For the majority of my life I was always exercising including practicing the martial arts for a great many years, which believe it or not, is the best training in the world to learn respect for others. You might think about it for your children.

Also that is where I would learn the yen and yang theory principles that would apply to most everything I would study and learn in my future life about health or government, for that matter.

The Yen and Yang principle is an Asian concept that says that for every action, there is an equal and opposite reaction. Can you visualize what opposite reaction spending creates? You guessed it, a deficit.

In my early life, steak and potatoes were my favorite meal, and vegetables were a little something in an obscure little pan on the table at Thanksgiving and Christmas. But this was also the norm for my family, my aunts, and uncles and so on.

My father as well as aunts and uncles were dying of what was determined to be "old age" diseases. Only they were dying in their late fifties and early sixties.

At about the age of thirty, I made this observation, I began to see that something was wrong in River City, and that meant Trouble with a capital T, which rhymed with P and that stands for Pool.

"Trouble in River City" is of course the story by Wilson and Franklin Lacey. I have often used the metaphor. But trouble meant problem and problem meant that a solution had not yet been applied to it.

The plot of Trouble in River City was; it concerns con man Harold Hill, who poses as a boy's band organizer and leader and sells band instruments and uniforms to naive townsfolk before skipping town with the cash, without delivering the goods. I don't know what comes to mind for you but possibly Enron might come to the mind for me; though there are thousands of such stories.

Observing my relative's health problems and those of my immediate family I said to myself, David, I don't know at this time what you are going to do, I just know you are going to do something; your health is the largest problem of which you will have ever found a solution for; but solve this you must.

Jumping forward in life, I was introduced to new problems from others and now it was up to me to find the solutions, in my wellness clinic.

The initial symptom I faced years ago was related to problems caused from stress, such as skin breakouts, and as I said, I was in my early thirties. I was fortunate to have met a physician who exercised with me at the same gym for years. We became friends over those many years and looking back, I can see that he was more of a naturalist and not of the mainstream pharmacy-medicine mold.

He knew quite a lot about my past from our conversations, as I did his. This gentleman was able to get my attention because of our mutual respect. He was a person not afraid to use the "A" word and introduced me to it; Alternative.

We spoke about stress and the physiology of stress. He explained to me that I had to learn how to vent my stress or I was going to occupy an early grave.

Before I speak further of the health solutions I pursued for my clients' health benefit, I want to introduce my beautiful wife of fourteen years, Stephanie whom I love dearly.

My wife Stephanie is the center of my life. In later years she joined my business as well. She has been an accomplished businesswoman who has applied her formal education brilliantly; she is a self-made woman and in some respects is enjoying the fruits of the clinic concept I have researched for more than twenty-five years. The concept is improving health before beauty, so that beauty would improve faster. She has become supportive of and involved with the clinic starting a few years after I opened the research and development center in 2001.

When you are fortunate enough to see her face you will never guess her age. Not only is she in the peak of health inside, but has impeccably beautiful skin on the outside. Good health happens to be the key to beauty on the outside; that is the essence of my health care concept.

Stephanie is a researcher in her own right and has a great head on her shoulders, which I count on daily. Here is to you my love, I love you dearly and you will make the country proud as a first lady who has no problem telling anyone that she loves her country even if her husband happened not to become elected and she has never felt disdain for it either.

Also, since our lives started out in the same manner, my sister Mary Ellen should be mentioned, because it explains several things about my past life.

Mary Ellen is an intelligent self-made woman; even though she did not get the opportunity to earn a college degree she has made a huge success of her life and has been the shining star in her family's life. Her light shined in my life as a boy growing up that in some degree pointed the way for some of my darkest childhood hours.

She and I are similar in some ways. We both loved learning starting at a very early age and both graduated high school even though we were not living at home and were supporting ourselves. Education was learning, not necessarily from a teacher or professor, which, due to life circumstances, did not happen for her and me; but now I see that as a good thing.

As we grew to be adults we never believed that we were deprived, because everything we accomplished came from our own passion and extraordinary effort. She started her life with marriage at age sixteen for some of the same reasons that I was in my first apartment living alone at sixteen, and was later able to split rent with my best friend Joe.

Anything my sister and I wanted to become could be in our grasp in life if we wanted to work for it in spite of those early life circumstances or, because of them, depending on how you look at it. We both took the cards dealt to us as though it was a royal flush and built a good life.

Without a blueprint to follow, as our childhood was a little rocky, and armed with passion to succeed, we are both successful today.

She is at the center of her family because of something else we have in common and that is our never give-up attitudes. I was constantly traveling the world in my business endeavors, making what I called a living for my family; possibly due to having no idea about parenting; I always issued tough love, making certain that each of my children would grow up to be self-reliant. Their mother and I were joined right out of high school because of our first child; but as the years went by she and I grew apart. But I raised our two children to become firm supporters of themselves and their families and not dependent on anyone.

My sister and I both worked hard to discover what a family could be and then applied astounding effort to accomplish that. We will wait for our judge in heaven to tell us if we were correct or not. I always remember the bible verse that went something like this: Thou shalt honor thy Father and thy Mother. I don't recall it saying thou shalt honor thy children of thou shalt spoil thy children.

Mary Ellen is an accomplished self-employed businesswoman who balanced the career superbly with the family, never losing sight of her family values, which she had to first become the architect of, certainly not patterned after our immediate family. My hat is off to my sister.

I believe everything happens for a reason as I have stated. I don't know why I was not chosen to jump off that helicopter with my best friend Joe and possibly suffer his same fate. I won't discover it looking in the rearview mirror of my life; and that is why I focus only on the windshield of life.

You can force your child to become something in life by paying for them to attend college and most will accomplish your dreams for them and obtain that degree; but some lack the passion and the drive that it takes to truly succeed because the passion was missing from the start, and without passion there can be no true success. That statement is always spoken eloquently by Donald Trump, who is unquestionably a great businessman says give me a person with passion over degree any day and I will show you success.

Every time I hear something that relates to passion I am reminded of my past and how passion and my never-give-up attitude have played such a vital role in forming who I am today.

As kids we did not perceive that we were building a path to greatness for ourselves through our passion and our thirst for knowledge. We had nothing against college we simply could not have afforded it. But not attending college did not prevent us from reading and writing extensively, sharing ideas with our friends, and learning from people who have excelled in their fields. We learned how to teach and learn for ourselves, which is by default what college is supposed to teach you.

In the beginning our passion and drive were sheer survival instinct. As kids we did not realize that the passion for learning far outweighed the simple degree handed to someone who was fulfilling a parents dream and not their own, who may have barely gotten that diploma.

Most have passion when they get their opportunity to go to college but if there is no passion for learning then the idleness of what should I do next presents itself when complete. The golf course or the new gadget will occupy time at that point, as they go about using up time, or spending life, which is often the outcome of non-passionate people, even those who did not attend college and who did not educate themselves tend to become entitlement-prone.

Digressing a moment to my friend the physician who I worked out with in the gym who suggested I get a handle on my stress. What I viewed as a lack of education always compelled me to not just do a good job but that I had to excel in everything I did to make up for that lack of a formal education, which I first saw as my handicap.

I felt in my own mind that people saw me as handicapped when I accomplished things in life even though certain things were recognized by others as being well above average; this was before I became truly aware as to what education that I truly was blessed with.

When I received compliments in my past, I received that praise with an unhealthy mental attitude, due to feeling that I did not deserve praise yet. I always felt I must study twice as hard and devote twice as much time or, I would be behind everyone who held the college degree.

I explained this to my friend the physician and to my amazement, he laughed a caterwauling laugh asking; what do you mean?

He began to explain that he was born into a wealthy family and was programmed to be a doctor when he came out of the womb. He said he was a good little boy and followed the path that was nurtured and paid for by his parents. He said, I had to be threatened a time or two to study and I had no passion for it.

What he said next nearly sent me through the floor. All of these years that I have known you, I have envied you and your successes in life; how you drink life in and study and research like your very life depended on it. You will learn more and accomplish more before you die than twenty people with degrees who lack passion

This was the right time in my life to have someone educate me as to what education really is; and to have someone point these facts out at that time was priceless.

What I have been able to accomplish through my research up to that point was going to help many people, and what I learned from him only accelerated my efforts, as the years would prove.

All the way to the development of the Aging Younger Research and Development Center that produced the technology and product combinations which are the success stories for our clinic concept from 2001 up to today. We help many people and we intend to help millions more, provided they choose for themselves to accept the help. Choice should always be yours and not the governments.

I intend to help all Americans by becoming your president in 2012, not by making your choices for you, but by removing government from your personal lives and returning it to its Constitutionally intended purpose, which is to protect America and Americans.

When I offer my suggestions in this book, they are put here with passion and a love for my country and my education is by and from others. I am asking you to make the choice of standing up with me and getting the word out about me; by getting as many people to read my book as possible; and by inventing venues and getting the funding for the venue so I can be invited to address people with my platform.

Together we win; divided we FAIL.

David's Final Word on the American Economy!

The American economy needs some fresh, non-ideological thinking, starting with defining the meaning of big government verses small government so that the American people can completely understand both. This will mean that, in the end, a government of the people and by the people and for the people can be created and can become a smarter, leaner government, geared more toward our Constitution.

Responsible, smart government must translate to responsible, smart people who will elect those who appoint governing agencies who enforce that governance of the people's will.

A smart government will stop inventing pipe dreams for the people, regarding what the American dream consists of and let each American decide and pursue for themselves their own dreams with as little government intervention as possible and with fewer government agencies. When government agencies create a job, the government must increase the amount of tax it takes from you to pay those agencies. That is not job creation it is simply increasing taxes on tax-paying Americans.

If that individual American has dreams that do not match his or her wallet then he fails and goes quietly after more achievable goals. America's failure at something does not mean that his neighbor or the government should come running to his rescue and take more money from taxpayers to bail him out

The same is true for business. Free enterprise will fill the voids left by failure and fix problems, as well as set wages and determine the future.

Education will ensure equality. Education could be an area where each American could contribute to his neighbor, through our tax dollars, because we care about our fellow Americans; however that does not mean expensive universities, it could be that we allow our government to take some of our tax money and offer job training to those who, for whatever the reason, find themselves always making the wrong decisions in life and keeping themselves in poverty.

Our tax dollars will not feed, clothe or house them; it will simply train them for a job. Feeding clothing and housing have the opposite effect from job training.

If someone, through his poor choices and bad habits, finds he is starving and has no roof over their head, he can turn to the church's compassion and ask for help and guidance to help him straighten his life out and begin to be a productive human capable of taking care of himself.

America is still the land of opportunity, but only with effort on our part and the absence of government intervention. Today the United States is perceived as a risky place to do business by foreign companies because of our government's role in our passive lives.

If we would begin to think outside the box and begin to offer a mix of tax incentives for new business and job-training services, as well as legal assistance to ensure they remain safe and profitable, this might persuade more foreign firms to invest in the United States thus creating jobs.

In an economy in which we are suffering from over-taxation and piles of tax codes and regulations, springing any new taxes on the American public or companies, foreign or domestic, verges on heresy; so tax incentives to start business should be part of the mix, as well as my graduated flat tax code, which means a tax never higher than say twenty five percent and never lower than say five percent, with increments in between, so that we are all responsible citizens without loop-holes.

In business, tax is nothing other than an expense and Guess who will ultimately being paying for that expense for goods or services? If you guessed American consumers would be paying fo them, then that would be accurate.

Throwing stones at large companies by taxing them at higher and higher rates would be self-defeating to the economy it is passed right back to the consumer and it incentivizes companies to move out of the United States. Make no mistake about it, economy means the American jobs, life and lifestyle.

Throwing stones at the wealthy would also be self-defeating, as the wealthy are the ones who create the most jobs.

To destroy business is to increase taxes which cause jobs to leave an area or the U.S. Another way business is destroyed is to have the wealthy create a company that creates jobs for the citizens of that community and then to have those who were given those jobs, to begin to unionize and dictate what the company owner will pay them and what the company owner will contribute to their retirement.

Americans must see it from both sides of the fence in order to realize how they are destroying their own lives, by their efforts to take over the company with unions. Free enterprise will dictate the wage and improved training and education will improve the wage.

From the website: truthwinds.com Nixon and the Watergate conspirators look like choirboys compared to the jokers that populate this Administration.

Some people seem to be incapable of getting their heads around the level of corruption in our government. I think it is simple. The first order of business is to restore values, honesty and integrity within our government by electing non-career politicians and start with the plan I have outlined in this book to rebuild our nation to its rightful place as being the strongest nation in the world. If we can't do that everything else is useless. Our government is so bought off by the lobbyists and the elite in this country that they don't file criminal charges against politicians or the elite white-collar criminals no matter how gross their crimes are against the people of America. I believe that if we continue to maintain the status quo, by continually voting for the career politicians we will see the end of this country, maybe even within our lifetimes. It is just to frustrating to listen to people babble about republican and democratic agendas. Both parties have corrupt politicians. Until we clean up the government by throwing the criminal bums out and separate our politicians from the god almighty dollar, because to the career politician only money talks and the people of America lose.

As for all of our Sovereign Souls answerable to no earthly authority other than Nature and Nature's God, who may not know the story---it has been removed from public education through the sophistry of John Dewey, financed by Rockefeller at the University of Chicago, also financed by Rockefeller. This must be reversed if only for our children's sake.

It is only though education that we can restore self-governance, and stop reliance on government, which begins with the Self as a Sovereign Soul. Liberty and Freedom are spiritual principles not measurable in physical, monetary terms. The very idea of a Spiritual Self and the Divine given Free Will, have also been removed from public education. In short, government authority, entrusted to the People, has been usurped by criminals through deception and censorship.

Yes, the 50s were the height of public education where we were number one in the world and that was the generation that took us to the moon. That generation was brimming full of job makers, not job seekers. The 60s saw the rise of the progressive destruction of education and a purge of faculty who are now minimally focused on academia and have a set agenda to dumb down our children. The 70s saw the institutionalizing of progressive social engineering techniques to shape young people to the needs of an industrial society, where they could not produce a job for themselves, they had to look for a job.

The early American epitaph is that each man and woman are free to follow the Will of God as it was seen to them, no priest, pope or king in between would decide for them, nor was religion and morals removed from the schools. Freedom of Speech, Religion, Association, and Assembly, secured for all the people, distinguishes American society as in no other country in the world, back then. But what about now with all of the erosion, control and regulations that have taken place. The return of these social precepts would allow all, not just the rich and powerful, to participate in local, state or national governance who promote peace & prosperity for all.

After 100-years of --Mis-education—we now have a –Mobocracy--created that elects a pseudo royalty who assume the authority to tell everyone what to do and how to live regardless of the laws and protections afforded us by our Constitution. Regular people are taught to obey the laws imposed instead of being the law to insure that our politicians abide by our Founding Fathers written law.

The Federal Reserve is totally unconstitutional and un-American as it gives a monopoly to a private enterprise that has the privilege to work in secret. Secret societies are the vehement denunciation to American social principles, because whenever a secret society is permitted to a position of social policy, those few in the club will have an advantage over the many. The success-ful State Bank systems that existed before the Federal Reserve, except S. Dakota, was destroyed by Federal Reserve agents after the Fed was created. The Federal Reserve and Income tax are major accomplishments of these (criminals (royalists, Federalists, known today as politicians Democrats and I am sorry to say—that includes Republican impersonators). Their major aim since the assassination of Lincoln has been the destruction of the republic and Republican Party, now pretty much accomplished I might add; which is why I chose to run as an independent. We the people do not need to compel any one to do anything for us. We have the authority to do for ourselves. It is about coalescing around common vision and common sense as a team. Liberty and Freedom can never be an aggressive force. You must first learn self-reliance and practice living in the Liberty of Self-governance and, once realized, defend it with the full force of life within you.

The personal line in the sand that should be drawn is to realize the un-elected bureaucrats and most of the elected politicians are criminals and declare, "I do not do business with criminals, and throw the bums out and put a patriot in each of their places." I like to call it—Term Limits.

It is good to point out how much is at stake in the 2012 election. I believe Obama is ultimately beatable, but he's not the only one seeking re-election that we must be concerned with. It is critical for America's survival that we keep the momentum of the Obama mid-term, by electing more Constitutional Congressmen and Senators. Increasing a conservative hold on the House and gaining a majority in the Senate should also be important goals for us to keep in mind.

Ultimately, regardless of the vote outcome, a district by district system in place of the Electoral College winner take all system, would render better and more equitable representation, for a while. In states like California, where two huge population centers comprised mostly of entitlement liberals, controls the largest number of electoral votes and that disenfranchises 96% of the state. In most districts there, the people are quite conservative, but under "winner takes all", a handful of districts effectively nullifies their votes and denies them representation.

Unfortunately, Gerrymandering eventually, would improve some of the affect of "by district" electors. Which brings us to the question of eliminating the Electoral College altogether. This action would require amending the Constitution. I believe we need to approach amendments with extreme caution. Original intent should never be violated and the wisdom of the founding fathers should be at the forefront in such discussions. These discussions and any conclusions need to be temporally contextual, with the old saying: If it ain't broke, don't fix it, and if it IS broke, USE the constitution as a tool instead degrading it with amendments for the sake of expediency.

District by district electors would fit nicely with the repeal of the 17th amendment, which establishes the direct election of United States Senators by popular vote.

By allowing State legislatures to choose Senators, voters at the state level would have more control over representation. If the people of a state become dissatisfied with their Senator(s), State elections become more important and participation at the state level would be more vigorous.

With more effective representation in the Senate and state governments which more closely mirrors majorities, the overall tone of national debate would change drastically. A more representative award of electoral votes would break the strangle hold of the handful of large cities on Presidential elections and would no longer control over a third of electoral votes. Presidential candidates would no longer slide into the White House by pandering to social activists and entitlement slaves in metropolitan areas. They would be forced to actually listen to the concerns of the majority.

Research accreditation:

Since every word in my life came from somewhere or someone, I can't claim ownership from any of them. I really can't remember how many books, articles and websites I have read to help me shape my ideas and ideals, as well as my opinions, even from opposing views and opinions and I have listed quite a few further on, and I put web links which are placed in my book also on my website so as to give you a quick place to access the many websites that I have reviewed. All have in some way helped me fashion thoughts into readable perspective. These will give you an idea of where to start searching for yourself for anything that agrees or disagrees with my line of thinking. I see no better way of delivering what I feel so passionate about than to list others who may feel the same way as I that I repeat their wording or who may disagree and I indicate why. If that will interest you, please go to this website http://www. LiveLonger123.com click on "book" and when it takes you to the book page find the title President 2012, Patriot or Puppet for Billionaires, then click on it and then click on "Research": Please give everyone of them, your utmost respect; for I believe each are patriots.

I also have in this book as many referenced websites as I could recall quoting, for your convenience, although you can simply click each for access on my website:

Links to some of the websites that I used for research of the book: President 2012, Patriot or Puppet for Billionaires

The Remittance Marketplace (2004) - Pew Hispanic Research on this website: http://pewhispanic.org/files/reports/28.pdf Where they speak of: Remittances and the Market, Banks and Remittances and U.S Government Initiatives

Billions in Motion: Latino Immigrants, Remittances, and Banking, the Pew Hispanic Center/Multilateral Investment Fund (2002) on this website: http://pewhispanic.org/reports/report.php?ReportID=13

Financial Access for Immigrants: The Case of Remittances (Fed. Reserve-Bernanke speech) on this website: http://www.youtube.com/watch?v=-xoU7N-LodIM

The Failure of Modern Public Education:

A great reference that I used for research of the failure of modern Education is: http://www.multiconsole.com/forums/archive/index.php/t-51563.html

Executive Orders

You can review many here: http://www.presidency.ucsb.edu/exectutive_orders.php as well as http://judiciary.house.gov or others such as http://comm docs.house.gov/committees/

Heritage memo calls Clinton's late Executive Orders 'improper, illegal'http://www.uhuh.com/laws/clinteos.htm

Executive Order– Establishing the National Prevention, Health Promotion, and Public Health Council http://www.whitehouse.gov/the-press-office/executive-order-establishing-national-prevention-health-promotion-and-public-health

The Shanghai Cooperation Organization SCO

I agree with this analogy from the Burning Platform on this website: http://www.theburningplatform.com/?p=7637

Cap & Trade

Cap and Trade research from Current TV: http://current.com/green/91637684_krugman-endorses-the-next-wall-street-bubble-cap-trade.htm and research from Right Soup http://rightsoup.com/cap-and-trade-debate-today-in-senate

Where does the borrowed debt money come from part of my research is from the Booman Tribune: http://www.boomantribune.com/story/2011/4/14/31024/6525and further research from msnbc; Just who owns our debt: http://www.msnbc.msn.com/id/17424874/print/1/displaymode/1098

Cap And Trade Debate Today In Senate http://rightsoup.com/cap-and-trade-debate-today-in-senate

The Fed Was Created in 1913

Some-research-from-Wikipedia-:http://www.Wikipedia.org/wiki/Federar-Reserve System The Federal Reserve System (also known as the Federal Reserve, and informally as The-Fed)

According to the Board of Governors http://www.federalreserve.gov the Federal Reserve is independent within government.

Speech by Governor Tarullo on industrial organization and systemic risk: an agenda for further research Esther George named president and chief executive officer of the Federal Re-serve Bank of Kansas City Opening remarks by Chairman Bernanke at the conference on the regulation of systemic risk Federal Reserve offers $5 billion in 28-day term deposits through its

Term Deposit Facility

Federal Reserve Board issues enforcement actions. http://www.federalreserve.gov

Banking Cushion Gone Because Of Fed

Banking Cushion from the Prison Planet website: http://www.Prisonplanet. com Here is what I was referring to earlier when I was referring to the banking cushion that must be enforced Fed-Federal Reserve is Aware of the Scheme review the Gold Seek Web- site http://www.news.goldseek.com and the Prison Planet website: http:// www.Prisonplanet.com both very helpful in my research.

FDA–The Medical-Pharmaceutical Industrial Complex - Corruption in Drug Research and in Medicine http://www.shirleys-wellness-cafe.com/ama.htm

Federal Reserve Shipped Billions to Iraq Which Were Then Stolen... Involved in Other Unsavory Activities http://www.globalresearch.ca/index.php?context=viewArticle&code=BLO20110623&articleId=25370

Federal Reserve System: The Federal Reserve System (also known as the Federal Reserve, and informally as the Fed). http://en.wikipedia.org/wiki/Federal_Reserve_Board_of_Governors

Federal Reserve Chairman Ben Bernanke Warns Congress That The Federal Reserve Will Not "Print Money" To Pay For The Exploding U.S. National Debt http://theeconomiccollapseblog.com/archives/federal-reserve- chairman-ben-bernanke-warns-congress-that-the-federal-reserve-will-not- print-money-to-pay-for-the-exploding-u-s-national-debt

One of the more mysterious areas of the economy is the role of the Fed. Formally known as the Federal Reserve, the Fed is the gatekeeper of the U.S. economy. http://money.howstuffworks.com/fed.htm/printable

Sherif Joe Arpaio

The website Barracuda Brigade 2012 was helpful in my Aheriff Joe Arpaio research: http://barracudabrigade.blogspot.com/2011/03/sheriff-arpaio-obama-and-aclu-are.html

China

Communist China's rise to power research, the website Archive was helpful: http://www.archive.org/stream/communistchinaan013656mbp/communistchinaan013656mbp_djvu.txt

General Electric got caught

Why don't companies like General Electric get caught hiding money offshore? Cleverly pointed out on this website Renes.com: http://www.rense.com/general59/usmid.htm & the website davar.net: http://www.davar.net/IT/Q-OTHER.HTM

Regan Vs. Obama on The Economy

Economics when Regan took office, worse than when Obama got elected-: http://theconservativepost.com/WordPress/?p=3380

What is so striking about Obamanomics is how it so doggedly pursues the opposite of every one of these planks of Reaganomics pointed out by the website American Civil Rights Union: http://theacru.org/acru/reaganomics_vs_obamanomics_facts_and_figures

Hospital Acuired Infections

Review-the-website-Medscape-:http://emedicine.medscape.com/article/967022-overview

Progressives and Government

Progressives want government intrusion into private life a good place to start review is the website Volusia 912 Project: http://volusia912.org/html/progressive_assault.html

From The Progressive Assault on the American Constitution By Ronald J. Pestritto, PH.D. Under the original system, the president was merely the leader of a single branch, or part of the government, and thus could not provide leadership of the government as a whole. Good research could start with, the website Discover the Net Works. Org Progressivism http://www.discov- erthenetworks.org/guideDesc.asp?catid=93&type=issue Also review Glen Beck's http://www.glennbeck.com/content/articles/article/198/23936/

Vague Sloppily Written Laws Are Bad Laws.

Obscure laws, vaguely interpreted by the Supreme Court, explained on the Ricochet website: http://ricochet.com/main-feed/Justice-Scalia-on-The-Lazy-Congress-and-Vague-Laws?amp

Introduction to 19th-Century Socialism http://public.wsu.edu/~brians/hum_303/socialism.html

Greece: They are the crown jewels of Greece's socialist state, and they are now likely to go to the highest bidder: the ports of Piraeus and Thessaloniki; prime Mediterranean real estate; the national lottery; Greek Telecom; the postal bank and the national railway system http://dealbreaker.com/2011/06/opening-bell-06-23-11

Why the Progressives are making us a God-free Nation http://imjustmusing.hubpages.com/hub/Why-the-Progressives-are-Making-us-a-God-free-Nation

Islam Muslims

Does the rise in honor killings co-inside with Islamic immigration analyzed on this website News With Views: http://www.newswithviews.com/Wooldridge/frosty526.htm

"Not all Muslims are terrorists"; Michael Savage said on his radio show, then falsely asserted that "all terrorists happen to be Muslim." Savage stated: "I am a believer in all five of the world's religions. http://mediamatters.org/mmtv/200810140003

Pakistan Court Temporarily Blocks Facebook on the Grounds That It "Spread[s] Religious Hatred" http://www.volokh.com

FORT DIX SIX, 9/11 AND MUSLIMS http://www.mortyscabin.net/modules.php?name=News&file=article&sid=1424

"Not all Muslims are terrorists, but all terrorists are Muslims," said radio talk show host Peter Boyles last week on http://www.khow.com in Denver, Colorado. http://www.aina.org/articles/mi21ca.jsp

Honor killings in USA raise concerns http://www.usatoday.com/news/nation/2009-11-29-honor-killings-in-the-US_N.htm

Americans fantasize that they remain safe from Islamic terrorists because U.S. military forces conquered Iraq and wage an endless war in Afghanistan. Except, last week five American Muslim terrorists surfaced in Pakistan-asking to be trained for jihad. http://www.rense.com/general88/mus11.htm

Greenhouse Gas

Over 97% of all greenhouse gases are natural and there is nothing we can do about them: Research on green house gas: http://www.akdart.com/warm-ing21.html

Illegal Act By Obama—Pulitzer Prize Acceptance

Research on Obama illegally accepting Pulitzer prize research on the Volokh-Conspiracy-:http://volokh.com/2009/10/28/can-obama-accept-the-nobel-prize-without-congressional-consent

Secret Rule of The Shadow Government

Shadow government by the website, constitution: http://www.constitution.org/shad4816.htm It is becoming increaseingly apparent to American citizens that government is no longer being conducted in accordance with the Constitution.

Release of the lockabie bomber

Review the website Lakewood 24/6 http://www.lakewood246.com/news/17728/ white-house-backed-release-of-lockerbie-bomber-abdel-baset-al-megrahi. html The U.S. government secretly advised Scottish ministers it would be far preferable to free the Lockebie bomber than jail him in Libya.

Illegal aliens

Mexican President Assails U.S. Measures on Migrants New York Times:http://www.nytimes.com/2007/09/03/world/americas/03mexico.html

Educating Illegal Aliens in Texa:shttp://www.minutemanhq.com/state/read.php?chapter=tx&sid=946

Immigration and Welfare: Although the United States' welfare rolls are already swollen, every year we import more people who wind up on public assistance immigrants-:http://www.fairus.org/site/News2?page=NewsArticle&id=16985&security=1601&news_iv_ctrl=1017

The Truth About Obama Health Care Reform

From America Rising website: http://logisticsmonster.com/2009/07/25/the-truth-about-obama-health-care-reform You Do Not Have A Choice In Health Care

Mom arrested because she was shielding her child from chemo and radiation from the website of CBS News: http://www.cbsnews.com/stories/2009/07/06/health/main5135062.shtml (CBS-reported) A woman accused of withholding cancer treatment from her autistic son has been charged with attempted murder.

Citizens sue feds to block Obamacare they contend they can't be forced to buy insurance, pay for abortions http://www.wnd.com/?pageId=131329

Obama Health Care, Codex, and Supplement Safety http://www.thenhf.com/article.php?id=2396

The Destruction of America

Read: The Destruction of America, by David Yeagley on the website bad eagle: http://www.badeagle.com/2008/11/04/obama-the-destruction-of-america How could America elect a foreign black communist? How could the majority of the population be so deceived? How could the nation commit treason against itself?

Also review Obama & Progressives Planed Destruction of America on the website USA Carry: http://www.usacarry.com/forums/politics/11742-obama-progressives-planned-destruction-america.html How could America elect a foreign black communist? How could the majority of the population be so deceived?

America waits with bated breath while Washington struggles to bring the U.S. economy back from the brink of disaster. But many of those same politicians caused the crisis, and if left to their own devices will do so again. http:// www.americanthinker.com/2008/09/barack_obama_and_the_strategy.html

Continuing Implosion of the World Economy The Chinese are using up their dollar reserves buying goods and services with them, knowing that the value of the dollar is falling and wanting to get rid of as many greenbacks as they can. Nations are purchasing gold and silver http://stevebeckow.com/2010/11/continuing-implosion-of-the-world-economy

Destruction of Capitalism in America - The Cloward-Piven Strategy: http://arcticcompass.blogspot.com/2010/01/destruction-of-capitalism-in-america. Html

America's debt crisis is due not to under-taxation but to overspending, not to "right-wing partisanship" but to bipartisan collusion. Spending profligates who demand "more revenue" on the occasion of an impending debt-lifting deadline are like thieves who turn back to their old victims upon the arrival of new bills. http://spectator.org/archives/2011/07/14/obamas-debt#

The combination of a $trillion bond fraud, dependence on inflating home equity for economic development, oversized cars, oil dependence, constant market intervention, insolvent banks, insolvent homes, outsourced indus-try, endless war, bud-get deadlock amidst runaway deficits, raided US gold treasury, mammoth future benefit obligations, and handing over the keys at U.S. Dept Treasury to Goldman Sachs has left the United States to fend off systemic failure. http://news.goldseek.com/GoldenJackass/1307649600.php

How Goldman Sachs Made Tens Of Billions Of Dollars From The Economic Collapse Of America In Four Easy Steps http://theeconomiccollapse- blog.com/archives/how-goldman-sachs-made-tens-of-billions-of-dollars-from-   the-eco-nomic-collapse-of-america-in-four-easy-steps

How Goldman Sachs has Engineered Every Major Market Manipulation Since the Great Depression http://www.dailypaul.com/98323/rolling-stones-taibbi-   how-goldman-sachs-has-engineered-every-major-market-manipula-tion- since-the-great-depression

Obama Supports Socialism – More Proof! http://bridgetdgms.wordpress.com/2008/04/07/obama-supports-socialism-more-proof

End of America: As We Know It-http://www.care2.com/news/member/246963792/2700248

Obama's Bith Certificate Not Valid

Nancy Goldfarb Thinks: State of Hawaii Says Obama "Birth Certificate" Not Valid http://ngoldfarb.wordpress.com/2009/05/15/state-of-hawaii-says-obama-birth-certificate-not-valid

Natural-born citizen. Who is a natural-born citizen? Who, in other words, is a citizen at birth, such that that person can be a President someday? http://www.usconstitution.net/consttop_citi.html

Barry Soetoro, alias Barack Obama, Imposter in Chief, Implements CODEX ALIMENTARIUS by Executive Order in the U.S.! http://survivingthemiddleclasscrash.wordpress.com/2010/06/14/barry-soetoro-imposter-in-chief-implements-codex-alimentarius-by-executive-order-in-the-u-s

Supremes get case against putative President Obama Petition: There exists possibility that he could be an illegal alien' http://www.wnd. com/?pageId=210521

Who Is Behind Barack Obama's Rise to stardom?

To deconstruct this Obama labyrinth-like network, you could start with this website America Free Press: http://www.americanfreepress.net/html/behind_barack_obama_188.html Is Obama the product of a vast socialist conspiracy designed to undermine the fundamental tenets established by our Founding Fathers?

Top Contributors to Obama in 2008 Election

Research of contributors from open secrets website: http://www.opensecrets.org/pres08/contrib.php?cycle=2008&cid=N00009638 This table lists the top donors to this candidate in the 2008 election cycle. The organizations themselves did not donate , rather the money came from the organization's PAC, its individual members or employees or owners, and those individuals' immediate families. Organization totals include subsidiaries and affiliates.

Poverty Means More Crime

Crime is explained to be Related to Poverty but Responsibility Starts Somewhere on Andy Blunden's website: http://home.mira.net/~andy/works/dependency.htm & The Heritage Foundation website: http://www.heritage.org/Research/Reports/1995/03/BG1026nbsp-The-Real-Root-Causes-of-Violent-Crime The Welfare State is under sentence of death.

Thirty years ago, when the welfare-state programs of President Lyndon Johnson's War on Poverty were first being implemented, the general consensus among the political elite and the intellectual community was that wise government, with sufficient funding, could lift the poor from their poverty. http://www.fff.org/freedom/0597f.asp

For the past 50 years there has been a national tragedy presented to the American Society in regards to fathers and their role within the American Family: http://www.angelfire.com/home/sufferingpatriarchy/chapters/Chapter01.html

Ward of the state is a term that usually refers to children who are under age 18 and retain a legal guardian from the court. In certain situations, adults, or those over age 19, can become wards of the state if they are mentally unable to care for themselves and do not have any family members or other guardians who could care for them. http://www.ehow.com/about_4576674_wards-state.html

America's Middle Class Becomes the New Working Poor http://www.rense.com/general59/usmid.htm

Policymakers at last are coming to recognize the connection between the breakdown of American families and various social problems. http://www.heritage.org/Research/Reports/1995/03/BG1026nbsp

The-Real-Root-Causes-of- Violent-Crime

The rise of fascism itself is a complex story, much less the rise of American fascism. http://www.rationalrevolution.net/articles/rise_of_american_fascism.htm

Unions

Union members swarm the Wisconsin capital, http://www.nationalreview.com/corner/260022/where-does-left-get-time-jay-nordlinger As I look at the union members swarm the Wisconsin capital, I have a familiar thought: A great advantage of the Left is that they are organized and determined and have a lot of time; Paid time. The taxpayer is funding these "days of protest," engaged in by the public-school teachers.

The Trouble with Public Sector Unions http://www.nationalaffairs.com/publications/detail/the-trouble-with-public-sector-unions

Is Boeing in trouble here? http://www.postandcourier.com/news/2011/apr/21/is-boeing-in-trouble-here

"The refusal of many federal employees to fly coach costs taxpayers $146 million annually." http://www.politifact.com/truth-o-meter/statements/2011/jan/18/newsmax/newsmax-courts-readers-statistic-about-federal-was

Are Postal Workforce Costs Sustainable? http://www.youtube.com/watch?v=BLoao23pJjs

Americas Does and Don'ts

See David Tippie's blog: http://davidtippie.blogspot.com/2006/08/new-america.html

Constitution

To review the Constitution refer to the Constitution Society website: http://constitution.org/c5/index.php

See also Congressional Issues 2012, the USA will be abolished from Craig for Congress:http://kevincraig.us/abolish.htm

I don't begrudge the progressive left its political power. They won. They are far from ashamed to say it, and I am not afraid to admit it. What I do mind is the left's obvious neglect and disregard for the Constitution as it is written. http://www.americanthinker.com/2009/11/a_progressive_constitution.html

Founding Fathers would have contempt for vision of today's Americans http://www.deseretnews.com/article/700046037/Founding-Fathers-would-have-contempt-for-vision-of-todays-Americans.html?pg=1

Does the Constitution Contain a Right to Privacy? http://www.harrybrowne.org/articles/PrivacyRight.htm

Since my 2008 campaign for the presidency, "How would a constitutionalist president go about dismantling the welfare-warfare state and restoring a constitutional republic?" http://www.lewrockwell.com/paul/paul647.html

Quantitative Easing 2

Quantitative Easing 2 Federal Reserve undertook quantitative easing back in November, 2010 http://archive.aweber.com/stockreport1ge/bfJA/h/QE_2_And_You.htm

Congressional Issues 2012 OCIETY The U.S.A. Will Be ABOLISHED! http://kevincraig.us/abolish.htm

Americans Love To Scream About Taxes Or Social Support, But Only Half Are Actually Paying Income Tax http://www.businessinsider.com/only-half-americans-actually-pay-income-tax-2010-4.htm

The Nationalization of GM and Chrysler http://www.akdart.com/obama122.

Government Crash

In the last week I've read at least four syndicated columns which contained the following argument: were the Congress to resist raising the debt "ceiling," the full faith and credit of the United States Government would be endangered. The financial system would inevitably crash; investors would send their capital to other safer, more stable havens; depression would follow. http://www.americanthinker.com/2011/04/do_we_really_need_to_raise_the.html

It is just another example of who rules our government, and why the only thing that will change it is a financial crash where all parties will be brought to heal and suffer proportionately. Any-thing less will be manipulated by those currently calling the shots and controlling our politicians. http://www.insidejob.com/profiles/blogs/bank-fine-hints-at-feds

Obama Vows to Battle for Tax Hikes http://barracudabrigade.blogspot.com/2011/03/sheriff-arpaio-obama-and-aclu-are.html

One of the most common – and often devastating – attacks launched by non-incumbent candidates against their opponents is the charge of being a "career politician." http://bearingdrift.com/2010/12/29/what-exactly-is-a-career-politician

Fixing America's Economy: Nine Ideas from Around the World http://www.businessweek.com/magazine/content/11_25/b4233053223432_page_3.htm

Hard Left Comment: The so-called "right" or "Tea Party" in this republic is being so thoroughly rolled and defeated that I am struggling to come up with an adequate violent submission metaphor that does not involve prison. http://www.americanthinker.com/blog/2011/08/we_the_stupid.html

From tech stocks to high gas prices, Goldman Sachs has engineered every major market manipulation since the Great Depression – and they're about to do it again http://www.rollingstone.com/politics/news/the-great-american-bubble-machine-20100405

Apparently, there is a big debate in the Michigan blogsphere regarding the law known as "right to work." http://www.rjkoehler.com/2010/09/14/the-kia-plant-in-georgia-and-michigans-debate-on-right-to-work

The Nationalization of GM and Chrysler http://www.akdart.com/obama122.htm

Davos Annual Meeting 2011 - The Next Shock: Are We Bet-ter Prepared? http://www.youtube.com/watch?v=i2WB-MLn43o

Recent Developments

Opposing Views between Bob Beckel and Sean Hannity http://lipskip.com/bob-beckels-elitist-exchange-with-sean-hannity

Can we bail out of the bailouts? OK until millions of dollars in executive bonuses were found out, after it was rescued with taxpayer cash. http://www.msnbc.msn.com/id/29762648/ns/business-eye_on_the_economy/t/can-we-bail-out-bailouts

WASHINGTON – President Obama is demanding a big long-term budget deal. He won't sign anything less, he warns, asking, "If not now, when?" How about last December, when he ignored his own debt commission's recom-mendations?-http://www.commercialappeal.com/news/2011/jul/14/charles-krauthammer-gop-should-seize-the/?partner=RSS

The confrontational New Jersey governor, appearing on a recent call-in show for a local public television channel, effectively shut down a caller who asked him why he sends his kids to private school. http://www.foxnews.com/politics/2011/06/21/christie-to-caller-none-your-business-where-my-kids-go-to-school

"Representation" remained the core issue for the Philadelphia Conven-tion. What was the best way for authority to be delegated from the people and the states to a strengthened central government? http://www.ushistory. org/us/15d.asp

Individual consumers have clear incentives not to be saddled with too much debt. Excessive use of credit can result in an arduous repayment proc-ess or bankruptcy. Certain cultures view personal debt as immoral. http://www.csa.com/discoveryguides/debt/review2.php

The corporate jet tax "loophole" – which Obama beat like a rented mule during his press conference yesterday – was actually part of Obama's failed "stimulus" plan. http://www.therightscoop.com/corporate-jet-tax-loophole -was- part-of-obamas-stimulus-package

How politicians who receive gifts or promise of jobs break the law: Sec.600. Promise of employment or other benefit for political activity. http://law. onecle. com/uscode/18/600.html

Fukushima is the greatest nuclear and environmental disaster in human history-http://www.stumbleupon.com/su/7sV24b/globalresearch.ca/index. php?context=va&aid=25327

New America & You Don't Have To Be Rich To Be President http://davidtip-pie.blogspot.com/2011/03/gold-secret-chinese-are-using-up-their.html

AC/DC – A Deliberation Regarding the Impeachment of the President of the United States of America http://samvak.tripod.com/impeach.html

Israelis view the Egyptian uprising with both fear and indifference http:// bikyamasr.com/25232/israelis-view-the-egyptian-uprising-with-both-fear-and-indifference

Mitt Romney's 'Jobs Record' Is A Sham http://politicalcorrection.org/fact-check/201106020002

Debt-Limit Chicken and the Spread of Political Fundamentalism http:// www.huffingtonpost.com/paul-stoller/cantor-debt_b_884321.html

WHY DO PEOPLE FAIL TO PRESERVE LIBERTY? WHY DO PEOPLE HAVE SUCH A DIFFICULT TIME RECOGNIZING ITS LOSS? http://www.joel-skousen.com/Philosophy/conservation.htm

Declaration of Independence

The Declaration and Its Importance http://www.factmonster.com/ce6/history/ A0857706.html The Declaration of Independence is the most important of all American historical documents.

Obama Strikes God from the Declaration Again, Inadvertent-ly Proves the Bible is True http://www.westernjournalism.com/obama-strikes-god-from-the-declaration-again-inadvertently-proves-the-bible-is-true

Democracy Versus Republic http://www.albatrus.org/english/goverment/ govenrment/democracy%20versus%20repubblic.htm

Democrats-Want-Illegals-to-Vote! http://nevadanewsandviews.com/2011/03/07/ democrats-want-illegals-to-vote

Is the United States a Democracy or a Republic? http://thecapitalist.news-vine.com/_news/2009/08/23/3184502-is-the-united-states-a-democracy-or-a-republic

In the days of the American republic, the only people allow-ed to partici-pate in 'democracy':- White men- Land-owning- over the age of 25–We can contrast this with today when "people" now includes virtually the entire adult population regardless of race, gender, religion, or other socioeconomic indica-tors. http://faculty.northseattle.edu/kleitich/notes.html

Radicals

Rules for Radicals: Obama's New Plan to Destroy America: Could voters be foolish enough to fall for Obama's new plan to destroy America? http://doc-stalk.blogspot.com/2011/02/rules-for-radicals-obamas-new-plan-to.html

Does Rev. Jesse Jackson truly represent the needs of African-Americans? http://www.helium.com/items/1180992-jesse-jackson-racial-segregation-rain-bowpush

This is taken from John Taylor Gatto's book, Dumbing Us Down: The Hid-den Curriculum of Compulsory Schooling http://www.sntp.net/education/gatto.htm

Eric Holder: Possible Racial Profiling Lawsuit against AZ http://www.thenewamerican.com/index.php/usnews/immigration/3999-eric-holder-possible-racial-profiling-lawsuit-against-az

Glenn Beck: Black Panther — Kill crackers and their babies http://www.glennbeck.com/content/articles/article/198/42683

Kill Some White Crackers; Kill their Babies - New Black Panthers; Holder drops charges http://www.youtube.com/watch?v=APZ3-Lcbwmc

Is Barack Obama Racist? http://newsflavor.com/opinions/is-barack-obama-racist

List of Obama's Czars http://www.glennbeck.com/content/articles/arti-cle/198/29391

Obama Surrounds Himself with the Most Extreme Appointees in Ameri-can History: http://www.westernjournalism.com/exclusive-investigative-reports/obama-surrounds-himself-with-the-most-extreme-appointees-in-american-history

Mexican President Calderon says: "Mexico does not end at its borders."http://www.minutemanhq.com/state/read.php?chapter=TX&sid=621

Left Wing: Van Jones building left-wing Tea Party, says the country 'isn't broke' http://www.freerepublic.com/focus/f-bloggers/2739456/posts

In Washington D.C. there is powerful and popular lobby called the Congressional Progressive Caucus which, at one time, openly espoused the principles of socialism and publicly signed onto the agenda of the Democratic Socialists of America. http://www.jeremiahproject.com/trashingamerica/progressive.htm

Supreme Court Justice–Elena Kagan–is Pro Sharia Law! http://www.gather.com/viewArticle.action?articleId=281474979569400

Secretary of Saving the World Tim Geithner's daunting to-do list at the Treasury Department. http://www.slate.com/id/2207073

A tort, in common law jurisdictions, is a wrong that involves a breach of a civil duty (other than a contractual duty) owed to someone else. It is differentiated from a crime, which involves a breach of a duty owed to society in general. http://en.wikipedia.org/wiki/Tort

Unbelievable: Obama NLRB Tells Boeing to Build Plant in Washington Not South Carolina http://www.thegatewaypundit.com/2011/04/unbelievable-obama-nlrb-forces-boeing-to-build-plant-in-washington-not-south-carolina

FDA: The Food and Drug Administration (FDA) is a government agency whose supposed job is to "protect" the public from dangerous drugs, foods, medicines, toxins, and medical procedures. In fact, the FDA is a Gestapo-type organization only serving the interests of the major drug companies and medical establishment. http://sntp.net/fda/fda_lynes.htm

US Banks Operate Without Reserve Requirements http://www.freerepublic.com/focus/bloggers/2218032/posts AND http://news.goldseek.com/GoldSeek/1238970345.php

For Year 2012 Federal Mandatory Budget http://useconomy.about.com/od/fiscalpolicy/p/Mandatory.htm

What is Political Correctness? http://wuphys.wustl.edu/~katz/pc.html

Democrats founded the KKK, fought the 13th, 14th and 15th Amendments, instituted Jim Crow Laws, fought the 1965 Civil Rights Act and continue to keep racism alive and blacks on their liberal plantation http://www.youtube.com/watch?v=nRM00LPWVLE

Why did Nixon take us off the gold standard? http://answers.yahoo.com/question/index?qid=20090513095002AA74jUQ

Gold certificate U.S. Dollar http://www.forward-usa.org/id2.html

New World Order Definition http://www.threeworldwars.com/new-world-order.htm

Black Gives Call To Arms For Whites

James David Manning, a black PhD gives a call to arms for white people of http://www.youtube.com/watch?v=e_alvfFq3BA&feature=related

The Republican Party in Texas was started in 1867 by 150 blacks and 20 whites. http://www.jewishworldreview.com/cols/elder111705.asp

www.ingramcontent.com/pod-product-compliance
Lightning Source LLC
Chambersburg PA
CBHW060245290526
45789CB00001B/197